THE FOURTH GOSPEL
in Recent Criticism and Interpretation

THE FOURTH GOSPEL
in Recent Criticism
and Interpretation

by
WILBERT FRANCIS HOWARD

Revised by
C. K. BARRETT

WIPF & STOCK · Eugene, Oregon

Wipf and Stock Publishers
199 W 8th Ave, Suite 3
Eugene, OR 97401

Fourth Gospel in Recent Criticism and Interpretation, 4th edition
By Howard, Wilbert Francis
Copyright©1961 Epworth Press
ISBN 13: 978-1-60608-720-6
Publication date 4/29/2009
Previously published by Epworth Press, 1961

Copyright © Epworth Press 1961
First English edition 1961 by Epworth Press
This edition published by arrangement with Epworth Press

TO THE MEMBERS
OF THE
BIRMINGHAM NEW TESTAMENT
SEMINAR

REVISER'S PREFACE

THE late Dr. W. F. Howard was to me an ideal of the Christian scholar and Christian gentleman. When therefore his family, and the publisher, invited me to undertake responsibility for a new edition of his *The Fourth Gospel in Recent Criticism and Interpretation* the honour was one that I could not refuse. If Dr. Howard had lived he would no doubt himself have given us his own comments on the literature which the Fourth Gospel has evoked during the last twenty years. That these comments were never written is not the smallest of the losses we have suffered in his death; yet even an *epigonus* may perhaps hope to provide a little information useful to those whose leisure for reading is limited.

It is important that the reader should know what to expect in this book. It seemed to me axiomatic that it should remain Dr. Howard's book, and that my own share in it should be confined to the smallest possible compass. The Introduction and Part I remain as Dr. Howard wrote them. So also do Parts II and III, but here the reader will find (*a*) occasional marginal signs drawing attention to notes (to be found on pp. 173 ff., 267), which either refer to more recent literature or suggest an alternative point of view; and (*b*) two short chapters (on pp. 164-72 and pp. 243-66) which give some account of the criticism and interpretation of the Gospel between 1931 and 1953. These notes and chapters are my work. Any one who has attempted to study the literary output on the Johannine writings will know how much more might have been said; if he thinks I have omitted much that I ought to have included I will plead only that I had determined that my contribution should be as brief as possible, and had to use my own judgement. The appendices are substantially as Dr. Howard wrote them, except that on the question of the common authorship of the Fourth Gospel and the First Epistle of St. John I have been able to reprint an important article contributed by Dr. Howard to the *Journal of Theological Studies* (Old Series, Vol. xlviii (1947), pp. 12-25). For permission to do this I am indebted to the Delegates of the Clarendon Press. The Bibliography has been revised. I have added books published since 1931, and omitted many earlier than that date. The list is now, I hope, up to date, and being also considerably shorter than it was may prove more useful to readers who were bewildered and discouraged, rather than helped, by the exhaustive list in earlier editions.

I wish to thank very warmly Mr. Maurice F. Howard, who has sent me those of his father's papers that bore upon this project (unfortunately they were very few), and the Rev. F. H. Cumbers of the Epworth Press, who has cheerfully acceded to every suggestion and request that I have made.

Were my own share in this new edition not so slight and insignificant, I should wish to offer it to the memory of the author, who was ever among the kindest of friends and wisest of counsellors.

C. K. BARRETT

DURHAM

ACKNOWLEDGEMENTS

The following publishers are thanked for permission to use copyright material:

A. and C. Black, London (A. Schweitzer, *The Quest of the Historical Jesus*, English Translation by W. Montgomery).

Cambridge University Press (C. H. Dodd, *The Interpretation of the Fourth Gospel*).

Faber and Faber, London (E. C. Hoskyns, *The Fourth Gospel*).

J. C. B. Mohr (Paul Siebeck), Tübingen (R. Bultmann, *Theologie des Neuen Testaments*); and the Student Christian Movement Press, who are publishing an English edition of this work.

Vandenhoeck und Ruprecht, Göttingen (R. Bultmann, *Das Evangelium des Johannes*).

PREFACE TO FIRST EDITION

WHEN the writer was asked to deliver the Fernley Lecture in 1931, he elected for his subject 'The Fourth Gospel in Recent Criticism and Interpretation.' The choice of this subject demands a brief explanation. Some years ago he wished to write a book about the Theology of the Johannine Writings, but found on closer study of the subject that the critical questions involved were not patient of the drastic solution proposed by many modern scholars, on the one hand, as, on the other, they surely could not be left with the answer offered with so great a mass of learning by the Cambridge school of the nineteenth century. The Johannine question has assumed many different forms within the memory of the present generation, and critical investigation is repeatedly turned into new directions, so that he who would guide others in the study of these sublime writings must first determine for himself the standpoint from which the Fourth Gospel is to be viewed. Under the pretext of 'originality' it would be easy to shirk the tedious task of studying at first hand the theories advanced by many scholars in this and other lands. But sound scholarship does not follow the line of least resistance. Professor Percy Gardner, in *The Ephesian Gospel*, writes: 'The date, the authorship, the composition, the tendencies, have been discussed at length by a multitude of able writers, many of whom have given their best years to the study of these problems. No one has a right to publish a book about the Gospel who has not in a measure surveyed this mass of literature. I say "in a measure," for to master it completely would be the work of many years, if not of a lifetime.' If this last sentence was true sixteen years ago, how much more does it mean to-day! Yet a serious attempt has been made to read the most important books and articles that have been written about the Fourth Gospel, and this book is the result of a wide and diligent, but far from complete, study of the relevant literature. The danger of such a book is obvious. It might easily degenerate into a catalogue of names. There is an even more deadly peril. It is possible to use the names of scholars whose work is only known at second hand from references found in books or articles. On this, as on many things, Dr. Johnson has said the final word. Boswell records the testimony of the Rev. Mr. Samuel Badcock: 'Speaking of Dr. P——, he said, "You have proved him as deficient in *probity* as he is in learning."—I called him an "Index-scholar"; but he was not willing to allow him a claim even to that merit. He said, "that he borrowed from those who had been borrowers themselves, and did not know that the mistakes he adopted had been answered by others."' Samuel Johnson may have been guilty here of a gross libel on the eminent Dr. Priestley, but the words serve as a general admonition. The present writer has guarded himself against this reproach by entering in the Bibliography no book or essay which he has not himself read.

The substance of two papers has been incorporated in this book. One, dealing with the Problem of the Fourth Gospel, was read before the Newcastle-on-Tyne Theological Society. The other, a linguistic study dealing with the unity of authorship of the Johannine Gospel and Epistles, was read before the Oxford Society of Historical Theology. Some of the material has been prepared for meetings of the Birmingham New Testament Seminar, of which the writer is Secretary. He wishes to take this opportunity of expressing his gratitude to the President, Professor H. G. Wood, and to his fellow members, especially to the Rev. F. Warburton Lewis, Greville P. Lewis, and V. Donald Siddons, for many happy hours spent in the study of this Gospel since September 1928, and more particularly for some fruitful discussions regarding the rearrangement of the text. Even though these friends may disagree with some of the positions adopted in this book, they will not deny the author the pleasure of dedicating it to our fellowship in sacred study.

The author returns his warmest thanks to two colleagues, the Rev. Dr. W. F. Lofthouse for reading the type-script, and the Rev. Henry Bett for reading the proofs. The text has gained in clarity of thought and of expression through the suggestions made by these most generous of friends. Last, but not least, grateful acknowledgement is made of help given in the correction of proofs and in the checking of the Index by his wife and his elder son.

HANDSWORTH COLLEGE,
July, 1931.

La règle élémentaire de la critique historique, universellement reconnue par tous ceux qui ont la moindre notion de méthode scientifique, veut, en effet, que partout où nous possédons des documents différents, relatifs à un même ensemble de faits historiques, nous commencions par une comparaison rigoureuse de ces documents, afin de dégager leurs relations réciproques et la valeur propre de chacun. Dans l'espèce, cette obligation n'existe pas seulement pour le savant qui aborde l'étude des évangiles avec l'unique souci de reconstituer une page capitale de l'histoire humaine ; elle est plus urgente encore et plus sacrée, dirai-je, pour le chrétien qui prétend fonder sa foi, la règle de sa vie morale et l'assurance de son salut éternel, sur la parole et l'œuvre de Jésus-Christ. On a quelque peine à se représenter l'état d'esprit de gens qui, d'une part, proclament l'autorité souveraine de la parole du Christ, le salut par Christ seul, et qui, d'autre part, se refusent à toute étude critique des évangiles : s'il s'agissait d'un fait quelconque de l'histoire moderne ou d'une affaire quelconque touchant à leurs intérêts matériels, ils ne manqueraient pas d'employer tous les moyens de contrôle dont dispose la science pour arriver à reconnaître la teneur exacte du fait ou la signification précise et originelle des textes. Et quand il s'agit de leurs intérêts spirituels les plus sacrés, ils négligent ces précautions élémentaires pour eux-mêmes et, trop souvent, crient au scandale parce que d'autres, plus soucieux de la vérité, plus sincèrement respectueux de la parole du Christ, mettent en œuvre toute leur intelligence et toutes leurs énergies pour en saisir la teneur originelle et la véritable signification ! La masse des fidèles alléguera sans doute qu'elle n'a ni le loisir ni les connaissances nécessaires pour se livrer à ce travail de contrôle. Mais que dire des conducteurs spirituels qui ont justement pour mission d'éclairer les fidèles et qui ne veulent pas se donner la peine d'appliquer aux documents mêmes sur lesquels ils fondent tout leur enseignement, les principes élémentaires en dehors desquels il n'y a plus, de l'aveu unanime, ni vérité historique, ni saine interprétation des textes !

Jean Réville.

CONTENTS

	PAGE
REVISER'S PREFACE	vii
PREFACE TO FIRST EDITION	ix
INTRODUCTION: THE PREACHER AND THE PROBLEM OF THE FOURTH GOSPEL	1

Part I: Historical Survey

THE FOURTH GOSPEL IN THE TWENTIETH CENTURY

I. IN BRITAIN AND AMERICA, 1901–1913	19
II. IN BRITAIN, 1914–1931	36
III. IN GERMANY, 1901–1918	53
IV. IN GERMANY, 1918–1930: IN FRANCE	70

Part II: Critical Investigation

I. THE UNITY OF THE GOSPEL AND ITS RELATION TO THE JOHANNINE WRITINGS	95
II. TEXTUAL DISLOCATIONS AND CHRONOLOGICAL ORDER	111
III. RELATION TO THE SYNOPTIC GOSPELS AND THE PROBLEM OF HISTORICITY	128
IV. THE BACKGROUND OF THOUGHT IN ITS RELATION TO THE JOHANNINE MESSAGE	144
V. CRITICISM OF THE FOURTH GOSPEL, 1931–1953	164

Part III: Problems of Interpretation

I. SYMBOLISM AND ALLEGORY	179
II. MYSTICISM AND SACRAMENTALISM	195
III. THE TEACHING OF JESUS IN THE JOHANNINE IDIOM	213
IV. THE FOURTH EVANGELIST: HIS MESSAGE AND ITS ABIDING VALUE	228
V. INTERPRETATION OF THE FOURTH GOSPEL, 1931–1953	243

Appendices

	PAGE
A. THE AUTHORSHIP OF THE BOOK AND THE ALLEGED MARTYRDOM OF JOHN	271
B. THE LINGUISTIC UNITY OF THE GOSPEL AND EPISTLES	276
C. THEORIES OF PARTITION AND REDACTION	297
D. THEORIES OF TEXTUAL DISPLACEMENT	303
E. EUCHARISTIC PARALLELS TO JOHN VI. IN IGNATIUS AND JUSTIN MARTYR	304
F. THE STYLE AND STRUCTURE OF THE TEACHING OF JESUS	306
G. NUMBERS IN THE FOURTH GOSPEL	310
BIBLIOGRAPHY	312
INDEX OF SCRIPTURE REFERENCES	317
INDEX OF NAMES AND SUBJECTS	321

Introduction

THE PREACHER AND THE PROBLEM OF THE FOURTH GOSPEL

THE FERNLEY LECTURER is required by the terms of the Trust Deed to write 'with special reference and adaptation to the necessities of the times, and with a view to the benefit of the Candidates who are about to be ordained by the Conference to the Ministry.' In other words, biblical and theological subjects are to be viewed in their vital relation to the Christian message, but in the light of modern knowledge. The religious and the scientific interests may sometimes appear to be in rivalry or even in conflict with each other. Still, the preacher who is more than a pulpiteer cannot be at peace within himself if he accept two standards of truth, one for the study and another for the pulpit. It is quite true that the function of the preacher is not that of the lecturer in Biblical Criticism. The Pauline canon of public worship still holds good, 'Let all things be done for edification.' Before, however, the expositor can handle a passage of Scripture, he must be fully persuaded in his own mind what kind of authority it is to which he can appeal in those words which he is to expound and apply. The need for such clearness of thought and an honestly wrought out working theory is felt especially in the use of the Gospels, but the difficulty becomes acute when the Fourth Gospel is under consideration.

Two quotations will illustrate the perplexity. The writers are both biblical scholars and preachers of high distinction, both reared under the same austere standards of sound learning and intellectual integrity in Scottish Presbyterianism. Dr. Lewis Muirhead,[1] writing of Marcus Dods and his commentaries on St. John in the *Expositor's Greek Testament* and in the *Expositor's Bible*, said : ' I confess to having found it difficult to forgive Marcus Dods from the heart for so completely ignoring (or, if you will, *evading*) the Johannine problem. But here again memory has come to my aid. I remember his chapter on the "Bread of Life," and I feel that everything should be forgiven to such a prince of exegetes and feeder of souls. At the same time one has confidence in saying to young ministers that the Dods attitude to the Fourth Gospel is one that is not honourably possible to *them*.' On the other hand, we have Dr. James Denney[2] writing about one of the most learned and ingenious books ever written upon the Fourth Gospel : ' The book taken altogether is both brilliant and wrong-headed : it would be a fine book to go through, a chapter at a time, in a seminary : but the idea of offering it to the lay public to initiate it into the debate is astounding. The only conclusion to which the lay mind could come—and it would come to it promptly and decidedly—would be that, if " John " is anything like what Bacon thinks, the less we trouble ourselves about him the better.' Thus we have the minister who revels in the spiritual insight of a great expositor but feels that the critical presuppositions are untenable, whilst the Professor of New Testament Criticism and Exegesis sees what benefit would come to a class of advanced students who worked through the brilliant speculations and arguments of the too imaginative critic, but recognizes that the effect of the conclusions offered would be for most readers of the Gospel to rob it, not merely of its spiritual message, but even of its living interest.

[1] *Expositor*, IX. i., p. 246.
[2] *Letters of Principal James Denney to W. R. Nicoll*, p. 158.

All the time we have before us the Gospel according to St. John, by most Christian believers regarded as the very summit of the biblical revelation. It contains within its chapters the very problems which the earnest seeker after historic truth is bound to unravel to his own satisfaction, unless he is prepared to leave that altogether on one side. The day has passed when the student could simply assume that it is a direct historical narrative of the ministry and words of Jesus from the pen of the Apostle John, and that any other theory of its character and origin is the product of ' unbelieving criticism.' Even the unprofessional Bible student entrusted with the preaching of the Word knows that this is not so. The three latest, most scholarly, and most popular one-volume commentaries on the Bible bear witness to the present situation.

In *Peake's Commentary*, Dr. A. E. Brooke has put the modern point of view with studious moderation, recognizing the indecisiveness of the external attestation, and the serious divergencies between the Synoptic and the Johannine presentation of the ministry and teaching of Jesus, but attributing the Gospel in its present form to the disciple of an eye-witness. In *Gore's Commentary*, Dr. Walter Lock presents the case in much the same light, although Dr. Charles Harris adds a long note in the attempt to show that the traditional position as to the authorship of the Fourth Gospel involves much less difficulty than any of the rival theories. Finally we have Dr. Garvie, in the *Abingdon Commentary*, interpreting the Gospel on the foundation of his well-known theory that we can distinguish three influences in the composition of the Gospel, the Witness, the Evangelist, and the Redactor, with varying degrees of historical value.

Thus the simplest and most accessible commentaries call the attention of the elementary Bible student to the existence of the Johannine problem. There is a sense in which this term is an obvious misnomer, for in its very complexity this problem is not one, but many. Yet, many as are the questions still under discussion, for most of us the essence of the problem can be put in one short sentence: 'How far is it possible for us to use the Fourth Gospel as a reliable witness to the earthly life and teaching of Jesus Christ?' This may once have been a question for the scholar in his study. It has long since become a matter of interest to the layman. One of the most remarkable signs of religious interest in the modern world is the ceaseless flow of books which attempt a fresh presentation of the life or teaching of Jesus. Even a popular study of Jesus must make some reference to the authorities upon which it is based. We have the recent case of Mr. Middleton Murry, whose widely read *Life of Jesus* revealed a strange inconsistency in his use of this Gospel. When replying to one reviewer, who had called attention to this critical caprice, he declared,[1] 'I am perfectly well aware that notable attempts have been made, particularly in the last ten years, to rehabilitate the partial historicity of the Fourth Gospel: I have studied the arguments with great care, and I have come to the conclusion that they are not really tenable.' On the other hand, we have Mr. Bernard Shaw, with characteristic perversity, staking the probability of the Johannine authorship upon the words in the appendix of the Gospel about the survival of the Beloved Disciple until the Second Coming of Christ. Mr. Shaw sees in this an obvious sign of an early date. There is shrewd insight here, but not many will be disposed to take the Preface to *Androcles and the Lion* very seriously as an incursion into the region of biblical criticism. Those who turn for expert guidance to the renowned scholars who have pronounced their judgements in the Home University Library and the latest edition of the *Encyclopaedia Britannica* will find divergent answers to our question. Professor B. W. Bacon, in his fascinating little

[1] *Methodist Recorder*, November 16, 1926

book, closes the chapter, 'The Spiritual Gospel,' with these words : ' The Fourth Gospel, as its Prologue forewarns, is an application to the story of Jesus as tradition reported it of the Pauline incarnation doctrine formulated under the Stoic Logos theory. It represents a study in the psychology of religion applied to the person of Christ. Poor as Paul himself in knowledge of the outward Jesus, unfamiliar with really historical words and deeds, its doctrine *about* Jesus became, nevertheless, like that of the great Apostle to the Gentiles, the truest exposition of " the heart of Christ." '[1] Professor Anderson Scott,[2] who also recognizes a singular blending of Pauline doctrine and striking originality of thought, lays more stress on the Evangelist's sound historical information. ' It is now generally understood that his work has much less the character of an historical record than of an interpretation of Jesus, an interpretation in the light of Christian experience and of the situation of the Church towards the end of the first century. That is not to say that " John " does not confirm, sometimes directly, sometimes indirectly, many points of the story of Jesus which are familiar to us from the Synoptic Gospels. There are even matters on which he appears to have preserved a more trustworthy tradition than in the Synoptic Gospels. But alike in the selection of the material and in the way in which it is handled the Evangelist is guided by the interpretation which has now been put upon Jesus and by his desire to put that interpretation to men.'

' Historical record,' ' interpretation.' Are these terms mutually exclusive? Therein lies the cardinal difference between the two positions just given. The element of interpretation in the Fourth Gospel is universally recognized. But a portrait painter is not necessarily less true to reality than a photographer. It may well be that G. F. Watts

[1] *The Making of the New Testament*, pp. 231 f.
[2] *Encyc. Brit.*, ed. 14, xiii. 25, art. ' Jesus Christ.'

has come nearer to a true representation of Robert Browning the poet than was possible to Messrs. Elliott & Fry. But, then, his interpretation took the form of a portrait to life ; it was not the personification of an idea. The Fourth Evangelist was certainly an artist ; some call him a dramatist. Does his genius lie in spiritual insight and sympathetic understanding of the historic life and message, or is it in the sphere of creative imagination ?

It is this fundamental distinction which is appreciated by those who have no leanings toward obscurantism, but have not interested themselves in the intricacies of scientific criticism of documents. So long as it was believed that this book was written by an intimate, personal disciple of our Lord, it had a value for the ordinary reader which could hardly belong to a study in the psychology of religion applied to the person of Jesus by a speculative philosopher imbued with theological Paulinism. Of course, this does not settle the question in advance. It supplies the preacher with an interest in the question which we have raised so vital that no disinclination for detailed examination of the Gospel can exempt him from studying the problem with all the means at his command.

Some may ask, What sufficient reason is there for raising doubts about a tradition of apostolic authorship which stood practically unchallenged for nearly seventeen centuries, and which has been sustained by the massive learning of scholars whose knowledge of early Christian history and literature is unsurpassed? The verdict of a Lightfoot or a Zahn is surely good enough for us ! And yet the fact remains that those whose earliest studies in the problem of the Fourth Gospel were influenced by the subtle reasoning of Westcott and the judicial marshalling of the evidence by Lightfoot are amongst those who feel the impossibility to-day of accepting their conclusions as a whole. Most significant of all is the fact that Sanday, whose early writings, *The Authorship and Historical Character of the Fourth Gospel* and *The Gospels in the Second Century*, established conclusions which were defended thirty years later in *The Criticism of the Fourth Gospel*, modified his opinion before the end of his life. In his last book[1] he wrote: ' I'm afraid there is one important point on which I was probably wrong—the Fourth Gospel. The problem is very complex and difficult ; and I have such a love of simplicity that I expect my tendency was to simplify too much, and to try too much to reach a solution on the ground of common sense. Perhaps I should say in passing that the contribution to this subject which has made the greatest impression upon me in recent years has been the article by Baron Friedrich von Hügel in the eleventh edition of the *Encyclopaedia Britannica*.'

The reason for the widespread abandonment of the full apostolic authorship of the Gospel is the clearer recognition that the external evidence is indecisive. It is not until we reach the last quarter of the second century that Irenaeus provides us with our first unambiguous witness in support of the traditional theory. The established position of the Fourth Gospel on an equality with the Synoptics at a considerably earlier date is proved by Tatian's use of all four Gospels in his Harmony. Echoes of the Gospel can be detected in Justin Martyr, and probably in Ignatius, whilst words from the First Epistle are almost certainly quoted by Polycarp. The ' longer ending ' of Mark shows dependence on John, and some of the ' double-bracket ' passages in the closing chapters of Luke are very early borrowings from the Fourth Gospel. Nevertheless, we are without any definite evidence to show that this Gospel was attributed to John by name in any writing before the time of Irenaeus. Of course, those

[1] *Divine Overruling*, p. 61. (1920. The earlier books named above were published in 1872, 1876, 1905.)

who accept the identification of the Beloved Disciple with the younger son of Zebedee as the obvious intention of the Evangelist can point to the editorial note of attestation in John xxi. 24 as a very early witness. The silence in early writers about the Apostle John and his residence in Ephesus probably accounts for the readiness with which so many modern scholars have accepted the slender evidence which is adduced for his early martyr death. If the external evidence is unconvincing, the contents of the Gospel itself raise difficulties for those who regard it as the work of one of the Twelve. It is not easy to imagine how one who was constantly present with the Master could record so much of His teaching without any recollection of the parabolic method. The discourses are stamped with the same style throughout, and it is not the style which marks the preaching and teaching of the earlier Gospels. Of such events as the Transfiguration and the Agony in the Garden, at which John was one of the favoured three allowed to be present, this Evangelist says not a word. Yet in some other narratives this writer shows a dependence upon Mark and Luke, neither of whom was an eye-witness, which defies explanation if he was himself on the scene. More striking still is the sharp contrast between the gradual unfolding of the conception of Messiahship in the Synoptic Gospels and the clear way in which Jesus is proclaimed from the beginning as Messiah by the Baptist, and recognized as such by His first disciples and even by the people of Samaria. Of course, it is possible to account for some of these variations by supposing that in advanced age the venerable Apostle looked at distant events through a golden haze of devotional reflection. But, if that is so, the value of apostolic authorship diminishes as a historical guarantee. It is therefore hardly a matter of surprise that the question of authorship has gone into the background, and other problems have come to the fore.

If the Gospel leaves us with no certain clue to the riddle of authorship, we may yet find in it many indications of the writer's purpose and aims. Thus it has come to be regarded as the work of a writer who has at the same time one eye fixed on the opponents or perverters of Christian truth at Ephesus at the close of the century, and the other fastened upon the historical Jesus who lived and died and rose again in Palestine two generations before. For the last twenty-five years every important study of this Gospel has given prominence to this apologetic or polemic purpose that is never for long out of sight. Of course, the Evangelist himself tells us plainly that his aim is theological. ' These are written that ye may believe that Jesus is the Christ, the Son of God ; and that believing ye may have life in His name.' [1] But that aim will be directed by the peculiar conditions which beset the Church in some definite region at some specific time. There is pretty general agreement that the Evangelist is putting the Church on guard against perils that come from Judaic, Gnostic, and sacramental tendencies within and without. Yet there is sympathy rather than hostility, and the correction is suggested and implied rather than flung down with a gage of defiance. Thus, the long discussions of Jesus are with opponents who are always classed together under the singular name of Jews. And yet Jesus is represented as saying to the Samaritan woman, ' Ye worship that which ye know not : we worship that which we know : for salvation is from the Jews.' The watchwords of Gnosticism are most carefully avoided (*pistis, sophia, gnosis*), but the same ideas are brought in under another guise. The Evangelist goes out of his way to state that Jesus Himself did not baptize, but His disciples ; and His disciples are ex-disciples of the Baptist, whilst he always appears as the forerunner whose light must fade before the increasing glory of the Christ. Yet

[1] John xx. 31.

the sacramental language of the conversation with Nicodemus is beyond dispute. In the long account of the events and conversation in the Upper Room, far longer than any record of that last supper in the Synoptists, there is not the slightest hint of the institution of the Eucharist. But who can deny that the discourse in the synagogue at Capernaum following the miraculous meal recorded in the sixth chapter is steeped in eucharistic thought and phraseology? Nevertheless, when the disciples were puzzled by this hard saying, Jesus added, ' It is the spirit which quickeneth, the flesh profiteth nothing: the words that I have spoken unto you are spirit, and are life.' There is still another subsidiary aim that can be detected in the Prologue and the earlier part of the Gospel. The emphatic way in which John the Baptist, whilst always spoken of with honour, is so pointedly subordinated to Jesus, has suggested that there were still at the end of the century, as there were at the time of Paul's first arrival in Ephesus, those who looked to John the Baptist as their religious leader, or even as the Messiah. Out of this element in the Gospel has arisen one of the most startling developments in recent speculation. Reitzenstein, who had done so much to explore the terminology and the affinities of the Hellenistic mystery-religions, devoted the last ten years of his life to research into the Iranian redemption-mystery. This subject he found reason to connect not only with the early history of Manicheeism and Mandaism, but also with the movement led by John the Baptist. The recent publication of a German translation of the ancient books of a small sect of Mandaean heretics, who still live in communities in Mesopotamia, has turned attention to their alleged origin as a sect founded by the Baptist. Rudolf Bultmann of Marburg even goes so far as to think that the Prologue to the Fourth Gospel was originally a document of these Mandaeans, and that the Evangelist has literally taken a leaf out of their book and introduced a few lines to turn it against them. I have given elsewhere an account of this most interesting theory, and have shown why some research into the Mandaean literature has convinced me that we shall look in vain there for the solution to our problem, although we may learn much on the way about Gnostic figures of speech and the theosophical speculations of an almost forgotten world of religious thought. But, instead of quoting from any published opinions on this subject, it is a privilege to be able to cite the words of an unrivalled authority in this field of research—Professor F. C. Burkitt of Cambridge [1]: 'I feel that Reitzenstein, and especially Professor Bultmann, are on a wrong track, and that the Fourth Gospel is not derived from Mandaism or pre-Mandaism. I venture to think that the Fourth Gospel is saturated with sacramentalism, but [the author] is insisting that the sacraments which the Christian practises shall be *understood*, i.e. the proper Christian is also the proper " Gnostic." Gnosticism was intensely sacramental—as one sees from *Pistis Sophia*. I also think Schweitzer is right in saying that the Jesus of the Fourth Gospel does not institute the Christian sacraments; but he prophesies their institution and expounds them.'

This brings us back to the point where we found ourselves just now—that the Fourth Gospel is an interpretation of Jesus as well as a record of His ministry. In their conflict with rival systems of thought Christian thinkers found a vocabulary, and even appropriated forms of thought, to set forth the relation of Jesus to the universe as a whole. But whereas at one time it was usual to trace the leading ideas of the Prologue to Greek philosophy, it is now more commonly recognized that we do not need to go beyond Judaism for the idea of the Logos, and that Hellenistic mysticism, rather than Stoicism, in its impact

[1] From a letter of February 8, 1927.

upon the life and thought of the Diaspora, had prepared the way for some of the notable phrases of this Gospel.

Still more significant is the trend of careful linguistic inquiry. Here, too, the weight of evidence seems to show that, though the writer of this Gospel wrote with simple ease in a style of the Greek *Koine* that bears many resemblances to modern vernacular Greek, there are yet many idioms which suggest that he thought in Aramaic, and fell quite readily into those vernacular idioms which are most closely parallel to Aramaic usage. The linguistic evidence lends striking support to the reasons we already have for thinking that, however familiar the writer was with the needs of a Hellenistic Church, he was also at home in Palestine. For nothing has ever really discounted the weighty evidence of the Gospel itself that the writer understood the topography, the manners and customs, the religious ideas and expectations of Palestine in our Lord's own time.

In fact, there is a dual strain which runs through the Gospel, and therein lies the essence of our problem. Side by side with an intense preoccupation with the values for which Jesus stood, the ideas represented by His name, we have the strongest emphasis upon the historic fact of the Incarnation and the reality of the experience of His human life upon earth. In this Gospel record we find the historical and the symbolical inextricably interwoven. The symbolical element attracts our notice by the regular use of the word 'sign' for miracle, and by the care with which the didactic purpose of the wonderful event is set forth. In the record of our Lord's teaching, the supersession of the parable by the allegory illustrates the same feature. But does symbolism take so large a place in the mind of the Evangelist as to displace history altogether? Few would go so far as this. The narrative of the trial and crucifixion cannot be dismissed in that fashion, though incidents in that part of the story are strongly coloured by the writer's sense of the harmony between outward form and spiritual meaning. But there are many difficulties that would be solved with some ease if we could treat the narrative as often the work of creative imagination, designed to carry some eternal truth. Some writers, such as the late Dr. W. R. Inge, even claim that the well-known contrast made by Clement of Alexandria between the ' bodily things set forth in the [earlier] Gospels ' and the ' spiritual ' Gospel produced by John is a contrast between the historical and the allegorical, and there is good evidence in several passages of Clement's pupil Origen to show that this was the view of the Alexandrian school. The best treatment of the Gospel on this basis of interpretation is in Heitmüller's commentary, which has been mediated in some degree to English readers in Dr. Lewis Muirhead's beautiful and reverent exposition, *The Message of the Fourth Gospel*. There are limits, however, beyond which this method of interpretation becomes too facile an escape from real difficulties inherent in the Evangelist's union of tradition, theological preconception and didactic method.

Our study of the Gospel will follow three lines of inquiry. First, lest we fall too readily under the sway of one attractive theory, or assume that one or two brilliant books have settled the case for us, we shall try to survey the ground that has been covered by a multitude of eager explorers within the last thirty years. We must not limit our outlook to books in one language, or to one school of criticism. By keeping to some rough sort of chronological order, we shall observe how solutions of the Johannine problem that at one period seem to be regarded as final are left behind a few years later as inadequate or misleading. Yet few theories have been advanced which have not contributed something to our general understanding of the structure or standpoint of the Gospel.

Our next inquiry concerns the Gospel itself rather than the changes in critical theory about it. Starting with clues that have been offered by various writers whose works we shall have glanced at in Part I, we shall try to arrive at some judgement on such questions as these: Is the Gospel the product of one writer, or are we dealing with a composite work, representing diverse points of religious outlook? Can we use the Epistles of John as emanating from the same writer, and therefore capable of throwing light upon obscurities in the Gospel? How does this Gospel stand in relation to the earlier Gospels which we possess? Are the divergences such as to vitiate its claim to be a historical witness to the life of Christ? Is the present form of the text such that an intelligible outline of events can be deduced, or is there good ground for believing that at certain places a rearrangement of passages would restore the writer's original scheme? With such restorations of material, do we find that the Fourth Gospel joins with the Synoptics in providing anything like an intrinsically probable order of events? Does the Fourth Gospel supplement, or even correct, the earlier Gospels at any points in the narrative? What bearing has all this upon the use of John side by side with the Synoptics as a source for the life and teaching of Jesus? Does our study of the Gospel itself show that external influences have played a part in shaping the thoughts and words attributed to Jesus, or affected the representation which is given of Him?

The third line of investigation concerns our interpretation of the Gospel. How far does the Evangelist's cast of mind bring him under subjection to dominant moods, or else stimulate visions which have for him, but not for us, the value of actual experience? When plainly symbolical language is used, is it because the event has suggested a hidden meaning, or has the story been fashioned as a vehicle for a creative truth? If sacramental language is used by the Evangelist in unexpected connexions, what are we to infer as to the writer's purpose and meaning? Is it possible for us to catch the very accents of the voice of Jesus behind the unfamiliar rhythm of the discourses which occupy so large a part of this Gospel? When we have considered all that is strange in the mind and method of this unnamed Evangelist, is there a positive conviction left upon the reader's mind that he has spoken to us as a revealer of the Jesus of history, and also as one who brings us into spiritual fellowship with the eternal Christ?

The task is long and the going is sometimes tedious, but he who endures to the end should find his just reward in a deeper knowledge of the ' spiritual Gospel.'

PART I: HISTORICAL SURVEY

THE FOURTH GOSPEL IN THE TWENTIETH CENTURY

CHAPTER   I. IN BRITAIN AND AMERICA, 1901–1913.
CHAPTER II. IN BRITAIN, 1914–1931.
CHAPTER III. IN GERMANY, 1901–1918.
CHAPTER IV. IN GERMANY, 1918–1930: IN FRANCE.

CHAPTER I

IN BRITAIN AND AMERICA, 1901-1913

As the nineteenth century came to a close, two standard works[1] appeared in this country which represented the main achievements of biblical research as they were appraised in Britain and on the Continent. The article on the Gospel of John by H. R. Reynolds in the *Dictionary of the Bible* was typical of the sturdy traditionalism of English biblical scholarship. The obvious aim of this essay was to vindicate the authenticity of the Gospel against the assaults of critical unbelief. This resolves itself into a vigorous defence of the traditional authorship of the five Johannine writings by the son of Zebedee. Following the lines laid down by Sanday, Lightfoot, and Westcott, the patristic evidence of the second half of the second century is marshalled with learning and skill, and the internal evidence is represented in the form of a series of concentric circles to prove that the author was a Jew, a Palestinian, an eye- and ear-witness, a disciple, the Apostle John. Principal Reynolds had a perfect mastery of the subject; he was fully acquainted with the critical work that had gone on in Germany for three-quarters of a century. His argument is closely knit and most impressive, until the other side is heard. It is only then that we recognize that this is not a judicial summary of all the evidence, but the passionate pleading of counsel for the defence, who feels that the honour of the Evangelist is

---

[1] Hastings' *Dictionary of the Bible*, vol. ii. (1899); *Encyclopaedia Biblica*, vol. ii. (January 1901).

at stake when the traditional theory regarding authorship and mode of composition is called in question. If, however, this was a one-sided presentation of the case, the balance was more than redressed a year later, when the *Encyclopaedia Biblica* offered English readers a remarkably lucid statement of the more radical treatment of the Johannine question by advanced critics in Germany. In this work the subject was divided between two very different writers. The article 'Gospels' was committed to Dr. Edwin Abbott and Professor P. W. Schmiedel of Zürich. Dr. Abbott was responsible for the descriptive and analytical section. In dealing with the internal evidence as to origin, he shows a far more flexible mind than Dr. Reynolds in recognizing the complexity of factors in the Gospel, and he throws much light on the style and method of the Evangelist. His excessive subtlety in finding recondite allusions in the most unlikely places by applying Philonic methods of exegesis is more ingenious than convincing. Schmiedel's treatment of the Fourth Gospel is postponed to the article 'John, Son of Zebedee.' This is a remorseless exposure of every difficulty that the traditional theory leaves unexplained. The argument in favour of apostolic authorship drawn from external evidence, which seems so strong in the familiar English apologetic, is shown to be very vulnerable. But the extreme scepticism of the writer weakens the argumentative force of the article. The Gospel is allowed no independent historical value, and its authorship is regarded as evidently distinct from that of the Epistles. The date is thrust far forward, after the revolt of Bar-Cochba in A.D. 135, to which an allusion is discovered in John v. 43. In one respect only is a conservative opinion strongly expressed. Schmiedel rejects all attempts at partition, for, although that method of critical treatment has been carried much further in the last thirty years, some theories, notably that by Wendt in its earlier form, had already been advanced. The impartial student who now studies these rival attempts to solve the Johannine problem will inevitably recognize the weakness of overstating a case, which is as manifest in Schmiedel, the counsel for the prosecution, as in Reynolds, who holds a brief for the defence.

Such was the state of critical debate on the question of the origin and value of the Fourth Gospel in this country when the twentieth century dawned. Nearly three years went by, and then, within two years, three books came out by leading English scholars[1] to show how premature was the assumption that the traditional position must now be evacuated. The first part of V. H. Stanton's massive work, *The Gospels as Historical Documents* (1903), was devoted to an exhaustive examination of such remains of early Christian literature as indicate the use of the Gospels and the manner in which they were regarded before the close of the second century. The result is a powerful argument in favour of the common tradition (which cannot, however, have been derived from a common source) that John the Apostle and son of Zebedee spent his old age in Asia, and was associated with the writing of the Fourth Gospel. Moreover, a strong point is made of the fact that this belief in the Asiatic residence of John the Apostle was unchallenged in the latter part of the century, even when in three different controversies, those with the Gnostics, with the Quartodecimans, and with the Alogi,[2] it was in the interest of one of the parties to support its case by disputing the apostolic authority of the Fourth Gospel. Dr. Stanton allowed for the possibility that in the Gospel we have the teaching of the venerable Apostle turned to account by another mind of larger grasp, whose own intellectual characteristics and

[1] These authors were the Ely Professor at Cambridge, the Principal of Manchester College, Oxford, and the Lady Margaret Professor at Oxford.
[2] The Alogi impugned the Fourth Gospel on theological grounds, not on the ground that the Apostle John had never settled in Asia.

training determined in some measure the form of the composition.

The internal evidence, which Dr. Stanton left over for treatment in the third part of his work, was weighed with the same care as the external evidence by Dr. James Drummond in *The Character and Authorship of the Fourth Gospel* (1903). The definite judgement of this learned Unitarian divine in favour of the Johannine authorship made a deep impression, for he could not possibly be suspected of apologetic bias, and his decision marked a singular departure from the published views of his venerated teachers, James Martineau and John James Tayler. Dr. Drummond held the external evidence for the early date of the Gospel to be so cogent as only to be set aside by an arbitrary exercise of judgement. That John was the actual author he regarded as less certain, but he is far less hospitable than Dr. Stanton to the theory of mediate authorship. After examining the internal evidence, he found a considerable mass to be in harmony with the external, and the residue to be insufficient to weigh down the scale.

Almost immediately after the publication of these two systematic investigations of the Johannine problem Dr. William Sanday gave a course of lectures in America which appeared under the title *The Criticism of the Fourth Gospel* (1905). Less detailed and exhaustive than his predecessors, Dr. Sanday had the advantage of discussing at large recent theories which received little more than a side-glance in the previous English works to which we have referred. This is notably the case with the suggestion thrown out many years before by Delff, that the John of ancient tradition was not the son of Zebedee, but a disciple living in Jerusalem, of a priestly family of wealth and standing, who later in life became one of the great lights of the Churches of Asia. This is taken in connexion with the curious statement found in some manuscripts of two late writers that Papias in his second book asserted that both the sons of Zebedee were slain by the Jews. Sanday does not definitely commit himself to this view, but plainly recognizes that, if the early death of the son of Zebedee could be proved, it would be easy to understand how the other John might have taken his place, as James the Lord's brother filled the vacancy left by the death of James the brother of John. While leaving this an open question, Sanday contended vigorously for an apostolic authorship (in the broader sense of the term) of the Gospel, which he regarded as the work of an eye-witness.

In these three books, which represent the finest type of English scholarship, cautious, competent, constructive, the reader could feel the swell of a strong conservative reaction. They not only defended the validity of the Gospel as a representation of the ministry and teaching of Jesus; they identified authenticity with the traditional theory of authorship—John of Ephesus, the beloved disciple of the Lord. It is strange to recall how quickly the tide turned once more.

The year after the appearance of Sanday's lectures a book written by a young minister trained in the United Presbyterian Church of Scotland roused a host of readers north and south of the Tweed from their dogmatic slumber. *The Fourth Gospel, its Purpose and its Theology* (1906), the first of many books by which Dr. E. F. Scott has enriched the study of the New Testament, made an immediate impression in this country, which remains after a quarter of a century. It was not a commentary; it was not a critical introduction. The critical debate was treated as settled in favour of the position ' which is now generally accepted by Continental scholars.' The indecisive character of the external evidence drives us to the Gospel itself. By assuming a date early in the second century, and an author who was in no sense an apostle or a contemporary of Jesus, Dr. Scott expounds the Gospel as a reinterpretation of Christianity to the larger world of Hellenic culture under the exigencies of controversy. In this narrative we are to recognize the work of one who identified the eternal Christ of inward religious experience with the Jesus of history, and who went back to the historical record to understand its deeper meaning, and to complete it and interpret it in the light of all that the Church had learnt by faith concerning the person and work of the exalted Lord. One of the most striking features of the book is the vivid way in which the Evangelist's subordinate aims are brought to light. Baldensperger[1] had advanced the theory that the Fourth Gospel was primarily intended as a polemic against the followers of John the Baptist. Professor Scott rejected this extreme theory, but carries his readers with him in the discovery of a polemical undertone throughout, uttered against a hostile Jewry, a rival sect of followers of John the Baptist, and an all-pervasive Gnosticism. On the positive side, one of the ulterior aims of the writer is to determine the nature of the true Church as constituted by the Lord Himself in His fellowship with His first disciples. This nobler ideal of the Christian Society is seen in its continual responsiveness to fresh revelation of truth through the Spirit of the unchanging Christ, in a spiritual appreciation of the two sacraments, and in a pastoral as opposed to an official conception of Church leadership. Authenticity is now detached from authorship. The Gospel will only reveal its eternal message to those who listen to the Evangelist undistracted by traditions and speculations which sprang up, we know not how, in the second half of the second century.

Close on the heels of this epoch-making book followed *The Gospel History and its Transmission* (1906). Earlier in the year the chapters of this book had been delivered in London by Dr. F. C. Burkitt as the Jowett Lectures,

[1] *Vide infra*, p. 57.

and afterwards as the Norrisian Professor's inaugural course at Cambridge. The seventh lecture is on the Fourth Gospel, and closes with these words: ' The Fourth Gospel is written to prove the reality of Jesus Christ. But the Evangelist was no historian; ideas, not events, were to him the true realities, and if we go to his work to learn the course of events we shall only be disappointed in our search.'[1] Like E. F. Scott, Dr. Burkitt thinks that the uncertainty of the external testimony compels us to read the answer to the riddle of the Fourth Gospel within the Gospel itself. The impossibility of finding a place for the raising of Lazarus in the historical framework of Mark decides against the historicity of that story. The eucharistic teaching of John vi. has been transferred from the Last Supper to the earlier Galilean miracle. But 'the most serious count against the Fourth Gospel, from the point of view of objective external history, is the attitude assigned to Jesus in His discussions with the " Jews." . . . There is an argumentativeness, a tendency to mystification, about the utterances of the Johannine Christ which, taken as the report of actual words spoken, is positively repellent.'[2] After describing the debates reported in chaps. v. and viii., Dr. Burkitt concludes: ' It is quite inconceivable that the historical Jesus of the Synoptic Gospels could have argued and quibbled with opponents as He is represented to have done in the Fourth Gospel. The only possible explanation is that the work is not history, but something else cast in historical form.'[3] It is evident, therefore, that the newer criticism of the Gospel may serve an apologetic purpose; and if the words just quoted suggest a harsh judgement upon the Evangelist, that would leave a totally wrong impression of the lecture as a whole. With remarkable freshness of treatment Dr. Burkitt builds up an argument which shows that the ideas in the Johannine discourses are the ideas which animate

[1] *Gospel History*, p. 256.   [2] *Ibid.*, p. 227.   [3] *Ibid.*, p. 228.

the Sayings in the Synoptic Gospels, and leads on to the inference that when here and there we find a wholly new idea, that also is not unlikely to represent the teaching of Jesus. With regard to the personality of the Evangelist, suggestions are offered to show that he was not only a Jew of Jerusalem, but a Sadducee, and therefore the well-known reference to him by Polycrates may have some foundation in fact. ' John, too, who leaned on the Lord's breast, who had been a priest, and worn the High Priest's mitre.'[1] An interesting point is made in support of the hypothesis of the Apostle John's early death. Professor Burkitt shows from a Syriac calendar dated A.D. 411 that among those who were celebrated as martyrs and victors, and the days on which they gained their crowns, we find 'On the 27th [December] John and James, the apostles at Jerusalem.' There can be no doubt that this curious theory of the early martyr death of the son of Zebedee gained further currency from this new and ingenious defence.

An utterly unexpected reinforcement of the critical treatment of the Gospel came with George Salmon's posthumous volume, *The Human Element in the Gospels* (1907). For twenty years before his death in 1904, *An Introduction to the New Testament* by the Provost of Trinity College, Dublin, had passed through edition after edition, and had no rival in its stout defence of the conservative position. In his last years, however, this veteran gladiator turned aside from polemical theology to study afresh the Synoptic Gospels, 'and, putting aside all Church doctrine as to their inspiration or authority, [to] discuss their mutual relations as a mere question of criticism, just as if they had been newly discovered documents of whose history we knew nothing.'[2] This study led inevitably to an examination of the Fourth Gospel,

---

[1] The letter of Polycrates of Ephesus to Victor, Bishop of Rome, is cited by Eusebius, *Hist. Eccles.* III. xxxi. 2, V. xxiv. 3.

[2] *Human Element*, p. 3.

and resulted in a modification of the position he had hitherto defended. Salmon found the Johannine story of the raising of Lazarus a great stumbling-block. It was inconceivable that any evangelist who knew of it would omit an event which, according to St. John's account, made so great a sensation. Yet Salmon remained convinced that the Fourth Evangelist knew the localities, and had trustworthy sources of information. His theory was that the author was John's *hermeneutes* and assistant. ' It remains for inquiry whether this assistant was not capable of ornamenting and making additions to the stories he heard from the Apostle.'

The publication of the first volume of Hastings' *Dictionary of Christ and the Gospels* in 1906 marked a perceptible change in critical orthodoxy. For whilst J. S. Riggs (art. ' John the Apostle ') maintains the traditional view, and R. H. Strachan, in the critical article on the Gospel, concludes that ' the Gospel is a genuine Johannine work from the pen of the Apostle, who wrote from Ephesus,' there are important qualifications even in Dr. Strachan's article, and still more in that by W. R. Inge. According to the former, the Gospel was not really the work of a single individual, but the testimony of a group of eye-witnesses. ' With John's as the guiding mind, they conjointly made themselves responsible for the statements contained in the book.' The dialogues with the Jews and the discourses of Jesus are expansions of fragmentary reminiscences. But while the mind of the writer had a part in the composition of the farewell discourse and the high-priestly prayer, the spiritual equipment of the Evangelist guarantees the fidelity of his psychological attitude as a ' witness,' and we may trust his peculiar and intimate knowledge of the mind of Christ. Nevertheless, W. R. Inge's article on the contents of the Gospel points definitely to the dominance of the symbolic or allegorical over the historical element in the narrative.

This method of treatment was more fully developed in Dr. Inge's contribution to *Cambridge Biblical Essays* (1909) on ' The Theology of the Fourth Gospel.' In this attractive essay the message of the Gospel is presented with great literary grace in what is virtually an epitome of E. F. Scott's notable book. The standpoint from which the Gospel is viewed is best described in Dr. Inge's own words: ' The whole book is a free composition by the writer himself, inspired, as he believed, and as we also have every reason to believe, by the Spirit of Jesus. The value of the Gospel, as an authority for the teaching of Christ, must depend for us, not on the apostolic authorship, nor on the existence of an oral or written tradition reaching back to Galilee, but on our view of the relation of the glorified Christ, or the Holy Spirit, to the Church. There can be no question as to the views of the evangelist on this subject. He believes that the incarnation did not come to an end at the Ascension, but was continued through the ministry of the Paraclete. Each generation might hope to have its message, adapted to its own needs, solving its own problems; a message new in form, but not new in substance and not less truly the words of the Logos-Christ than those which He actually uttered while He tabernacled among men in Galilee and Judaea.'[1] This passage is quoted at length to show that, however satisfactory we may find the exposition of the Johannine theology, the essayist contents himself with the facile solution of our main problem by dismissing any claim the Gospel makes to historical value. In the next essay, Dr. A. E. Brooke boldly faces this difficult question of ' The Historical Value of the Fourth Gospel,' and he shows courage in refusing to be impaled on either horn of the fashionable dilemma—either Synoptic or Johannine, either historical or allegorical—arguing that these alternatives are not mutually exclusive. Probably this

[1] *Op cit.*, p. 254.

discriminating essay did as much as any other English contribution to check the tendency to abandon the historical element in both narrative and discourse in the interest of uniform and consistent exposition. The closing paragraphs call attention to recent attempts of German scholars to distinguish between an original writing and the large-scale interpolations worked into the fabric of the Gospel in the second century.

Two more books on the conservative side came about the same time. Professor Peake's *Critical Introduction to the New Testament* (1909) gave a masterly summary of the debate at that stage. In such matters of criticism Peake always showed the qualities of a judge rather than of an advocate. This gives the more weight to his personal opinion in the matters under discussion, which remained, in spite of his unsurpassed familiarity with all that was written at home and abroad, his definite conviction until his death twenty years later. E. H. Askwith's *The Historical Value of the Fourth Gospel* (1910) is a defence by means of internal evidence of its historical trustworthiness against the attacks of Schmiedel and the arguments of Burkitt. It is avowedly apologetic, but the case is weakened by failure to recognize any departure from historic probability.

So far we have restricted our survey to books by English writers. But it would be impossible to leave out of account the most ingenious, brilliant, and persistent writer on the Johannine problem, even though other American contributions must be omitted from this record.[1] Professor B. W. Bacon, of Yale University, for more than thirty years has written with a fullness and fertility on Johannine criticism in periodical literature,

---

[1] Dr. Bacon is a host in himself; still, the writer regrets that he has not found room for a reference to H. P. Forbes, *The Johannine Literature* (1907), and that he has not yet met with B. W. Robinson's *The Gospel of John* (1925). Professor B. S. Easton has touched upon the Fourth Gospel incidentally in *Christ in the Gospels* (1930).

and the crown of all these studies is promised[1] in a volume, *The Gospel of the Hellenists*. No historical survey of the Fourth Gospel in the twentieth century could possibly ignore *The Fourth Gospel in Research and Debate* (1910), which stood mid-way between the same writer's *Introduction to the New Testament* (1900) and his *Jesus and Paul* (1921). The germ of most of Dr. Bacon's later work is to be found in the twenty-five vivid pages of this little Introduction. At that time he recognized three hands in the Gospel : (*a*) To the ' witness ' may be traced the conscious authority and superior knowledge displayed in a number of passages where the Johannine narrative is to be preferred to the Synoptic. This is the ' Beloved Disciple ' whom Bacon apparently identified with the son of Zebedee. (*b*) The original reporter of the Apostle's testimony, the ' Elder,' is the profound and cultured mind to whom we also owe the Epistles. (*c*) The author of the appendix (chap. xxi.) who compiled the Gospel as we now read it, is responsible for many comments through the book, for the insertion of several narratives which show misunderstanding of the original author's aim, and, above all, for the grave dislocations of the material which led Tatian to make a number of rearrangements within Johannine passages when constructing his Diatessaron. Two features which characterize this account of the origin of the Ephesian Gospel were developed more fully in the two closing lectures in *Jesus and Paul*. The structure of the Gospel is said to consist of the story of the public ministry in Synoptic outline, upon which a scheme of the great religious festivals is superimposed with typical ' signs ' and discourses of Jesus. Also the Pauline mysticism and doctrines of grace are represented as interfusing the record of the teaching of Jesus.

Though this is the book in which Dr. Bacon most

[1] See B. W. Bacon, *Studies in Matthew* (1930), p. x.

beautifully unfolds the Johannine message, the weightiest contribution he has made to the critical discussion is that brilliant but intensely and even scornfully polemical work, *The Fourth Gospel in Research and Debate*. In this exhaustive study the son of Zebedee vanishes altogether from the picture. Neither will Dr. Bacon give any place to 'John the Presbyter'—that shadowy figure—the Jerusalem disciple, who migrated to Ephesus and there carried on the apostolic tradition. The name of John has been attached to the group of Ephesian writings on the strength of the Apocalyptist, who followed a conventional usage in assuming a venerable name of the past to win a hearing for his prophecies. The author of the Gospel and Epistles was neither a contemporary of Jesus nor a Palestinian, but an Ephesian whose topographical details ' bespeak not the companion of Jesus' walks about the villages of Galilee and Peraea, but the pilgrim antiquary of a century after, whose starting-point is Jerusalem.'[1] In the original Gospel, 'the disciple whom Jesus loved' is the ideal disciple who has entered into mystic union with Christ in the fellowship of His suffering and the power of His resurrection. A real man sat for that portrait. He was the Apostle Paul, who in Gal. ii. 20 confesses crucifixion and resurrection with Christ, and a life of faith in the Son of God, '*who loved me* and gave Himself up for me.'[2] But the author of the appendix, desiring to gain apostolic rank for this anonymous work of edification, implied an identification of the unnamed disciple with the son of Zebedee by his skilful touches in xix. 35 and xxi. 20 ff. Yet this is only part of a far-reaching revision of the Gospel by a Redactor whose aim was to establish a place for it beside the other well-known Gospels. Writing at Rome about A.D. 150, he not only insinuated Johannine authorship, but worked over the document, rearranging the material

[1] *Fourth Gospel*, p. 389.   [2] *Ibid.*, pp. 325 f.

to conform more closely to the Petrine Gospel of Mark, which was honoured in Rome, and inserted the story of Peter's denial in order to recount the incident of Peter's rehabilitation and commission, and thus secure authoritative recognition from the see of Peter's successors.[1] Bacon's examination of the alleged dislocations in the text was the fullest treatment that this problem had yet received. He not only found that Tatian often furnishes external support for the belief that the material once stood in the revised order, but contends that a Redactor can be traced at every point where dislocation is evident, and often in passages which by their direct connexion with the appendix give independent evidence of having been introduced by the author of chap. xxi.[2]

James Moffatt's *Introduction to the Literature of the New Testament* (1911) provided the English-speaking world with an exhaustive survey of all the tangled mass of critical theory that surrounds the Johannine writings. No book or brochure or article of any importance, written in English, German, French, or Dutch, can have escaped Professor Moffatt's searching eye. But he who works steadily through the 150 pages given to this part of the New Testament will gather many indications of the results at which Dr. Moffatt has arrived, though definite judgements are not always possible, as he warns us. ' In the literary criticism of the Fourth Gospel one has to jump for conclusions—if one is eager for them—and that is usually to land in a bog of confusion.'[3] He accepts the theory of the early martyrdom of John, son of Zebedee; inclines to the view that he may be identified with the Beloved Disciple and so have been the original authority for some of the special traditions upon sayings and deeds of Jesus; but that neither the Gospel nor the First Epistle was written either by John the Apostle or by John

---

[1] *Fourth Gospel*, pp. 219 ff.   [2] *Ibid.*, p. 523.
[3] *Introduction to the Literature of the New Testament*, p. 617.

the Presbyter, author of the Apocalypse and the Second and Third Epistles towards the end of the first century. He even doubts whether Gospel and First Epistle come from the same hand. The ascription of Johannine authorship is later than the wide diffusion of the Gospel, which can be proved as early as the first quarter of the second century. Paulinism, Jewish Alexandrian philosophy, and Stoicism have all contributed to the Ephesian Gospel, and, though the Logos-idea is confined to the Prologue, its spirit interpenetrates the subsequent narratives and speeches. Yet the theological aim and presuppositions of the writer must not disqualify his work as a historical contribution. In a number of ways the superior accuracy of the Johannine information must be allowed, though the general dependence upon the Synoptic narratives illustrates the derivative character of his work. More remarkable is the way in which the dramatic and creative genius of the author has drawn upon sayings of Jesus, attested as such by their originality and profound depth, in composing the meditations and illustrations of Jesus that are so characteristic of the Gospel. Dr. Moffatt gives some space to discussing the various schemes of ' partition ' and of ' revision ' which are so striking a feature of Bacon's researches.

The examination of the Gospel for evidence of textual dislocation was the subject of a monograph by F. Warburton Lewis, *Disarrangements in the Fourth Gospel* (1910). Working on the suggestion made by Spitta, but covering the ground independently, Mr. Lewis, in this little book, and in some supplementary essays in the *Interpreter*,[1] attempted a reconstruction of the original order of the Gospel. He showed by internal evidence that a number of passages are now found in positions which they cannot have been intended by the writer to occupy. With Spitta, he observes that each of the transposed passages

[1] See Appendix D.

is approximately a multiple of the same unit of length, which proves to be almost identical with the length of the shorter form of the *Pericope Adulterae*, which has been inserted in the Codex Bezae at vii. 53–viii. 11. Supported by this objective corroboration Mr. Lewis postulates a primitive disturbance of the leaves of the manuscript of the Gospel, and shows that the acceptance of his rearrangement opens up lines of agreement between the Synoptic and the Johannine chronology of the life of Jesus. This book and its German predecessors stimulated investigation, and within the last few years this subject has come to the fore in the most recent English commentaries upon St. John.

The eleventh edition of the *Encyclopaedia Britannica* came out in 1911, with an article upon the Gospel of St. John by Baron F. von Hügel, which is important by reason of the author's fame as a religious philosopher thoroughly conversant with the psychology of mysticism, who was also the most distinguished lay member of the Roman communion within the English-speaking world. His theory of authorship is that John the Presbyter wrote the Apocalypse (or the more ancient Christian portion) about A.D. 69, and died at Ephesus about 100; that the author of the Gospel wrote the first draft here about 97; that this book was expanded by him and circulated within a select Ephesian circle, and that the Ephesian Church officials added the appendix and published it in 110–120. Four great characteristic tendencies are traced throughout the Gospel: (*a*) 'A readiness to handle traditional, largely historical, materials with a sovereign freedom, controlled and limited by doctrinal convictions and devotional experiences alone.' (*b*) 'The mystic's deep love for double, even treble, meanings.' (*c*) 'The influence of certain central ideas, partly identical with, but largely developments of, those less reflectively operative in the Synoptists.' (*d*) 'A striving to contemplate history *sub specie aeternitatis*, and to englobe the successiveness of man in the simultaneity of God.'[1]

The emphasis which von Hügel lays upon the all-pervasive symbolism of the Gospel recalls the eagerness shown by E. A. Abbott[2] to find Philonic allegory everywhere in St. John. It was therefore all the more significant that this veteran scholar should register a reaction from this extreme position. Writing in 1913, in the preface to the introductory volume in the series entitled *The Fourfold Gospel* (1913-1917), Dr. Abbott declares: 'Comparing the present volume with my articles on the Gospels in the *Encyclopaedia Biblica* (1901) and in the *Encyclopaedia Britannica* (1880) and with earliest parts of *Diatessarica*, I find that the Fourth Gospel, in spite of its poetic nature, is closer to history than I had supposed. The study of it, and especially of those passages where it intervenes to explain expressions in Mark altered or omitted by Luke, appears to me to throw new light on the words, acts, and purposes of Christ, and to give increased weight to His claims on our faith and worship.'

[1] *Encyc. Brit.*, ed. 11, xv., p. 454.   [2] *Vide supra*, p. 20.

Chapter II

IN BRITAIN, 1914-1931

DURING the next six years, owing to the upheaval of war, only three books were added to the long list: one a popular treatment of the purpose of the Gospel and its message to our times, one a brief exposition for student circles, the third a conspectus of critical theory.

Professor Percy Gardner wrote as a scholar deeply versed in ancient literature and religion, who modestly disclaimed an exhaustive study of the literature of criticism, but came to the study of a few recent works after a careful independent examination of the Gospel itself. In *The Ephesian Gospel* (1915), Dr. Gardner's general treatment resembles that of E. F. Scott. But while he emphasizes the author's freedom in handling his material in the interest of contemporary needs of the Church, translating events from a temporal and spatial setting into one which is spiritual and ideal, and reading back on to the lips of Jesus the Church's experience of the exalted Christ, he does fuller justice than many of his predecessors to the historical factor in the Gospel. He is convinced that 'the writer had in his mind an oral tradition of the life of Jesus which had hitherto flowed apart from the ordinary channels of Evangelic composition.'[1] The Evangelist is conceived as a man of philosophic mind and high religious genius, converted

---

[1] *The Ephesian Gospel*, pp. 74 f. This is really an endorsement of some words quoted on p. 67 from Moffatt, *Introduction to the Literature of the New Testament*, p. 562.

in early life by the preaching of Paul, whose teaching deeply impressed him. He afterwards became an attentive and admiring hearer either of John the son of Zebedee or of one of his immediate disciples, whose traditions, as coming from the Beloved Disciple, he regarded as of special sanctity. Nevertheless, the dazzling vision of the incarnate Jesus had blinded the earliest disciples to the deeper meaning of His life and teaching. To the writer of the Fourth Gospel only those like Paul himself, who had not seen and yet had believed, were in a position to understand the true majesty of Christ after the Spirit. The First Epistle was the work of extreme old age.

Dr. R. H. Strachan's *The Fourth Gospel, its Significance and Environment* (1917), marks a definite stage of the progress from his essay in *D.C.G.*[1] to his more important work, which will be described later.[2] He considerably modifies his earlier argument that the Gospel as it stands is the work of the Apostle John. Following up some essays in the *Expositor* and the *Expository Times*, he offers as his solution of the Johannine problem a hypothesis of editorial revision and recasting. The memoirs or preaching notes of the Apostle were originally arranged ideally. An editor has superimposed on this original scheme a chronological one to bring the work into closer relation with the Synoptists. In addition to the redactional work involved in thus rewriting the Gospel, the editor wrote chap. xxi.

Dr. Latimer Jackson, in *The Problem of the Fourth Gospel* (1918), offered a very full summary of critical processes and theories, and withdrew from several positions taken up in his earlier book, *The Fourth Gospel and Some Recent German Criticism* (1906). The view finally adopted, in language of extreme caution, is that the Gospel, after long and careful preparation in collaboration with an inner circle, was left unfinished when the author died.

[1] *Vide supra*, p. 27. [2] *Vide infra*, p. 46.

He may possibly have been the Beloved Disciple, but was certainly not the son of Zebedee. Internal evidence points to Jewish penmanship, but not to the first-hand information of an eye-witness. After his death the original treatise of the Evangelist was supplemented, interpolated, and perhaps modified, by editorial hands. Yet these Redactors, differing in mental calibre and trend of thought, who belonged to the Johannine school at Ephesus, lent a semblance of unity to the expanded work. The Gospel may only with cautious reservations be used as a source for the life of Jesus, but there is a deposit of genuine reminiscences, both of deed and word, embedded in it. The chief value lies in the spiritual affinity of the Evangelist with Jesus. ' In his spiritual Gospel the Christ of his experience is accordingly invested with a personality which, tremendous in its impressiveness, cannot for a moment be regarded as naught but the mere creation of pious fancy.'[1]

Two books of lasting importance reopened the Johannine discussion shortly after the war. Archdeacon R. H. Charles's monumental commentary on Revelation (*International Critical Commentary*, 2 vols., 1920) made a valuable indirect contribution to our problem in his ' Short Grammar of the Apocalypse,' which deserves to rank with E. A. Abbott's *Johannine Vocabulary* (1905) and *Johannine Grammar* (1906). It offers philological support to the theory of a separate authorship of Gospel and Apocalypse. The latter is ascribed to a prophet John, a Galilean disciple who reached Asia Minor, but left his work unfinished, to suffer clumsy editing at the hands of a disciple. The Gospel and three Epistles are credited to the presbyter John, the Apostle of that name having died a martyr's death before A.D. 70.

Within a few months Dr. Charles's book was followed by the third volume of that massive work, *The Gospels as*

[1] *Problem of the Fourth Gospel*, p. 133.

Historical Documents (1920),[1] in which Professor Stanton gives a masterly examination of all the critical problems that gather round the Fourth Gospel. His main conclusions are that the author was a disciple of John the Apostle, and that he embodied the oral tradition which his beloved master had given so often in his later years at Ephesus. This author was possibly a Palestinian Jew, who, while still a boy, had seen and heard Jesus, and therefore adds his personal testimony to the Johannine tradition. The last chapter was added shortly after by another member of the Johannine circle at Ephesus. The author of the Gospel had already written the First Epistle, and had written the body of the Gospel before he composed the Prologue. This was not a philosophical thesis which the main part of the Gospel was written to illustrate. On the contrary, after years of meditation and teaching and brooding over those reminiscences of St. John (which were wrought into the Gospel), he discovered at last in the Logos idea the worthiest expression of his belief regarding the Person of Christ. After carefully considering the various theories of interpolation and dislocation, Dr. Stanton decides against any displacement on a large scale, but recognizes that the structure of the Gospel is looser than was at one time supposed; and 'that in a few instances editorial remarks have been introduced, and sayings added in a manner inappropriate to the context.'[2] The perplexing arrangement is partly accounted for by emphasizing the formative influence of oral teaching and preaching in the shaping of the Gospel.[3] A good instance is the explanation offered for the position of the eucharistic discourse in chap. vi.: 'We may then reasonably

---

[1] *Vide supra*, p. 21.   [2] *G. H. D.* iii., p. 73.
[3] This anticipation of the method of the *formgeschichtliche Schule* was independent on Dr. Stanton's part. There is no evidence that he had read the two books which started this new movement in Gospel criticism, M. Dibelius, *Die Formgeschichte des Evangeliums* (1918), and K. L. Schmidt, *Der Rahmen der Geschichte Jesu* (1919).

conjecture that he was led to place the whole of this discourse-matter where he does, just after the miracle of the feeding, from his having been accustomed to use that miracle in his instruction of Christian assemblies as a text for setting forth Jesus as the living bread.'[1]

In *The Beloved Disciple* (1922), Dr. A. E. Garvie finds a solution of the problem by tracing three hands in the composition. First, and in the background, stands the Witness, here identified with ' the disciple whom Jesus loved,' but not with the son of Zebedee. He was a Judaean, a wealthy citizen of Jerusalem closely connected with the family of the High Priest, acquainted with the secret machinations of the hostile party as well as with the currents of popular opinion. He was probably the host who provided the guest-chamber for the Last Supper and gave hospitality to some of the disciples. In the foreground stands the Evangelist, a disciple of the Witness, who wrote the Prologue and preserved the mingled reminiscences and reflections of the Witness, sometimes incorporating his own comments. The Evangelist may be identified with John the Presbyter. Hovering near is the elusive figure of Bacon's Redactor, whose activities have been considerably reduced by Dr. Garvie, though chaps. vi. and xxi. are assigned to him, as well as a few other passages varying in length from seventeen verses to a single verse. Dr. Garvie holds the historical value of this Gospel in high esteem. ' The Witness has reproduced the thought of Jesus in his own speech, and the Evangelist may have further modified the language. And yet, making all due allowance for these changes, surely reminiscences were preserved and developed by the Spirit of Truth in the reflections of the Witness, which warrant our feeling that we are really getting closer to the very mind and heart of the Christ of our faith than we do in the Synoptics.'[2]

[1] *G. H. D.* iii., pp. 239 f.   [2] *Beloved Disciple*, p. 240.

Just before the appearance of this stimulating criticism of recent theories, with its attractive solution, a new direction was given to Johannine criticism by Professor C. F. Burney's *The Aramaic Origin of the Fourth Gospel* (1922). It had always been seen that internal evidence favoured a Palestinian source, but the linguistic argument for Jewish authorship had been considerably shaken by Deissmann's parallels from the papyri to the Johannine sentence-structure.[1] Now, not long after Dr. Rendel Harris[2] had marshalled afresh the evidence for a Jewish rather than a Greek origin of the Logos doctrine of the Prologue, Dr. Burney flung horse, foot, and artillery into the fray, to the confusion of those who believed themselves secure in the victory of Hellenism. Against such a mass of linguistic detail no casual impressionism could stand its ground. Unfortunately, Dr. Burney carried his victory too far. That the Fourth Evangelist thought in Aramaic as his mother-tongue may be regarded as established. That the Gospel was actually written in Aramaic and later translated into Greek is a very doubtful assertion.[3] The author claimed that his theory, if soundly based, 'must surely effect something like a revolution in current Johannine criticism; for, while cutting at the roots of the fashionable assumptions of a particular school of critics, it may be held to go even farther, and to demand a re-examination, if not a reconstruction, of certain fundamental postulates which have hitherto been accepted by all schools of criticism.'[4] On the linguistic question Dr. Burney, as a great Aramaic specialist, spoke with authority. On other points of criticism his views are

---

[1] *Light from the Ancient East* (English trans.), ed. 1, pp. 127 ff.; ed. 2, pp. 131 ff.
[2] *The Origin of the Prologue to St. John's Gospel* (1917).
[3] On this subject see the writer's 'Semitisms in the New Testament,' an appendix to J. H. Moulton's *Grammar of New Testament Greek*, vol. ii., esp. pp. 483 f.
[4] *Aramaic Origin of the Fourth Gospel*, p. 126.

interesting. He regarded the Gospel as a product of Palestinian thought, written in Aramaic by one who was thoroughly familiar with rabbinic speculation, and knew his Old Testament, not through the LXX, but in the original language. Alexandrian influence is to be dismissed as a figment, the place of writing suggested is Antioch, and the date about A.D. 75-80. Dr. Burney follows many other recent scholars in accepting the early martyrdom of John, son of Zebedee, as proved, identifying the author of the Gospel with that of the three Epistles, and inclining to the theory that the same author also wrote the Apocalypse. This man is supposed to have been a young disciple of our Lord, of a priestly family living in Jerusalem, whose rabbinical training and home circumstances were not unlike those of Saul of Tarsus, so that the teaching of that great Apostle would make a special appeal to him in later years. After writing the Gospel, he moved to Ephesus. Here he may have written the Apocalypse in the Greek, which was not yet a familiar tool, whilst the amanuensis to whom he dictated the Epistles corrected the Greek and translated the Gospel.

Two little books should now be mentioned, which stand in a class by themselves. They are not concerned with the kind of critical discussion of which we have been thinking, where it is quite possible not to see the wood for the trees. One is a posthumous essay by Canon Scott Holland, *The Fourth Gospel*, which first appeared in 1920 as the second part of a composite book,[1] and was republished separately in 1923. The other is by Dean Armitage Robinson, containing two lectures on *The Historical Character of St. John's Gospel*, originally published in 1908, of which a second edition was issued in 1929, with the addition of a lecture delivered in 1922 on ' The Present

---

[1] *The Philosophy of Faith and the Fourth Gospel*. This book was edited by Canon Wilfrid J. Richmond, whose work, *The Gospel of the Rejection* (1906), deserves mention.

Value of the Fourth Gospel.' The two authors are alike in their firm conviction that internal evidence proves a general faithfulness to historic fact, and leads to the discovery that it is the Fourth Gospel which gives coherence and intelligibility to the Synoptic narrative of the ministry. They share the belief that ' St. John the Apostle is the actual author, or, at any rate, that his memories, collected and guaranteed for us by one of his disciples, lie behind the book and render it an historical document of the first importance.'[1] Dr. Armitage Robinson allows much to theological interpretation and reflection, but demands at the source ' a great mind and a great experience, an intimate discipleship, and a long life of brooding over the amazing events of the world's greatest tragedy.' In view of this scholar's life-long studies in the second century, great weight attaches to his statement, ' I cannot find a place for this document there.' The dim figure of ' John the Presbyter ' at Ephesus makes no appeal to him, nor can he conceive that the Church could have been led to confuse him with St. John the Apostle and the writer of the Fourth Gospel. ' That mole never made such a mountain.'[2]

Canon B. H. Streeter's *The Four Gospels* (1924) is notable rather for its valuable contribution to the early history of the text of the New Testament, and for its exposition of the Proto-Luke theory and of the Four-Document hypothesis as a solution of the Synoptic problem, than for a complete survey of the Johannine problem. But emphasis is laid on the local origin of the form of the tradition, which finds expression in the different Gospels, and this prepares the way for a study of John. A careful examination of the relation of this Gospel to the Synoptics shows that Mark and Luke have influenced the writer, but not Matthew. The difference between the Johannine

[1] Robinson, *Historical Character of the Fourth Gospel*, p. 93.
[2] *Ibid.*, pp. 101 f.

chronology and that of the Synoptics is found to be merely a difference from Mark, whose arrangement is said to be not chronological. The Johannine chronology, however, is based upon an attempt to piece together scattered bits of information picked up in Jerusalem. Dr. Streeter attributes the Gospel to the Elder, whose signature is found in the Second and Third Epistles, which, together with the First, are manifestly by the same writer as the Gospel. We may infer that he was a disciple of the Apostle John, one who knew Jerusalem and may even, when very young, have seen and heard Jesus. The most distinctive feature is Dr. Streeter's treatment of the Evangelist's mysticism. The Gospel is held to belong rather to the Library of Devotion than to the class of works definitely historical in intention. The Evangelist regarded himself as a prophet inspired by the Spirit of Jesus; his subconscious mind worked with a creative activity that was marked by great dramatic force. He does not invent narratives as an allegorical vehicle for imparting spiritual truth, but uses, because of their symbolical worth, stories like the raising of Lazarus, which came to him orally or in some documentary form, and which, rightly or wrongly, he believed to be historical. Miss Evelyn Underhill is quoted in support of a suggestion that some of the scenes described had been seen by the Evangelist in a mystic trance.

Excellent examples of expository interpretation, based upon a full knowledge of critical discussion, are Professor Manson's *The Incarnate Glory* (1923) and Dr. Lewis Muirhead's *The Message of the Fourth Gospel* (1925). Though each might claim, with Horace, ' *nullius addictus iurare in verba magistri,*' we might say that if the former in some measure reflects the teaching of the Holtzmann-Bauer commentary, the latter to an even greater extent mediates Heitmüller's commentary through a pulpit ministry. They serve to show how an expositor whose critical position is liberal, or even radical, may yet unfold the doctrinal and devotional treasures of this Gospel.

Within a month of Dr. Muirhead's expository study being published three other books saw the light. Lord Charnwood, a historian of renown coming to the problem with a fresh mind trained in other fields of research, arrived at conclusions in his *According to St. John* (1925) which remind one of the impression made two generations ago upon two other men of letters, Matthew Arnold and R. H. Hutton. Much water has flowed under the bridge in the last sixty years, but the conservative conclusions are not widely removed from those which are still worth reading in *God and the Bible* and *Theological Essays*. The trained historian, after a fashion that recalls Matthew Arnold's famous protest against professorial 'vigour and rigour,' derides the evidence which has led so many scholars in recent years to accept the statement that the Apostle John suffered early death as a martyr. 'There could be no better example of a vice which microscopic research seems often to induce, that of abnormal suspiciousness towards the evidence which suffices ordinary people, coupled with abnormal credulity towards evidence which is trifling or null.'[1] The Gospel he attributes to a follower and pupil of the Apostle (not John the Presbyter, who is regarded as a mythical figure), the three Epistles to the Apostle himself. Patient study of the Gospel has convinced Lord Charnwood that it is replete with actual history, although 'the poetry of devotion may have deflected the writer's historical interest in regard to secondary matters.'[2] He also misses certain notes in the teaching familiar to us from the Synoptics ' which we believe to have been the accents of our Lord.'[3]

In *The Fourth Evangelist* (1925), Dr. C. F. Nolloth essays a task like that of Dr. Latimer Jackson, but

[1] *According to St. John*, p. 35.   [2] *Ibid.*, p. 101.   [3] *Ibid.*, p. 116.

arrives at opposite conclusions on most points. The statement that 'the case against the old tradition of authorship is overwhelming' provokes the avowal that study has convinced the writer that 'this verdict is borne out neither by the witness of history nor by the literary and psychological considerations which emerge in the course of a critical investigation of the Gospel.'[1]

The last of the books whose simultaneous publication in 1925 has been referred to is Dr. R. H. Strachan's *The Fourth Evangelist: Dramatist or Historian?* This is an expansion of the thesis set forth in his earlier book, with a courageous attempt to enlist the aid of linguistic evidence on the side of his redactional theory. The title fairly sets forth an antithesis which is vital to the writer's view of the Evangelist's method and aim. The historical value of the Gospel is not minimized, provided that we recognize that historicity is more than antiquarian exactitude, and rests upon 'the assurance brought by the Fourth Evangelist's work that the Christ of Paul and of the Christian Faith is congruous with belief in an historic personality.'[2]

With *The Johannine Writings* (1927) that great scholar and saint, Dr. J. Estlin Carpenter, gave to the world the last harvest of his fruitful life before he passed to rest. The chief value of the section devoted to the Gospel lies in the discussion of its relation to the background of syncretistic mysticism. In the sober and restrained account of critical theories, Dr. Carpenter will not commit himself on the subject of the Apostle's early death. He gives reasons for believing that some dislocation has taken place, and recognizes disparate elements, due partly to composite authorship and partly to some later redaction. Little favour is shown to recent attempts to

---

[1] *The Fourth Evangelist*, p. v.
[2] *The Fourth Evangelist: Dramatist or Historian?* p. 26 n. See further, *infra*, p. 99.

claim considerable elements of historical value in passages where the Fourth Gospel either supplements or corrects the Synoptic narrative.

Professor A. H. McNeile's *Introduction to the New Testament* (1927), while by no means following the lines of ancient tradition, places a higher historical value on the Gospel than does Dr. Carpenter. The main divergences from the Synoptic order are set forth, with the conclusion that on some points the Fourth Evangelist 'probably had the more trustworthy information; in other cases alterations and rearrangements were the result of his use of the events as falling into line with the spiritual scheme of thought which the Gospel presents.'[1] The general unity of the book is affirmed, but dislocations are allowed for, some scribal and accidental, but others editorial and deliberate. Authorship is attributed to John the Elder at Ephesus near the end of the first century. The Palestinian colour of the Gospel is due partly to the Aramaic language, in which the writer habitually thought, partly to his having been at one time in Jerusalem, where he obtained some of his material from local tradition. In his boyhood he had witnessed the crucifixion, and he had at some time known John the son of Zebedee, 'whom he deeply revered, and thought of as the ideal disciple of Jesus, him whom He loved; and from him he gained some more material.'[2] The differences between the Gospel and the first Epistle seem to impress Dr. McNeile more than the similarities, and on the whole he inclines to the view that the Epistle belongs to 'a slightly earlier stage in the development of Christian theology—more ethical, eschatological, soteriological.'[3]

The two books which we shall next consider are the

---

[1] *I. N. T.*, p. 259. [2] *Ibid.*, p. 264.
[3] *Ibid.*, p. 284. For fuller treatment of the relation between Gospel and Epistles see the same writer's *New Testament Teaching in the Light of St. Paul's*, pp. 303-9. Also Appendix B.

most original and independent contributions which have appeared in English within the present century. Dr. Vacher Burch's *The Structure and Message of St. John's Gospel* (1928) offers the astonishing suggestion that John the Apostle wrote the Gospel soon after the crucifixion as a historical record of the ministry and teaching of Jesus as Revealer of God. The work was written in Aramaic, whereas the First Epistle was written in Greek. Then a Redactor, steeped in the language of the Epistle, translated the Gospel into Greek that was more Johannine than his own,[1] adding chaps. xvii., xx., and xxi., the post-resurrection material being taken from the lost ending of Mark![2] The reason given for this last remarkable assertion is the alleged 'Petrine material, with its striking evidence of Roman provenance.'[3] Having determined that these three chapters are additions by the Johannist editor, Dr. Burch discovers traces of his handiwork here and there in the Gospel, for the Evangelist himself is a recorder of what he sees and hears, and is not a theorist upon the facts of Jesus. 'John does not borrow from the Synoptics. John records the Revealer. The Johannist editor borrows for the simple reason that he is not a recorder, and is editing John's record.'[4] Dr. Burch finds a key to the just appreciation of the Evangelist's selection of material. The predominance of Jerusalem in the Johannine narrative is due to the influence of the Festivals upon 'the didactic and episodic contents of the Gospel.' In these we see primarily 'Christ's attitude towards, and religious valuation of, the capital expressions of Hebrew religion.'[5] Four other incidents, which lie outside Jerusalem, are reported because 'they display, either for the first time or so luminously as to thrust themselves out in the course of the ministry of Jesus, the greater principles of His revelation.'[6] Dr. Burch is inflexible in

---

[1] *Structure and Message*, p. 222. [2] *Ibid.*, pp. 173 ff., 186–189.
[3] *Ibid.*, p. 173. [4] *Ibid.*, p. 226. [5] *Ibid.*, p. 66. [6] *Ibid.*, p. 139.

his refusal to see any theological purpose or any Hellenistic influence at work in the shaping of narratives. The language of Mandaean Gnosticism often closely resembles the Johannine phraseology; but this only proves that the Gospel must be put earlier than A.D. 70, the *terminus a quo* in dating the earliest strata of the Mandaean *Johannes-Buch*.[1] Even the term *Logos* owes none of its meaning to Heraclitus or to Philo, but only to ' the list of names Jesus used for Himself that the ordinary folk might understand His revelation.'[2]

The other really original contribution to the Johannine question has been made by a Swede, Dr. Hugo Odeberg, and his book was printed and published at Uppsala. But inasmuch as it is written in English, and originated in studies carried on in the University of London under the inspiration of Canon Box, it rightly finds a place in this chapter. The title indicates the angle of approach: *The Fourth Gospel interpreted in its Relation to Contemporaneous Religious Currents in Palestine and the Hellenistic-Oriental World* (1929). The first part deals with chaps. i.-xii.; a second part will cover chaps. xiii.-xx.; whilst a third will investigate the narrative portions of John and of the Prologue and Epilogue. The value of this instalment of a very learned work is in the marshalling of a mass of evidence to show that in the comparative study of religious ideas the Fourth Gospel will receive light, less in the *milieu* of the Western world of Hellenism than in an Oriental environment. Dr. Odeberg's ample equipment in Aramaic and late Hebrew enables him to show that John has affinities with rabbinical theology, but even more with other elements of Palestinian thought and feeling.

A return to the partition theories of twenty years ago seems to be indicated by Mr. E. S. Hoernle's *The Record of the Loved Disciple* (1931). The Gospel, according to

[1] *Structure and Message*, p. 54.   [2] *Ibid.*, p. 35.

this writer, was a compilation made in the Ephesian Church of two distinct sources, R—the Record of the Loved Disciple, St. John ; and P—a Gospel according to St. Philip. The main theme of P was that by a constant series of miracles Jesus declared His divinity, whereas the aim of R was to reveal the character of Jesus. The source R was in two volumes, RD—a collection of sayings setting forth the doctrine of the Father and the Son ; and RN—a narrative of the disciple whom Jesus loved. Further, this document RN was in two parts, one dealing with the ministry of Jesus, the other with the Passion of Jesus. There were two stages of compilation. In the first, each *work* of Jesus taken from the Gospel of Philip was illustrated with *words* of Jesus taken from the spiritual discourses recorded by John (RD). In the second, this new edition of P was again enlarged by incorporating the whole of RD, some of the first part of RN, and the whole of the second part of RN, except some portions (such as the account of the institution of the Eucharist), which were missing through loss of papyrus leaves. In this second stage of compilation, when the story of the disciple was incorporated, mutual illustration of passages rather than chronological accuracy was the chief aim. Ingenious calculations are made to show the average number of letters on a papyrus page. But Mr. Hoernle goes further, and thinks that he has good reason for suggesting that RN was written in poetical stanzas, which, while not conforming to any classical metre, have a definite beat and rhythm.

This survey must close with a brief reference to two commentaries on the Fourth Gospel which have done much to remove the reproach that has lain so heavily upon British exegesis for a generation past. Apart from the slight and inadequate treatment given to the Gospel by McClymont in the *Century Bible* thirty years ago (with a perfunctory revision in 1922), no commentary on St. John had been produced in English since that of Marcus Dods in the *Expositor's Greek Testament*. In other words, we were without a fair-sized commentary that advanced beyond the standpoint of Westcott in 1881. In 1928, Dr. G. H. C. Macgregor brought out a useful exposition in the *Moffatt New Testament Commentary*, and at last, in 1929, Dr. J. H. Bernard's long-expected work in the *International Critical Commentary* was published in two volumes. Scotsman and Irishman are found in agreement in denying the authorship to the son of Zebedee, in affirming the authority of an eye-witness behind the Gospel, in recognizing disarrangements of the text and certain editorial comments embedded in the text. But whereas Dr. Bernard thinks that the Apostle is the Beloved Disciple and eye-witness, and that the Elder John actually wrote the Gospel, Dr. Macgregor argues that the author is John the Elder, a Jew of Palestine, a young contemporary and admirer of the Beloved Disciple, and that as a boy he may have seen Jesus. (It is left an open question whether he or the Beloved Disciple is the unnamed disciple referred to in xviii. 15.) He wrote the three Epistles. Apparently Dr. Macgregor thinks that chap. xxi. was written by a Redactor, who may also have translated the Gospel into Greek from Aramaic, at the same time introducing a number of additional passages. Is the Gospel to be regarded as history or didactic drama? On the side of history it is described as 'a didactic meditation on the drama of Christ's life.'[1] In the discourses the author is said to be drawing upon the treasury of authentic sayings, and seeking ' as he meditates upon Jesus' word, to fill in also " His silences," and so interpret to his age the mind of his Master. But he would claim that his interpretation has come to him through direct inspiration from the risen Christ.'[2] Dr. Bernard, while allowing much to the

[1] Macgregor, *op. cit.*, p. 22.   [2] *Ibid.*, p. xxiv.

literary style of the Evangelist, finds in the Last Discourses the teaching of the Master Himself, whose last words had been preserved in the memory of the Beloved Disciple, the last of the Apostles. He rejects the allegorical method of interpreting the narratives, with which von Hügel's name is often associated (though it really goes back to Origen), and its implication that in some stories the Evangelist is concerned not so much with the truth of the narrative itself as with the truth which the story symbolizes. Nevertheless, room is left for the possibility that miraculous stories have grown out of non-miraculous events, and in matters of chronology a comparison with the Synoptics leads to some verdicts in their favour, and others on the side of the Fourth Evangelist.[1]

[1] For a further account of Bernard's position, *vide infra*, p. 193.

CHAPTER III

IN GERMANY, 1901-1918

IT is, of course, a glaring anachronism to start with an account of British studies in any department of New Testament investigation and then to turn to the Continent to pursue the inquiry there. For Germany has led the way in biblical criticism, and from the appearance of Bretschneider's epoch-making work[1] in 1820 there has been a ceaseless flow of critical discussion on the Fourth Gospel.

At the close of the nineteenth century the debate seemed to have been fought out in every aspect of the problem, and German scholarship had come with comparative unanimity to conclusions which then appeared radical to the majority of British divines. It is true that Theodor Zahn[2] gave the support of his immense erudition to the extremely conservative position which he still, in his tenth decade, maintains with unabated courage. John the Apostle is credited with the authorship of all the five Johannine writings. The Gospel, properly interpreted, does not diverge from the Synoptic tradition about the Last Supper and the date of the Crucifixion. The last chapter was written after the death of Peter, but during the life-time of John, by persons closely associated with him, with his consent and on the basis of his oral statements. They testify that John was the author of

[1] *Probabilia de evangelii et epistolarum Johannis apostoli indole et origine eruditorum iudiciis modeste subiecit C. T. Bretschneider.*
[2] *Einl. in das N.T.*, ed. 1, 1897-1899; ed. 3, 1907 (English trans., 1909). *Kommentar zum N.T.*, ed. 1, 1908.

the whole work. The veteran Bernhard Weiss,[1] not quite so extreme in his conservatism, conceded that in the speeches the Evangelist has to some extent allowed his own ideas to colour the words of the Master. The leading representative of the established critical view was H. J. Holtzmann,[2] who rejected the tradition of the Ephesian sojourn of the Apostle John, and declined to recognize in the Gospel bearing his name a primary source for the historical life of Jesus. He distinguishes the author from the writer of the Epistles, regards him as one who in the first quarter of the second century wrote a theological work in which, under the influence of Pauline and Philonic thought, he created with great freedom the picture of Christ, the speeches as self-witness of the Logos, and the narratives as symbolical events. The incisive criticism of P. W. Schmiedel has already been referred to in an earlier chapter.[3] It became available for German readers in two popular pamphlets.[4] A younger scholar, Adolf Jülicher,[5] differed from Holtzmann and Schmiedel in attributing the Gospel and Epistles to the same writer, but declared that ' the one unassailable proposition ' which internal evidence can set up regarding this Gospel is that its author was not ' the disciple whom Jesus loved.' By that title the author idealized either the son of Zebedee, or else that distinct but venerable figure, the aged John of Ephesus. To him he attributed the authorship of the Gospel, because in it he was giving the witness of him to

---

[1] *Das Johannesevangelium* (Kritisch-exegetischer Kommentar, von H. A. W. Meyer), ed. 1, 1893 ; ed. 2, 1902. *Das Johannesevangelium als einheitliches Werk*, 1912.

[2] *Einleitung in das N.T.*, ed. 3, 1892. *Hand-Commentar zum N.T.*, IV., ed. 2, 1893 ; ed. 3, revised by W. Bauer, 1908.

[3] *Vide supra*, p. 20.

[4] Religionsgeschichtliche Volksbücher, 1. Reihe, Hefte 8 u. 10, 12. *Das vierte Evangelium* (1906), *Evangelium, Briefe und Offenbarung des Johannes* (1906). English trans., with author's additions, translated by M. A. Canney, *The Johannine Writings* (1908).

[5] *Einleitung in d. N.T.*, ed. 2, 1900 (English trans. by J. P. Ward, 1904).

whom the whole Asiatic Church of that time owed its knowledge of the divine character and absolute redemption of the Son of God. The Gospel was an apologetic against the assaults of contemporary Judaism. Thus the Gospel was in aim not only historical but imaginative, and when its historical tradition differs from that of the Synoptics, as in the date of the Supper and the Crucifixion, it is invariably wrong. There is, however, one matter in which Jülicher shows himself very independent of the ordinary assumptions of the critical school. He insists that chap. xxi. is an integral part of the Gospel. Not even are the last two verses assigned to a different hand, for they are by the same interpreter to whom we owe verse 19a. The last two verses of chap. xx. were not originally intended as the ending of the Gospel, but rather, like xix. 35, are a sort of editorial note after the manner of the Synoptic ' He that hath ears to hear, let him hear.'

But the most commanding figure at that time in the world of New Testament scholarship was Adolf Harnack,[1] with his unrivalled knowledge of early Christian literature. After a careful examination of the external data, he concluded that there was evidence of the use of the Gospel and Epistle so early as to make A.D. 110 the latest date for its publication. But he did not find the same evidence in favour of its attribution to the son of Zebedee. This general belief from the end of the second century he held to be due to a confusion in the mind of Irenaeus, who had mistaken what Papias wrote about John the Presbyter for an allusion to John the Apostle. Not that Harnack favoured the very late story of the martyr death of the Apostle. He accepted xxi. 1–23 as an integral part of the original Gospel, and regarded this as evidence of the recent death of the son of Zebedee, as well as of the impossibility that he could have written the Gospel.

[1] *Chronologie der altchristlichen Litteratur* (1897), i. 320–381, 656–680; *Erforschtes und Erlebtes* (1923), pp. 36–43, Zum Johannesevangelium.

Those, however, who added v. 24 did not think or see that the death of the son of Zebedee was indicated. In these additional words they stamped the Fourth Gospel as the written work of the Apostle John. Their warrant for this incorrect statement is that the writer of the Gospel had attached himself very closely to ' him who witnesses these things,' and tried to bring this out by the remarkable way in which the son of Zebedee is identified four times over as ' the disciple whom Jesus loved,' and is given a position of unusual prominence in the Gospel. It may therefore well be styled ' the Gospel of John (the Presbyter) according to John (the son of Zebedee).' It is thus clear that Harnack recognizes behind the Gospel, not only the author, himself in some sense ' a disciple of the Lord,' but also the more distant figure of the most intimate of all the personal followers of Jesus. The evangelist's aim is to carry over to others the divine life which he has experienced in Jesus. To do this he deals quite freely with his material, which is sometimes taken over from the older Gospels, sometimes drawn from a parallel tradition. At other times he creates the material himself, as a vehicle for higher truth. A characteristic of the Fourth Evangelist is to introduce circumstantially the material and external form, only to surrender its significance in a closing sentence. Thus the raising of Lazarus leads but to the declaration, ' He that believeth on Me, though he were dead yet shall he live '; and the appearance of the Risen Lord to Thomas is followed by the assertion, ' Blessed are they that have not seen, and yet have believed.' It is not always easy to say whether the objective quality of the narrative is historical or is to be taken symbolically. Harnack goes so far as to say that much of the historical and geographical detail ' serves only the poetical purpose of placing the supratemporal and eternal in the midst of space and time.' This prevents the Evangelist from bringing out the development and progress in the earthly life of Jesus. He meets with full opposition from the beginning, and so the cleansing of the Temple is placed at the beginning of the ministry. For the writer the end is already present from the beginning. Even the speeches in the Gospel, as they stand, are the spiritual property of the author, as we see clearly from the First Epistle, which should be read constantly side by side with the Gospel. But the themes of a considerable part of the discourses must be attributed to Jesus Himself, as we can tell by comparison with the earlier Gospels. ' John has composed fugues from the themes of Jesus.'

These were the scholars who carried greatest weight in the field of critical introduction at the beginning of the century : Zahn and Bernhard Weiss, standing for the full apostolic authorship as guarantee of authenticity ; Holtzmann, Schmiedel, and Jülicher, denying any independent historical value in the Gospel as a source for our knowledge of Jesus ; whilst Harnack represented a mediating position.

We should now notice two monographs which made a deep impression on all subsequent study of the Gospel. Baldensperger[1] insisted, as against Harnack,[2] that the Prologue is the key to the right understanding of the whole Gospel, and of the Johannine literature. It is a carefully composed unity, in which the strophic construction is unmistakable, and the antithetic clauses about John the Baptist and the Logos place the purpose of the Gospel in the forefront. So far from striking out those allusions as an obvious intrusion in the hymn of the Logos, he regards them as cardinal to the true interpretation of the Gospel. That is first and foremost a polemic against the sect which exalted John the Baptist at the expense

[1] *Der Prolog des vierten Evangeliums*, 1898.
[2] *Zeitschrift für Theologie und Kirche*, II. (1892), 189–231. ' Ueber das Verhältniss des Prologs des vierten Evangeliums zum ganzen Werk.' See Stanton, *G. H. D.*, iii. 167–179.

of Jesus. This apologetic aim is discovered not only in every direct reference to the Baptist, who is always subordinate to Jesus, but in many subtle suggestions throughout the Gospel. When once we have remarked the significance of the Baptist's consistently subordinate rôle in the Fourth Gospel, as merely a witness to Jesus and no longer the hero of a great prophetic movement through the land, it is impossible to deny this defensive purpose in the writer's mind. Baldensperger, however, pressed his theory too far, and that may partly account for failure on the part of many who followed to give due heed to one admirable suggestion in his book. He surmised that an apologist who aimed at winning over converts from a rival sect, however free might be his handling of the material, would be careful not to create material, the historicity of which would be immediately challenged.

Wrede, who also discussed the character and tendency of the Gospel,[1] does not advance a thesis and subject the whole Gospel to its sway, but offers an incisive critical study of the Evangelist's method and aims. The Gospel owes its distinctive character to a group of features. The narrative is didactic throughout. The miracles have an allegorical or ideal meaning, but are treated as having had an actual effect in creating faith. Whereas in the Synoptics faith is the condition of a miraculous cure, in John faith is the intended result. The discourses are long, coherent expositions on the same pattern, with the object of setting forth a Christological dogma. Jesus and the Baptist speak in the style of the Evangelist himself, which is also the style of the First Epistle. Two stereotyped qualities in the narrative style are the constant insertion of short explanatory comments, and the repeated misunderstanding of the simplest words of Jesus. There is a noticeable absence of dramatic progress in the controversies

[1] *Charakter und Tendenz des Johannesevangeliums* (1903), republished posthumously in *Vorträge und Studien*, pp. 178–231 (1907).

with the Jews. Again and again an unsuccessful attempt is made to seize Jesus. The failure is due to the same supernatural cause. ' His hour was not yet come.' The teaching of the Gospel centres in the doctrine of Christ, who is set forth in terms that give Him a meaning, not only for Israel, but for the whole world. Jesus is described in a series of striking metaphors: Logos, Light, True Vine, Good Shepherd, Door, Bread of Life. The Holy Spirit is called the Paraclete. There are sharply dualistic antitheses, Light and Darkness, birth from above and from below; believers already have eternal life, unbelievers already suffer judgement. All these ideas and figures bear witness to the special background of religious thought and phraseology in the *milieu* of the Evangelist. Though he does not use the philosophic terminology of Gnosticism, he breathes its atmosphere.

The aim of the Evangelist was not to supplement the other Gospels, or he would not have reported much that was in them. The Gospel was born from a conflict and written for the conflict. Judaism is a rival whose attacks upon Jesus as Son of God and Messiah are met by emphasizing miraculous powers beyond those of Moses, by explaining the Galilean life as an escape from the hostility of the religious leaders in Jerusalem, by bringing out the Procurator's recognition of the innocence of Jesus and the failure of His enemies to convince Him of guilt, by displaying the freedom of Jesus in all His resolves and actions, especially as regards the passion and death, so that even the treason of Judas was foreseen. A defence against heathen attacks is not a conspicuous aim, and the fact that Gnosticism, so clearly opposed in the First Epistle, is not refuted in the discourses of Jesus, shows that this opposition was not in the foreground when the Gospel was written. All the references to John the Baptist show an unmistakable apologetic interest. It is, however, an open question whether the Evangelist had in view a sect of followers of the Baptist who exalted his figure unduly, or a form of Jewish antagonism which played off John the Baptist against Jesus. The writer was at any rate forced by the struggle in which he took a leading part to compose the life of Jesus, for this had already become an important and favourite literary form. Miracle and prophecy, passion and crucifixion, origin and resurrection, relation to John the Baptist—all were in the centre of the debate, and were best dealt with in the form of a representation of the life of Jesus. To understand this Gospel aright we must look at what the author, with a superb indifference to material historicity, wants to teach and defend. This alone has made his work one of the most significant and noble writings of early Christianity.

The next group of writers to be considered contains those who evolved theories of partition or of extensive editorial revision. The general subject will be discussed in a later chapter, and an outline of the principal attempts at documentary analysis is given in an Appendix.[1] In this historical sketch it will suffice to indicate briefly the significance of these scholars in the literary criticism of the Gospel.

H. Delff is best known as the writer who linked the traditions of Papias and Polycrates and elaborated the hypothesis of a young and intimate disciple of Jesus, trained in scholarly Rabbinism, a relative of the High Priest, who lived at Jerusalem, had special knowledge of the visits of Jesus to the city, and was present at the Last Supper and the Crucifixion. It is not so often remembered that Delff[2] tried to establish the historicity of a genuine Johannine narrative by striking out as later interpolations a large number of passages throughout the Gospel. The passages thus excised are suspected of trying to assimilate

---

[1] *Vide infra*, Part II., chap. ii., pp. 111 ff.; Appendix C.
[2] *Das vierte Evangelium wiederhergestellt* (1890). See *Th.R.* ii. (1899), pp. 259–262, by A. Meyer.

the Gospel to the Galilean tradition, to current millennarian expectation, and to Alexandrian philosophy—a sufficiently varied assortment of motives! Delff conjectured that these additions were taken from an apocryphal Gospel belonging to the Galilean circle of tradition by one who explained it allegorically. As a finishing-touch, the Prologue was added to bring the whole Gospel under the standpoint of theosophical metaphysic. Delff was so eccentric a thinker that he has never been treated seriously. This reference to his theories is given here because not a few of his ideas have reappeared in several recent books on the Fourth Gospel.

H. H. Wendt[1] was a scholar of very different calibre, and for forty years he maintained with courage a theory that sought to secure a portion of the Gospel as a genuine work of the Apostle John. This apostolic written source is preserved in the Prologue and in the longer discourses. The distinguishing feature of these is the absence of appeal to ' signs,' which dominate the narrative sections of the Gospel. The proof of Messiahship is based upon an appeal to the ' works ' of Jesus, or to his ' works and words,' or even to his ' words ' alone. These discourses originally belonged specially to the closing period of our Lord's public ministry, but have been dispersed through the whole ministry by the elaborate historical framework supplied by the Evangelist. The obvious relationship between Gospel and First Epistle is discovered to lie in a common authorship of the letter and the discourses. In his last book Wendt offers a most interesting treatment of the situation that called forth the Second, Third, and First Epistles to the same Church in that order, and emphasizes once more the different conception of the

[1] *Lehre Jesu*, i. (1886), ii. (1890). Vol. ii., English trans. (1892, with new Introduction, summarizing critical results reached in the German vol. i. of 1886). *Das Johannesevangelium* (1900, English trans., 1902). *Die Schichten im vierten Evangelium* (1911). *Die Johannesbriefe und das johanneische Christentum* (1925).

character and purpose of the ministry of our Lord in the Johannine discourses and letters as compared with the narrative portions of later date.

F. Spitta[1] is mentioned next, not only because of his early work on the structure of the Gospel, which started the modern theories of displacement in the original text, but because, like Wendt, he looks for a genuine Johannine source behind the present form of the Gospel. Unlike Wendt, however, Spitta discovers the Johannine record in a document containing both sayings and deeds of Jesus, written with a purely historical interest. This source, earlier and more trustworthy even than our Synoptic Gospels, was transformed into a theological treatise by an elaborator, who added chap. xxi., introduced material from other sources, sometimes in the wrong chronological context, and interpolated many expository glosses which tended to obscure the primitive meaning. This elaborator, by conceiving everything in the light of his Logos-doctrine, has dimmed the original picture of Jesus as a devout Jew who observed the Jewish festivals, has magnified the miracles, has obscured the eschatological tinge of the teaching, and by his lengthy commentary has often changed the form of the pithy sayings of Jesus.

The more thorough and systematic treatment of this subject by these two writers in the years 1910 and 1911 was due to the interest aroused by two Göttingen professors, whose main achievement lay in other fields of learning: Eduard Schwartz and Julius Wellhausen, the one a classical philologist, the other the famous Semitist.

Schwartz[2] began by observing that the four passages in the Passion story in which 'the disciple whom Jesus loved' appears (by that or some other title) are evidently not an original part of the Gospel. (a) In xiii. 21 ff. the

[1] *Zur Geschichte und Literatur des Urchristentums*, i. 156–204 (1893). *Das Johannesevangelium als Quelle der Geschichte Jesu* (1910).
[2] *Aporien im vierten Evangelium.* A series of articles in *Nachrichten der Göttinger Gesellschaft der Wissenschaften*, 1907, pp. 342–372; 1908, pp. 115–148, 149–188, 497–560.

indication of the traitor at the Supper has taken the place of a sign at the foot-washing. He discovers a contradiction between verses 21 ff. and 28 f. and between vv. 27 and 2. (*b*) In chap. xx. the story of Mary Magdalene at the sepulchre is strangely interrupted by the episode of the two disciples who ran to the tomb. (*c*) In chap. xviii. the incident of Peter's denial, after he had been introduced by ' the other disciple ' into the High Priest's court, confuses an account which otherwise tells only of a Roman arrest and trial. (*d*) In chap. xix. the story of the mother and the disciple before the cross is said to disagree with the statement (xviii. 8) that all the disciples fled. Another mark of contradiction is discovered at vii. 3 ff., which assumes that only Galilean signs have been wrought so far. With this clue to guide him, Schwartz suspects that the chronological scheme, which depends on the festal journeys to Jerusalem, is not an integral part of the Gospel. In the discourse passages of chaps. xii.–xiv. only fragments of the original account can be recognized, whilst chaps. xv.–xvii. may be cut out as a later addition. The Gospel in its original form was a dramatic poem, unfettered by historical tradition, which represents Jesus from the beginning in His divine nature, with unreserved use of miraculous power, who seeks out His enemies the Jews and goes heroically to His death dispensing with any defence. In the double redaction which this basic document received Synoptic narratives were introduced, and it was brought into closer accord with the general tradition of the Church. The ' proto-John,' as we might call it, was first worked over by a ' Redactor,' to be identified with the author of the Johannine Epistles, who amplified the discourses until their primitive form was entirely lost. He it is who first brought in the ideal figure of the disciple. Then came an ' Interpolator,' who added chap. xxi., identified the disciple whom Jesus loved with the Ephesian John, and represented him as an eye-witness and the author of the entire Gospel. To this 'Interpolator' Schwartz attributes the festal scheme of chronology in the Gospel and the anti-Gnostic additions in the First Epistle. Various retouchings may be traced to still later hands.

Wellhausen,[1] working at the problem simultaneously, and not without communications with his colleague, arrives at a solution not unlike that of Schwartz. He stumbles at a number of discrepancies and doublets both in narratives and in discourses. Like Schwartz, he is puzzled by the suggestion in vii. 3 that Jesus has worked hitherto in Galilee, but accounts for the statement by eliminating from the original document most of the Judaean and Jerusalem scenes which have appeared in chaps. ii.-vi., and regarding others as incidents which have been wrongly transposed from their place at the close of the ministry of Jesus. The original document described a ministry in Galilee, followed by a journey through Samaria, with closing scenes in Judaea and Jerusalem. Two typical examples of Wellhausen's critical method may be given. In Mark xiv. 42 we read, 'Arise, let us be going: behold, he that betrayeth Me is at hand.' If we compare with this John xiv. 30, 31, 'I will no more speak much with you, for the prince of the world cometh: and he hath nothing in Me; but that the world may know that I love the Father, and as the Father gave Me commandment, even so I do. Arise, let us go hence,' we must recognize that the Marcan narrative is being followed closely. 'The prince of the world' is embodied in Judas Iscariot, who at the beginning of chap. xviii. appears in the garden to betray Jesus. Therefore chaps. xv.-xvii. are a later interpolation, and the word 'much' in John xiv. 30 (which is not found in the Sinaitic Syriac version) was inserted in this verse because of xvi. 12: 'I have

---

[1] *Erweiterungen und Aenderungen im vierten Evangelium* (1907). *Das Evangelium Johannis* (1908).

yet many things to say unto you, but ye cannot bear them now.' In the next place, divergent views are found in chap. xiv. regarding the Paraclete and the Parousia, whilst one of these views is consistently maintained in chaps. xv. and xvi., according to which it is the exalted Jesus who returns to abide in His Church, and the Paraclete is subordinate to Christ. Wellhausen postulates a basic document which was worked over by a series of Redactors, as we may infer from the many repetitions of parallel incidents and sayings.

Soltau[1] with vivid imagination traced the composition of this Gospel through the successive stages by which three distinct sources were slowly combined and extended. First came the Johannine 'legends,' oral accounts by the Apostle himself. Some time after A.D. 80 these were supplemented by a second source, consisting of passages borrowed from the Synoptics, and thus the basic document was formed. Then about A.D. 130 the Evangelist composed the text of the Gospel from this document, with the addition of some 'anti-Synoptic sagas' and many sayings drawn from the Discourses according to the oral communications of the Presbyter. A decade later, the whole of this third source, the Discourses, was worked into the Gospel. Some time after A.D. 150 a Continuator added chap. xxi., and an Interpolator inserted two further allusions to the 'disciple whom Jesus loved' (xiii. 23, xx. 2 ff). The reason which Soltau gives for the distinctive elements in his theory is that we have (*a*) narratives entirely independent of Synoptic tradition, (*b*) others that closely follow the Synoptics, (*c*) others again that show unmistakable acquaintance with the Synoptics but are given a radically different context. The explanation offered for regarding the Discourses as a separate document inserted

[1] *Das vierte Evangelium in seiner Entstehungsgeschichte dargelegt* (1916). This is the latest and most convenient statement of Soltau's theory, previously worked out in various articles contributed to *Th. St. u. Kr.* (1908, 1915) and *Z. N. T. W.* (1910, 1915).

at a late date is that fragments from the Discourses can be found in other parts of the Gospel.

Needless to say, a brisk debate followed this concentrated attack upon the integrity of the Gospel. We need only mention four of the replies. C. R. Gregory, the well-known textual critic, issued a racy pamphlet, *Wellhausen and John*[1]; the veteran Zahn wrote another, *The Gospel of John under the Hands of its Latest Critics*[2]; another veteran scholar, Bernhard Weiss, added to all his previous books on St. John a substantial volume of 365 pages, *The Gospel According to John as a Unitary Work, Historically Explained*[3]; and a pastor named Heinrich Appel wrote a very lucid critique under the title *The Genuineness of the Gospel According to John, with Special Consideration of the Latest Critical Investigations*.[4]

The next group of writers to be considered contains three names of the highest distinction in biblical exegesis and the history of religious ideas. Although they had all contributed in some special way to the discussions about the Johannine writings, in their later work they made concessions to the arguments of the analytic school.

Bousset, Johannes Weiss, and Heitmüller are alike in accepting the early death of the Apostle and in identifying John of Asia, whose name is attached to the Apocalypse, with John the Presbyter. The two former approached the Johannine question first by way of the Apocalypse. Each was impressed by the affinities between the Gospel and the Revelation. Johannes Weiss[5]

---

[1] *Wellhausen und Johannes* (ed. 2, 1910).
[2] *Das Evangelium des Johannes unter den Händen seiner neuesten Kritiker* (1911).
[3] *Das Johannesevangelium als einheitliches Werk, geschichtlich erklärt* (1912).
[4] *Die Echtheit des Johannesevangeliums mit besonderer Berücksichtigung der neuesten kritischen Forschungen* (1915).
[5] *Die Offenbarung des Johannes* (1904), *Literaturgeschichte des N.T.*, R.G.G., ed. 1, iii., 2199–2201 (1912), *Das Urchristentum* (pp. 611–624, ed. by R. Knopf, 1917; E. T. (1937), pp. 786–803).

offered an ingenious explanation of the relationship. He postulated an apocalypse written by this John shortly before A.D. 70. In later years his apocalyptic ideas receded into the background, and he wrote the Epistles and the reminiscences of Jesus. A disciple of this John combined his master's apocalypse with a Jewish apocalypse written about the same time, together with additional material of his own composition. In like manner, after John's death another disciple of his added chap. xxi. to the Gospel, and expanded the text with additions, comments, and expositions of the words of Jesus. It was probably this Redactor who brought in the narratives of the marriage-feast at Cana, the lame man at Bethesda, the man born blind, the raising of Lazarus, and the anointing at Bethany. The strangest feature about this theory is the suggestion that the original author was John Mark, whilst the Second Gospel was written by a Roman Mark.

Bousset[1] is alive to traces of textual dislocation, and suspects that the passages in which the 'disciple whom Jesus loved' is mentioned did not belong to the Gospel in its original form. He also finds a number of homiletical amplifications throughout the discourses, numerous short glosses, and traces of attempts to correct the text to bring the Johannine story into agreement with the Synoptists. While dismissing the idea that we have behind the present Gospel a uniform work in one piece, independent of the Synoptics, Bousset none the less lays stress on the unity of religious ideas in the Gospel and Epistles, with the possible exception of the passages emphasizing the bodily resurrection. If the Epistles are not from the same hand, they were probably written by one of the Redactors of the Gospel. Indeed, Bousset closes his essays on the literary

[1] *Die Offenbarung Johannis*, in Meyer's *Krit.-exeg. Kommentar*, ed. 1 (1896), ed. 2 (1906). 'Ist das vierte Evangelium eine literarische Einheit?' *Th.R.*, xii. 1-12, 39-64 (1909); 'Johannesevangelium,' *R. G. G.*, ed. 1, iii. 608-636 (1912).

unity of the Fourth Gospel with the sentence: 'Perhaps we must accustom ourselves to treating the Gospel as the work of a school, not of an individual.'

Heitmüller[1] is decidedly more cautious than Schwartz and Wellhausen in attempting a literary analysis of the book. He declares that apart from chap. xxi., and small glosses that can easily be separated, the Gospel as we have it now, even if different hands have contributed to its formation, shows a unity of design. We can probably recognize that literary materials were used and edited. But the whole in its present form was in essentials shaped by the hand of one writer working with a method. The chief feature of Heitmüller's commentary is the stress which he lays on the Evangelist's exclusive interest in teaching and doctrine. History is regarded as only a form of the teaching. 'Everything transitory that is here, everything historical, is only a parable.'[2] It follows from this that the allegorical key is used throughout to expound the events narrated in the Gospel.

The names of many scholars who contributed to the vast literature of Johannine criticism in pre-war Germany must be omitted, but an important book by Paul Wendland calls for special notice, as it dealt with 'early Christian literary forms,'[3] and thus points the way to a line of research which has been followed up with zest in the last dozen years. In the section devoted to the Fourth Gospel, Wendland shows himself to be chiefly dependent upon Schwartz. His own researches into ancient fables and superstitions had brought him to the conclusion that in the writings of Phlegon, a Greek writer in Asia Minor of the second century A.D., miraculous stories could be distinguished

---

[1] *Das Johannes-Evangelium*: in *Die Schriften des Neuen Testaments*, ed. 1, ii. (1906); ed. 3, iv. (1918).

[2] For Goethe's well-known saying, thus adapted by Heitmüller, see p. 234.

[3] *Die urchristlichen Literaturformen* (1912). (Lietzmann's *Handbuch zum N.T.*, I. 3.)

as a secondary strain in the narrative. Applying his principles of form-criticism to our Gospel, he discovered here a similarity in the technique of narration to what he had observed in Phlegon. The constant use of the evidential method, and the conception of miracle, which he had pointed out in different sections, belong to the very passages which on other grounds have been rejected as not being part of the basic document. Nevertheless, while quite convinced by Schwartz and Wellhausen that we must distinguish between basic document and redaction, he finds far more evidence of purpose and deliberation on the Redactor's part, and less confusion, than those two scholars have allowed. Another point made in this book is that the heavenly Christ speaks in John from a supraterrestrial standpoint. 'The process of separating the words of Jesus from the situation, their combination into longer discourse-passages, and the projection of the faith of the Church into the sayings of Jesus, has advanced to poetic freedom in the composition of speeches, as it had passed from ancient epic and fiction into historical writing. But John has not, like Thucydides, a historical interest in putting into the mouths of his heroes what best accords with his idea of the contemporary situation. His purpose is much rather to expound his Christology and his metaphysic effectually by the lips of Jesus.'[1] Wendland looks upon 1 John as a homiletic tractate, which in ideas and in stylistic peculiarities so closely resembles the Redactor of the Gospel that we can hardly doubt that this Epistle was written by the Redactor.

[1] *Die urchristlichen Literaturformen*, p. 308.

Chapter IV

IN GERMANY, 1918–1930: IN FRANCE

In the years that immediately followed the war, no book aroused more widespread interest than Eduard Meyer's three volumes on the Origin and Beginnings of Christianity.[1] In Germany the critical standpoint of the author was looked upon as unduly conservative, though this can hardly be urged against his conclusions about the Johannine writings. Meyer distinguishes the Apostle, the Presbyter, the author of Revelation, and attributes Gospel and Epistles to an unknown author. This is not the Apostle, whose early death at the same time that his brother James was slain by Agrippa is assumed on the strength of the speculations of Schwartz and Wellhausen, even though this assumption involves us in a further assumption that Luke's text has been tampered with in Acts xii. 2. After this, it is rather surprising to read that the identification of the Beloved Disciple with the author of the Gospel, and, further, with John the son of Zebedee, is the manifest intention of the author, who has assumed his mask. ' How this could be denied is one of the many things which remain incomprehensible to me in the assertions of modern criticism.' Although the closing chapter, together with a few additions, are the work of an editor, the Gospel as a whole is bound together by a unity of thought and design which is recognizable in the Prologue. The Evangelist is a mystic rather than a logically

[1] *Ursprung und Anfänge des Christentums*, i. (1921), pp. 310–340; iii. (1923), pp. 174 ff., 633–648.

consistent philosopher, and the fundamental defect of such critics as those named above is their failure to put themselves at the standpoint of such a writer. He made use of the Synoptics and of another written source, from which he derived many facts of considerable historic value, but throughout he exercises the freedom of a dramatist in shaping his rough material to suit his design. Meyer derives the Johannine Logos from Jewish sources. In the first volume he commits himself to the precarious position that John v. 43 dates the Gospel as later than Bar-Cochba's revolt,[1] but in an additional note at the end of the third volume this is abandoned.[2]

Although the name of H. Windisch is not identified with the school of younger investigators who have made *Formgeschichte* the ruling interest in Synoptic criticism, he it is who alone has applied this method to the study of the Fourth Gospel in his famous essay[3] on ' The Johannine Style of Narrative.' Like Eduard Meyer, Windisch calls attention to the dramatic structure of this Gospel. Whereas in the Synoptics we find a chain of pericopae (i.e. self-contained sections), the Fourth Gospel is a unitary composition put together with artistic skill, in which the elements are (*a*) detailed and dramatically presented stories, (*b*) a blending of stories and polemical speeches and (*c*) a series of related single scenes. Examples of the first type were given by J. M. Thompson from the narratives of the Man born Blind (chap. ix.) and the Trial before Pilate (chap. xviii.). Windisch carries out the same treatment for the Samaritan Woman (chap. iv.), the Raising of Lazarus (chap. xi.), and the Epiphany at the Sea of Gennesaret (chap. xxi.). The Healing of the Lame Man (chap. v.) is a dramatic story mingled with a polemical address, whilst the Feeding of the Multitude and

[1] *Vide supra*, p. 20.
[2] *Ursprung und Anfänge des Christentums*, iii., p. 650.
[3] *Eucharisterion*, ii. (1923), pp. 174-213, ' Der Johanneische Erzählungsstil.'

its sequel, the Walking on the Water, are miraculous stories followed by the explanatory discourse in the Synagogue at Capernaum (chap. vi.). These two illustrate the second type. The third type of Johannine narrative method finds an excellent example in chap. i, verses 19–34 and verses 35–51. Here we have two acts : (1) The Witness of the Baptist, consisting of three scenes, two series of dialogues, and an address of witness ; (2) The Winning of the First Disciples, consisting of quite short dialogues which are organically connected. There are other types, such as the great speeches and controversial discourses, the farewell discourses, the passion-narrative, which is more compact and unified than that of the Synoptics, and the resurrection-narrative, which shows the pericope structure more than any other part of the Gospel.

The same writer again chose a Johannine subject for another *Festgabe*.[1] The five Johannine sayings about the Paraclete[2] are carefully examined, and declared to be taken by the Evangelist from a different context and inserted in the Farewell Discourse. Originally they referred to a Paraclete who was to represent the absent Christ, and thus to stand by believers to help them in special need. By identifying the sending of the Spirit with the promised return of Jesus it has been possible to incorporate these sayings in the framework of the Farewell Discourse —but at the cost of doing violence to the original sense of both promises, that of the return of Christ and that of the gift of a Paraclete.

Professor Windisch has made his fullest contribution to this field of studies in his exhaustive discussion of the relation of John to the Synoptics.[3] His general position regarding the origin of the Gospel is that it arose about

---
[1] *Festgabe für Adolf Jülicher* (1927), pp. 110–137, 'Die fünf johanneischen Parakletsprüche.'
[2] John xiv. 15–17, 25–26, xv. 26–27, xvi. 5–11, 12–15.
[3] *Johannes und die Synoptiker* (1926).

A.D. 100, that Palestinian traditions connected with the son of Zebedee, or with a Jerusalem disciple of the primitive circle, may have been worked up and incorporated in it, and that the actual author must have been a Christian of the second generation, who, living in Syria or Asia Minor, clothed the Gospel in the form of an Oriental-Hellenistic message of Redemption. The Fourth Gospel as a whole must be regarded as the work of a single author. Most of the additions and interpolations which have been marked by the discriminating eye of the analyst are probably the author's own additions. The few which strike the eye of every reader may be tentatively assigned to another hand.[1] When we examine John's use of Synoptic sources, it is evident that he knew Mark, and probable that he brought Marcan expressions into non-Marcan, and even into non-Synoptic, sections. He must also have known in some textual form a few Galilean and several Jerusalem narratives (chiefly connected with the Passion) as we read them in Mark, possibly also as they are recorded in Matthew and Luke. He was also familiar with a collection of the words of our Lord as Matthew and Luke have taken them into their Gospels. Of still greater influence with the writer was a non-Synoptic source, whether oral tradition or written, containing a collection of ' signs.'[2] In his main concern of working over these he also drew upon Synoptic material, but only in an auxiliary capacity. Windisch discusses four theories of the relation in which John stands to the Synoptics. It may supplement them, or be independent of them, or interpret them, or supersede them. We may thus sum up Windisch's results : The Fourth Gospel is no collection of paralipomena. There are no gaps into which we can insert the Synoptic narratives omitted by John. Over against a few passages where correction of

[1] John i. 15, ii. 17, v. 28 f., vi. 39*b*, 40*b*, 44*b*, vii. 39 (?), xix. 35, xxi. 24.
[2] John ii. 11, iv. 54, vii. 31, ix. 31 f., xii. 37, xx. 30.

Synoptic narratives might be inferred we must set other important passages, where a clearer reference would have been necessary but is disdained by the Evangelist. The Fourth Gospel is autonomous and sufficient. No passage with Synoptic parallels in John requires a comparison with the Synoptic story to explain and complete it. Any connexion with the older tradition would be rather of a polemical nature. Some Synoptic narratives are omitted because they contradict leading ideas of John.[1]

Though Windisch offered the first systematic examination of the Johannine narrative style, a detailed discussion of one such narrative had already been published by Professor Karl Ludwig Schmidt, whose essay[2] on ' The Johannine Character of the Narrative of the Miracle at the Marriage-feast at Cana ' raises many questions of wider significance. Unlike the other great miracles in this Gospel, it seems secular, and even humorous in character. Obviously it is taken over from popular tradition as an historical occurrence. Its relation to the other miracles recorded by John is found in the principle of religious identification. Christ is that which He dispenses. Here the allegorical element enters into the writer's purpose. The water represents the Jewish ritual religion, with its purifications, the wine being the Gospel, with its spirit of fire. Side by side with the polemical motive against Judaism there may be an implied contrast between John, who baptized with water, and Christ, who baptizes with the Spirit. Interesting analogies are quoted from Philo and the Dionysiac mysteries. Jesus not only dispenses wine, but is the true vine. This principle of identification is happily illustrated from the Odes of Solomon (xvii., 1, 8, 10).

The method of *Formgeschichte* inevitably suggests the

---

[1] *Johannes und die Synoptiker*, pp. 87 f.
[2] *Harnack-Ehrung* (1921), pp. 32–43. ' Die johanneische Charakter der Erzählung vom Hochzeitswunder in Kana.'

name of Martin Dibelius, who devotes the last section of an essay on ' The Structure and Literary Character of the Gospels '[1] to the question of style in the Fourth Gospel. Like K. L. Schmidt, he sees that the Evangelist did not create the miracle-stories which are peculiar to his Gospel; he made use of traditions which belonged essentially to the type of *Novellen* (i.e. popular stories, marked by strong colours and concrete detail). But all these stories receive a peculiar illumination by means of parentheses and appended dialogues, in which the inner experience of the Evangelist interprets the event as a momentary presentation of the abiding power of the exalted Lord. Thus, instead of resorting to the hypothesis of a late Redactor to account for the interweaving of primitive descriptions of miraculous events and inspired interpretation, Professor Dibelius finds the interweaving to be the author's own redaction of a ' novellistic ' tradition.

An essay[2] in Deissmann's *Festschrift* applies the same method to a popular saying. Dibelius examines the saying in xv. 13 (' greater love hath no man than this ') with special reference to the distinction between tradition and composition in the Gospel, and concludes that the Evangelist makes use of definite traditions which he does not attempt to preserve as secret lore for a Christian mystery, but to make known to every one who believes in the name of Jesus. The Christianity of the Fourth Gospel is the Christianity of the Church, concerned at the same time with coming to know the deep things of God and with refreshing the weary and heavy-laden.

But the greatest service that Dibelius has done for the understanding of this Gospel is his admirable article[3] upon it in the new edition of the religious encyclopaedia in which Bousset's article formerly held that position. It

[1] *Harvard Theological Review*, xx. (July 1927), pp. 151–170.
[2] *Festgabe für Adolf Deissmann* (1927), pp. 168–186.
[3] *R. G. G.*, ed. 2, iii. 349–363 (1928).

is significant that whereas Bousset, when he wrote that essay, was drawn towards the then popular theories of partition or far-reaching redaction, his successor emphasizes the fundamental unity of the Gospel, with the exception of the last chapter. Even the comments so often accounted for as explanatory glosses by an editor are found to be more probably insertions by the writer himself. The discontinuities, the parallel versions of sayings, the statements made at one place in a good context, then repeated irrelevantly, are all examined and put down to tendencies which form part of the individuality of the Evangelist. Above all, Dibelius emphasizes Bousset's principle, laid down in the article just mentioned, that from the religious-historical standpoint the whole Gospel is an indivisible unity. On the question of authorship, we find the usual reasons given in favour of John the Elder. But the most important section is that in which the latest theories about the religious-historical position of the Gospel are expounded. Certain terms and points of view which distinguish this book from the other Gospels are due, not to the idiosyncrasy of the Evangelist, but to the world of thought in which his readers lived. The prominence given to such conceptions as Logos and Truth has led many to look to Philo as representing the philosophical sphere in which such ideas played their part. But there are three important points of difference. There is no speculative purpose in John's use of Logos. The cosmic status of the Redeemer is presupposed, not described. All the stress lies on God's revelation to men in the historic Jesus. This same emphasis upon the historical person of the Redeemer distinguishes the writer from Hellenistic mysticism and the world of the Mysteries. No exact examples have yet been found in those analogies which have been adduced from the writings of Hellenistic syncretism. Gnosticism in its narrower sense is separated by its more radical dualism, radical rejection of the Old Testament, and radical correction of the historical picture of Jesus. Gradually a world of thought has been discovered which shared many of the characteristics of that for which the Fourth Gospel was written. This is found in the letters of Ignatius, the Odes of Solomon, the Hermetic writings, and parts of Philo. The tendency to-day is to look for the source of these common ideas, which are connected with Gnosticism in the broader sense, in Iranian religion. It is the Manichaean and Mandaean texts which have lately come to light that point the way to an unorthodox current within the Persian religion. There are four groups of thought in which Dibelius traces this relationship to Iranian Gnosticism: (*a*) Jesus came from Him who sent Him. He is ' the Sent ' of the Iranian texts. In place of the sayings and parables of the Synoptics, in John we constantly meet with metaphors for which parallels can be found in these Oriental Gnostic writings, and such as depend on them. Most striking are the ' I am ' words, e.g. Shepherd, Vine, Door, Way. The divine nature of Jesus can be described in the expressions, ' whence I come,' ' whither I go.' (*b*) So also in these texts we find the Revealer sent into the world as a stranger, whom the world does not recognize, but constantly misunderstands; for He comes from another world, and returns to it, when men will look for Him in vain. (*c*) One of the most striking thoughts in the Fourth Gospel is that Jesus, though possessing all divine power, must yet be perfected by God. He must be ' lifted up ' or ' glorified,' and must ' consecrate Himself.' This exaltation involves in some sense a vindication of the Redeemer, but also the downfall of the Cosmos, and at the same time the redemption of believers. Many scholars at the present time think that the prominence given to this idea in the Gospel is related to the Iranian myth of the Primal Man, which tells how the divine ' Sent ' was ensnared in the Cosmos and then liberated. That this myth played a part in early Christian thought we know from the Odes of Solomon and the Song of the Pearl in the Acts of Thomas. (*d*) The commission which Jesus received from the Father is to reveal. Hence the revelation contained in the ' I am ' discourses. Only in two passages in Matthew (xi. 25 ff., xxviii. 18 ff.) is there a parallel to this in the Synoptics, though many can be found in the Mandaean texts. In the world of thought represented by the Odes of Solomon, the Hermetica, and some parts of Philo, we also find such specially Johannine ideas as the antithesis of Truth and Falsehood, and the association of Light and Life. All this raises a twofold problem. There is the literary task of finding in what form these thoughts reached the author of the Fourth Gospel, and whether, in the Prologue, for instance, he may have taken up an actual text. There is also the historical task of ascertaining what connexions this kind of Christianity has with the type of Christianity ruling in Jerusalem, and also how it stands in relation to the Baptist's sect (the germ-cell of Mandaism), to Philo, to the Mysteries, and to Gnosticism, both non-Christian and Christian. Such studies, however, only deepen our sense of the greatness of the Fourth Evangelist's achievement in translating the message of Jesus into a message for all the world to understand. Yet, while entering sympathetically into the forms of thought that were common to these various religious movements, the Evangelist sounds a note of exclusiveness which warns against the danger of syncretism. ' First in John does the Gospel gain a firm footing in the world (xvii. 15) ; first in John has it reached a form which enables it to win the world, and also to conquer it (xvi. 33).'

This newer attitude to the religious-historical background was first adopted by two other scholars, Rudolf Bultmann and Walter Bauer. Under the influence of Reitzenstein's researches into the Iranian redemption-mystery, and with the powerful stimulus provided by

Lidzbarski's translations into German of the three sacred books of the Mandaeans,[1] they attempted to unify the phraseology and the conceptions which are common to Johannine, Ignatian, Syrian, and Egyptian mysticism by postulating a common origin in Gnostic myths and cults which rose in Persia and spread westwards, leaving a deposit on the soil of Palestine and Syria.

Bultmann first aroused interest by his two surprising essays in the *Festschrift* for Gunkel and in the *Z.N.T.W.* In the former[2] he boldly advances the theory that the Prologue to the Fourth Gospel was originally a document of the Mandaeans which the Evangelist appropriated for Christian use by simply interpolating verses 6–8, 15 and 17. In the latter[3] he ransacks the Mandaean books for parallels to thoughts and phrases in John. He arrives at the conclusion that the Baptist's teaching was strongly influenced by the Gnostic ideas which found literary form in the Mandaean writings; that Jesus, whose public career carried on in independent form much that was first received from the Baptist, proclaimed a doctrine of the same type; that the Johannine Christianity represents an older type than the Synoptic, for, though John is later than Mark, Luke, and Matthew, they have been more influenced by the Christianity that kept closer to orthodox Judaism.

As an indication of this writer's general views on recent discussions about the Gospel we may give this outline of

[1] Reference may be made to the present writer's essay, ' The Fourth Gospel and Mandaean Gnosticism,' first given before the Oxford Summer School of Theology in August, 1926, then published in the *London Quarterly Review*, January 1927.

[2] *Eucharisterion* ii. (1923), pp. 1–26, ' Der religionsgeschichtliche Hintergrund des Prologs zum Johannes-Evangelium.'

[3] *Z.N.T.W.*, xxiv., pp. 100–146 (1925), ' Die Bedeutung der neuerschlossenen mandäischen und manichäischen Quellen für das Verständnis des Johannesevangeliums.'

an article[1] in which he briefly summarized the present situation. (*a*) The older attempts at source analysis have been discredited. The present need is for a more thorough stylistic examination of the alleged strata in the Gospel and a comparison with the First Epistle. (*b*) The point of view of the Evangelist is to be explained from the tradition, not of Greek philosophy, but of Hellenistic mysticism, always remembering that this amalgam contains many mythological speculations from the East. (*c*) The ' Word,' like the hypostatized ' Wisdom,' belongs ultimately to an Oriental cosmological and soteriological mythos, the influence of which appears in the Christian Gnosis, in the Pauline anthropology, and in the eschatology of the Synoptic Gospels. (*d*) The Mandaean sect, whose writings are supposed to show such close similarities to some leading ideas in the Fourth Gospel, probably started in Syria, where Bultmann would find the home of this Gospel, as well as of the related writings, the Odes of Solomon and the Ignatian Epistles. (*e*) Burney's theory of an Aramaic Gospel translated into Greek he cannot accept, but believes some passages were actually translated from Aramaic, and that an Aramaic-speaking source lies behind other parts. (*f*) But, however far the watchwords of the Gospel carry us back in the history of religious speculation, ' The Gospel of John itself is no mythology ; it only employs with sovereign certainty the thought-forms of a mythos, just as it uses the forms of the older evangelic tradition to set forth its conception of the revelation of God in Jesus.'

Bauer first won his right to high rank amongst the expositors of the Johannine writings by his revision of

---

[1] *Die Christliche Welt*, xl. Nr. 11 ; 502–511 (2 Juni 1927) 'Das Johannesevangelium in der neuesten Forschung.'

As an illustration of the kind of investigation which Bultmann desiderates under (*a*) we may draw attention to his essay in *Festgabe für Adolf Jülicher* (1927), ' Analyse des ersten Johannesbriefes.'

H. J. Holtzmann's Commentary[1] and of the New Testament Theology[2] by that same scholar. His own labour produced the exposition of the Gospel in Lietzmann's series,[3] but, when the revised edition appeared, it was discovered to be entirely recast, with copious parallels from the Mandaean books. His latest contribution is a comprehensive summary of work done in this field of New Testament research which appeared in the first volume of the revived *Theologische Rundschau*.[4] In this he expresses doubt about the validity of attempts to determine sources by analysis of style; and writes with general approval of Windisch's contention that the Evangelist wrote to supersede all the Gospels current in his time, but made use of non-Synoptic material in both narrative and discourses. He rejects Lohmeyer's elaborate theory that the Gospel is dominated by the number seven, also Bert's ingenious proposal to regard the narrative of the life of Jesus as only a symbolical representation of the natural life—marriage, birth, childhood, food and drink, sickness, death. Neither will Bauer accept Bornhäuser's thesis that the Gospel was intended to be a missionary manifesto to Israel. Though distrusting Burney's linguistic argument, he agrees with him that the Evangelist and his work belong to Syria, for Bauer himself finds evidence in the Gospel of that syncretistic Gnosticism which is believed to have been prevalent in the regions nearest to Palestine at this period. For this reason he attacks Büchsel, who rejects syncretistic influence because of the scanty fragments and late date of our Gnostic documents. He commends Goguel's *Introduction to the New Testament*, where it is suggested that the Gospel was written at Antioch by the Presbyter John, who used the Synoptic Gospels and a

[1] *Hand-Commentar zum Neuen Testament*, iv. (ed. 3, 1908).
[2] *Lehrbuch der Neutestamentlichen Theologie* (ed. 2, 1911).
[3] *Handbuch zum Neuen Testament*, II. ii. (ed. 1, 1912; ed. 2, 1925).
[4] *Th.R.* (neue Folge), i. (1929), pp. 135–160.

number of other sources, but was edited (with additions) and published by another at Ephesus. Bauer is unconvinced by Wendt's theory of the relation between Gospel and Epistles, agreeing rather with Bultmann that the author of 1 John (not to be identified with the Evangelist) had made use of the anonymous document which was worked up by the Evangelist into the discourses in the Fourth Gospel.

We cannot close this survey of German work on the Fourth Gospel, slight and incomplete as it necessarily is, without referring to three other books which deal with the problem of the religious background. Professor Julius Grill brought out the first part of his learned investigations into the origin of this Gospel[1] early in the century, the second part twenty-one years later. There is a marked contrast between the two volumes. In the first, the key to the Gospel is found in the Prologue, and the message of both is to be found in John i. 4. Light and Life are the cardinal conceptions throughout. The consciousness of Jesus all through is a Logos-consciousness, and thereby he brings light and life to men. With unequalled fullness Grill musters every Philonic parallel to every clause in the Prologue, and provides an astonishing array of parallels to verses throughout the Gospel. At the same time he clearly states the differences that must strike the reader who compares the two conceptions of the Logos—in Philo a philosophical abstraction, in John the creative word of God of biblical tradition, personally conceived. In the second volume, with all its learning, we miss the saving common sense which preserved some kind of proportion in the earlier instalment. The story of the Marriage-feast at Cana gives Dr. Grill a clue. It is the aim of the Fourth Evangelist to set up beside the Old Testament typology, which has its place everywhere in the New Testament, a

[1] *Untersuchungen über die Entstehung des vierten Evangeliums*, i. (1902), ii. (1923).

Hellenizing typology. He ransacks the myths of antiquity for his types, but the main characteristics of the picture of Christ are drawn from Dionysus. Sometimes Asclepius comes in. So Jesus is represented as the bringer of joy to mankind, as the dispenser of the water of life and the personified Vine, as the wonder-working wedding-guest, who is also the bridegroom, as the fanatic who appears as a madman, as the one who is threatened with stoning, as the imperious inspirer of terror (in the garden), as seer, liberator, purifier, saviour, shepherd, as one who calls back from the grave, as victor over death. The influence of the mysteries upon the New Testament is traced, with special reference to the Lord's Supper. The word mystery itself as used in the New Testament is free from any significance. The Supper was first regarded as a farewell meal, where Jesus was host. The historical passed over into the ideal in the Epistle to the Hebrews, where the Supper was typologically associated with the meal of Melchizedek. Then in the sixth chapter of John we see the introduction of the mystical meal in the cult of Dionysus. One last fantasy appears almost as a postscript to Grill's book: the discovery of Parseeism in Matthew, especially in the Lord's Prayer, as a step towards the universalistic Hellenism of the Fourth Gospel!

A much shorter book has already been referred to, which reminds one in some respects of Grill's earlier volume. Apart from the fantastic element which Bauer deprecated, G. Bert[1] offers much interesting interpretation in the light of the Hellenic Logos-idea. But the chief value of the book is its ample list of parallels between this Gospel and the Odes of Solomon.

The remaining book on which a word must be said is one that does not directly deal with the Fourth Gospel. But

[1] *Das Evangelium des Johannes. Versuch einer Lösung seines Grundproblems* (1922).

in his series of essays[1] dealing with the problems of Palestinian late-Judaism and primitive Christianity Professor Gerhard Kittel enters a solemn protest against the scandalous neglect of the most obvious source of thoughts and phraseology in the Fourth Gospel. Writing as a rabbinical scholar, he speaks in high praise of Adolf Schlatter's neglected work of nearly thirty years ago, and indicates the loss which so learned a commentary as that of Bauer's suffers from the author's unfamiliarity with a field so much nearer than those remote regions to which he goes for parallels. When the Swedish scholar Odeberg completes his important work already mentioned,[2] we shall be in a better position to assess the value of the Jewish contribution to the true interpretation of the Gospel according to St. John.

If the survey of French books dealing with the Johannine problem is very meagre, there are two reasons to account for this seeming disparity. For one thing, the Roman Church, while producing many great scholars, does not encourage critical studies in the field of biblical research, and those books which appear with the official imprimatur are rather directed to the defence of established positions than to the contribution of new materials for discussion. On the other hand, the champions of Liberal Protestantism are numerically far weaker than in Germany.

The two writers who aroused most attention at the beginning of the century were Professor Jean Réville, who represented the left wing of Protestant scholarship, and the Abbé Loisy, still at that time a loyal member of the Roman communion. In many respects their attitude was the same. For both of them the Evangelist was a theologian, and history was not to be looked for in

---

[1] *Die Probleme des palästinischen Spätjudentums und das Urchristentum* (1926).
[2] *Vide supra*, p. 49.

such a composition as his. Réville[1] despaired of deriving any trustworthy information from ecclesiastical tradition about the author's name. The name John is due to the self-designation of the Apocalyptist, who claims the rank of prophet, not of apostle. The writer of the Second and Third Epistles calls himself an Elder, but his treatment of Diotrephes does not indicate apostolic authority. The very slow progress of the Gospel into acceptance as of apostolic authorship is hard to explain if it came from the last survivor of the Twelve. The Gospel itself must be interpreted in the light of the Prologue, and is seen to be steeped in the Philonic philosophy. There is a sense in which the Evangelist treats of historical data, but to accept his symbolical interpretation as though it were reliable history would be like treating Philo as a fresh historical source for our knowledge of Moses.[2] Therefore any non-Synoptic narratives must be rejected as of no documentary value. In a book which is entirely concerned with spiritual perception, and which offers drama rather than history, we must not try to base our theory of reliability upon the words of an eye-witness. ' The Fourth Evangelist is not an historian ; he is a seer.' The writer wished for anonymity, and it is only the addition by a later hand of the Appendix (chap. xxi.) which has identified him with the Beloved Disciple. Even this editor did not intend to equate him with the son of Zebedee, for the phrase ' the sons of Zebedee ' has simply been imported into this story from Luke v. 10. The millenarianism of the author of Revelation, and also, according to Papias, of the Presbyter, rules both of them out in our unprofitable search for a name. Réville would date the Gospel between A.D. 100 and 125, as there is no trace of the Gnostic developments which soon after that time came to a head.

[1] *Le Quatrième Évangile, son origine et sa valeur historique* (1901).
[2] *Ibid.*, pp. 297, 335.

Loisy's great volume[1] of nearly a thousand pages appeared within a year or two of Réville's, and in many respects follows the same critical line. The question of authenticity gives way to that of historicity. In this respect we find that 'the theology of the incarnation is the key to the entire book, and that it dominates it from the first line to the last.' It is useless to look, as many writers have done, for doctrine, historical tradition, and symbolism, as three distinguishable factors lying side by side in the Gospel. 'Tradition supplied the author with data which he uses as symbols, while modifying their form more or less, sometimes very considerably.' The book throughout is an allegory of the Logos. As for the writer, one cannot identify him either with the Apostle or with the Presbyter John, nor think of him as a companion of Jesus. He was an Alexandrian Jew, a man of the third Christian generation, who had studied the writings of Paul. The date of the Gospel is before A.D. 125, for it is older than the Gnostic systems of Basilides and Valentinus, and from the letters of Ignatius we infer that a date nearer A.D. 100 is required.

Within a year of its publication this book was condemned by the Roman Church. It is therefore interesting to observe that Loisy, long since untrammelled by any ecclesiastical obligations, brought out an entirely new edition eighteen years afterwards, in which some of his positions were modified. Whereas formerly Loisy accepted the Gospel as a unity except for the last chapter, he now adopts a theory of extensive redaction. The Gospel in its original form was a series of meditations on the theme of Christ, His manifestation, His teaching, His death, and His subsequent glory. It was neither a consecutive story nor a collection of discourses, but consisted of mystical speculations expressed in the form

[1] *Le Quatrième Évangile*, ed. 1 (1903); ed. 2, *Le Quatrième Évangile: Les Épitres dites de Jean* (1921).

of symbolical narrative, of which a theological sentence provided the key, at other times in the purely didactic form of a more extended discourse. The author of this was a profound mystic, converted from paganism like the masters of Gnosticism, but more profoundly religious than Marcion, and less speculative than Valentinus. He was instructed in Judaism, and had perhaps travelled in Palestine. Well versed in Hellenistic-Jewish monotheism he had been won to the faith of the Saviour Christ as a salvation-mystery, and he had completed for his own satisfaction a definition of it in terms of a mystery. The complex work of redaction was first directed to bringing the Gospel into accord with the traditional type represented by the Synoptics. The next purpose was to give a chronological outline of three and a half years (a figure borrowed from apocalyptic symbolism), and to give to the earthly life of Jesus a duration of forty-nine years, so that he should enter into glory at the end of the seventh week of years, after having taught for a half-week. This chronological redaction meant rearrangement and additions, including incidents touching John the Baptist, as well as a considerable ministry in Jerusalem. While retaining some of the mystical spirit of the original meditations, the Gospel has lost in the process of adaptation not a little of its doctrinal transcendence and simplicity.

The controversy stirred up by the publication and condemnation of Loisy's first edition calls for no description here. But four works by Roman Catholic scholars deserve mention. Père Calmes, in the *Études Bibliques*, edited this Gospel in a learned work[1] which allowed for a large subjective element in the discourses, and attempted to combine the historical and the symbolical elements in the narratives. The Johannine authorship was only claimed in a mediate sense. Professor Lepin devoted

[1] *L'Évangile selon Saint Jean* (1904).

himself, in two considerable works,[1] to the refutation of critical theories, with special reference to those of Réville and Loisy.

When 'a fruitful and very absorbing ministry in South America' prevented Père Calmes from bringing out the new edition of his excellent commentary, the duty of writing a new work devolved upon Père M.-J. Lagrange,[2] whose unusual equipment on the linguistic side gives to all his discussions of grammar, especially on questions where a Semitic background is in dispute, an unsurpassed authority. It is unfortunate that the Biblical Commission of May 29, 1907, has prevented a really unbiased discussion of the critical points at issue, for the great learning and sound judgement of this scholar, who lives in Palestine, would carry weight beyond that of any ecclesiastical committee. But the second sentence in the Introduction reads: 'It is no longer a question of knowing if it had as author the Beloved Disciple, John, son of Zebedee. This point is fixed by ecclesiastical tradition.'

Another book of great value by a Roman Catholic writer is the *Life of Christ* by Père Léonce de Grandmaison, in three volumes, of which the first is an introduction to the Gospels,[3] displaying a remarkably wide knowledge of all the critical work done upon the Fourth Gospel. In many ways it is the best summary we have of the modern position of the debate from the conservative side.

Undoubtedly the best account of the Johannine problem in all its modern developments comes from a representative of French Liberal Protestantism, Professor Maurice Goguel.[4] Amongst other preparatory studies, he had

---

[1] *L'Origine du quatrième évangile* (1907). *La Valeur historique du quatrième évangile* (1910).
[2] *Évangile selon Saint Jean* (1925, ed. 2, 1928).
[3] English trans., *Jesus Christ*, vol. i. (1930).
[4] *Introduction au Nouveau Testament :* Tome ii. *Le Quatrième Évangile* (1923).

written a valuable brochure dealing with the sources of the Johannine story of the Passion.[1] This prepares us for Goguel's argument in favour of the author's use of a number of non-Synoptic sources of varying value. The Presbyter John may have taken part in the production of the Gospel, but it was published by an editor who added chap. xxi. and inserted xix. 35. A few redactional glosses are also indicated. The Gospel was possibly written at Antioch and edited and published at Ephesus.

Finally, as a curiosity of critical credulity, we should mention the theory advanced by Henri Delafosse[2] that the Fourth Gospel was a Marcionite document written about A.D. 135, worked over by a Catholic Christian after A.D. 170, and then given currency under the name of the Apostle John.

SUMMARY

In the First Part we have watched the course of critical investigation during the first third of the twentieth century. The result must be disappointing for those who have looked forward to definite progress along a clearly marked route. It cannot be claimed that there is unanimity amongst those who have devoted the best years of their life to the pursuit of this most fascinating problem in the region of biblical studies. Agreement does not even run along lines of national temperament. In each of the countries considered in this survey there are critics of the right and critics of the left. In Germany, ever the home of rigid scientific inquiry, a host of pioneers have been searching all the time in new directions for some clue to encourage an altogether fresh start in Johannine criticism. Originality rather than probability has been the guide of life, and in the desire to sustain a

---

[1] *Les Sources du Récit Johannique de la Passion* (1910).
[2] *Le Quatrième Évangile* (1925).

novel hypothesis important factors are often sacrificed, not because they are disproved, but because they are old-established. At the same time, these keen-scented sleuths of the chase keep scholarship on the move, and open up many a field of study for those who would otherwise seldom leave the beaten track. On the other hand, a comparatively small band of conservative scholars bring immense learning to the defence of the more traditional positions, and so prevent the mere quest for novelty from doing serious injury to scientific soundness of judgement. In Germany, Biblical Criticism is almost a pure science. Great learning and a high standard of thoroughness mark the work done by those alike who are defenders of tradition and those who are detached from the doctrinal consequences of their theories. In France the line of distinction is between Catholic and Protestant, for since the Biblical Commission of 1907 fixed the bounds of orthodox opinion in matters of Biblical Introduction, free inquiry in any true sense of the term has been impossible. Yet even within the prescribed limits a work of great value is done, for the fresh and stimulating theories of radical critics are exposed to a remorseless examination by those who are committed in advance to disprove every novelty that conflicts with ecclesiastical pronouncement. On both sides logical incisiveness is combined with perfect lucidity of expression, and the student who follows the debate is bound to gain something in clarity of mind. In England and America we find that almost every pioneer has gone to school in Germany. Yet when he propounds a novel hypothesis there is usually a difference of tone, and a stronger sense of perspective. He generally weaves the new colour into a pattern where older colours are still an integral part of the design. To some it may seem a reproach ; others will regard it as a chief glory of British scholarship in biblical research, whether on the liberal or on the traditional side, that the religious value of the book is seldom out of sight. The questions which raise the greatest interest and liveliest discussion are not those which lie on the circumference of linguistic or archaeological research, but those which touch most deeply the religious meaning, value, and use of the Fourth Gospel. For this reason the question of direct apostolic authorship has faded from the discussion, but the validity of the testimony given in the Gospel is what supplies keen interest to the special questions now most often debated. We shall, therefore, in the Second Part study in order four of these problems. Is the Gospel substantially from the mind and pen of one writer, and which of the other Johannine books came also from his hand? Does this Gospel furnish any information which helps us to understand the course of the ministry of Jesus, and have we good reason to rearrange any sections of the text in the attempt to find this chronological order? When the Synoptic Gospels and the Fourth Gospel are at variance, is it to be assumed that the Fourth Evangelist is always in the wrong? Is there any underlying agreement between them in the framework of the narrative? To what extent is the course of the story and the cast of the teaching determined by religious and philosophical conceptions which were current in the time of the Evangelist, but which were not likely to have influenced the life and thought of Jesus?

The reader will be prepared for a certain degree of repetition. This is inevitable. Names and topics that have already occurred in the historical survey will now return in a new setting. But whereas so far we have been interested in the contribution which each scholar has made to the Johannine discussion, we shall henceforth consider, not the historical development of the debate, but the several ways in which help may be sought in the solution of the Johannine problem.

PART II: CRITICAL INVESTIGATION

CHAPTER I. THE UNITY OF THE GOSPEL AND ITS RELATION TO THE JOHANNINE WRITINGS.

CHAPTER II. TEXTUAL DISLOCATIONS AND CHRONOLOGICAL ORDER.

CHAPTER III. RELATION TO THE SYNOPTIC GOSPELS AND THE PROBLEM OF HISTORICITY.

CHAPTER IV. THE BACKGROUND OF THOUGHT IN ITS RELATION TO THE JOHANNINE MESSAGE.

CHAPTER V. CRITICISM OF THE FOURTH GOSPEL 1931–1953

CHAPTER I

THE UNITY OF THE GOSPEL AND ITS RELATION TO THE JOHANNINE WRITINGS

THE integrity of the Fourth Gospel is said to have been called in question at an early age. The critical discussion of its literary unity in Germany, from Alexander Schweizer's investigation in 1841 until the year 1908, is fully described in two articles by Bousset in the *Theologische Rundschau*, vol. xii. (1909). It is clear that, though Strauss's famous metaphor[1] of the 'seamless robe' was repeated with conviction for at least half a century, yet all the time the way was being prepared for a new critical treatment of the Gospel. For the last generation it has been usual to regard it rather as an elaborately fashioned garment that has passed through several hands in the process, or, at the worst, as a patchwork quilt.

Yet in fairness it must be recorded that it was an apologetic impulse that started this movement of analytic criticism. Weisse and Schweizer in the early middle of last century, no less than Wendt and Spitta more recently, were moved by a desire to save as much Johannine material as possible. It is perhaps worth noting that, so long as this was the motive behind the analysis, all such efforts were treated as eccentricities of devout scholarship. But, when in the hands of Schwartz and Wellhausen the same method was employed, many

[1] See Appendix C.

critical scholars hailed it as a legitimate weapon scientifically applied. Dogmatic bias was by no means the sole reason for this change of demeanour. Any one who turns to Spitta's *The Fourth Gospel as a Source for the History of Jesus* will find the text of the whole Gospel (in German) with typographical aids to separate, not only editorial additions from the *Grundschrift*, but even the editor's personal reflections from material drawn from other written sources. In the same way, when he turns to Wendt's *The Strata in the Fourth Gospel*, he will again find the text of the Gospel (in German), with typographical discrimination between the two layers, as they have been determined by Wendt. But what a contrast between the two analyses of the text! Spitta has attempted to recover a *Grundschrift* of great historical value written by the Apostle John, which was afterwards worked over by the author of chap. xxi. and enlarged. Wendt, on the other hand, tries to distinguish between an older and a later tradition, attributing the genuine words of Jesus, together with the Prologue, to the Apostle John. It is not that all the 'Sayings' are to be regarded as belonging to the original document, and all the narrative as forming the later stratum. Wendt recognizes that some narrative cannot be separated from a number of sayings of Jesus and must therefore belong to the original layer. At the same time he descries in some sayings attributed to Jesus characteristic elements of the secondary layer of narrative material. We have seen in an earlier chapter that Wendt believes that the Johannine Epistles are from the same hand as the primary layer of the Gospel. For, throughout the narrative portion, 'signs' are emphasized as giving evidence of the Divine Sonship of Jesus, and so creating faith. In the Epistles, as in the discourses of the Fourth Gospel, it is rather the revelation of the ethical nature of God as love that fills the writer's mind.

We see, thus, that in different ways both Spitta and Wendt divide the Gospel into two portions, attempting to conserve from the ravages of criticism considerable sections of genuine tradition, to which apostolic authority may be ascribed. But the results are so dissimilar, we may even say so contradictory, that they cannot both be right. Is it not probable, then, that they are both wrong?

Schwartz and Wellhausen, on the other hand, both start from certain real or apparent discrepancies and contradictions in the narrative. In the result, their solutions of the problem differ in detail rather than in fundamental theory. Nevertheless, every fresh attempt to show by what different hands the various parts of the Gospel were written adds to the inherent improbability that any solution will be found along these lines. There are too many cross-divisions. Some start from the Prologue, some from the Appendix, others from chap. vii., others, again, from the Farewell Discourse. To some there is a clear line of demarcation between discourses and narratives, for others the dividing line cuts across both. Sometimes the seeming contradictions or repetitions are a clear token that separate hands have taken part in the composition of the Gospel. At other times we are assured that the chronological scheme is manifestly a later device. Now it is evident that, if the Gospel is a composite work, the validity of these various criteria will be shown by the convergence of their evidence towards one definite result. This is certainly not the case. It is surprising to observe that none of the writers named so far has made any attempt to apply so obvious an objective test as a comparison of linguistic characteristics.

In one of the most thorough investigations of the questions relating to the literary unity, B. W. Bacon rejects all attempts to resolve the Gospel into documents similar to those blended in the Pentateuch. Bacon classes himself with the 'Revisionists,' not with the

'Partitionists.' '"Revisionists,"' in his words, 'regard the phenomena as indicating a *redactional* process, whose latest undulations only are traceable in the textual transmission, but which centres in the Appendix. This implies a method of critical scrutiny which approaches the problem from the side of the Appendix, taking careful account of the textual phenomena, but without the delusion of those who imagine that there is no history of the evangelic writings behind that furnished by the textual critic.'[1] The method followed by Dr. Bacon seems decidedly subjective. He regards chap. xxi. as the work of a Redactor, a contemporary of Papias, Polycarp, and Justin, whose aim was to adjust the Asiatic tradition to that of Rome. In order to do this, the story of Peter's rehabilitation is necessary, and this further requires the insertion of the story of the denial. It is also his aim to identify the author of the Gospel with ' the disciple whom Jesus loved,' and thus to give this Asiatic Gospel an authority not less than that attaching to the Roman Gospel of Peter-Mark. Other passages also are assigned to the Redactor. The principle of determination is thus set forth: ' Passages connected with the Appendix, if really due to redactional insertion, may be expected to show traces of the fact: (1) in greater or less disturbance of the context; (2) occasionally in a continued reflection of this disturbance in the textual history; (3) in a specially close relation to the synoptic narrative.' It is significant that Bacon reprints from an earlier article his criticism of those who try to discover ' sources ' in the Fourth Gospel. ' Certainly,' he writes, ' the search will not be promoted by the ready-made theories as to the personality of the author and his relation to the Apostle (an allusion to Delff), nor by artificial devices of separation, whether by sweeping classifications, like Wendt's, into narrative material (secondary) and discourse material (Johannine),

[1] *The Fourth Gospel in Research and Debate*, pp. 481 f.

or by fine-spun distinctions of style and catch-words of vocabulary.'[1] With all its critical acumen and fertile ingenuity of analysis and reconstruction, Bacon's great work would be more convincing if some attention had been given to considerations of lexical and grammatical usage. Once without comment he quotes Scholten (on the use of ἐγερθείς in xxi 14),[2] and once he quotes Wellhausen (on the use of μέντοι) where the evidence actually refutes him. Apart from these two unfortunate glances in the linguistic direction, we are put off with a perfunctory reference to a short paragraph in Schmiedel's article on John, Son of Zebedee, in the *Encyclopaedia Biblica* (col. 2543).

In *The Beloved Disciple*, Dr. A. E. Garvie analyses the Gospel into three sources; the Evangelist, the Redactor, and the Witness. But, inasmuch as the Witness is an authority whose reminiscences are worked into the narrative by the Evangelist, we are really concerned here only with two hands in the actual composition of the Gospel in its present form. Thus the theory is a variant of Dr. Bacon's, from which it differs in attributing fewer insertions to the Redactor, and, even more, in tracing the Witness in many parts of the Evangelist's record as well as in some of the more important additions by the Redactor. A more radical theory is that which Dr. R. H. Strachan sets forth most fully in his latest book, *The Fourth Evangelist: Dramatist or Historian?* He discovers in the Gospel two apparently disparate plans of construction. First we have what is called the Johannine material (J), incidents and discourses grouped according to what might be called an ideal or logical arrangement. Then, superimposed upon this, is a chronological arrangement, which aims at giving a chronological form to the Gospel. This scheme is assigned to R—the inevitable

[1] *Op. cit.* p. 480.
[2] See note on this word in Appendix B.

Redactor. A noteworthy feature of this book is a series of appendices in which the author attempts to justify his findings by notes on words and constructions peculiar to R. Whether R is identical with the author of the *Appendix (chap. xxi.) is left open for discussion.

Is it possible that this chameleon-like R has at last come to an end? This is perhaps too much to expect. At any rate, Archbishop Bernard's great commentary, the fruit of a quarter of a century's brooding over the problems of this Gospel, argues powerfully for the conclusion that the whole Gospel comes from the same hand that wrote the Epistles. Even the Appendix is regarded as Johannine, and editorial glosses from another hand are reduced to a bare minimum. Thus iv. 1, 2 has been re-written for clearness, but with non-Johannine touches. It shares with vi. 23 and xi. 2, which also have the appearance of explanatory glosses, the phrase ὁ κύριος, which is not elsewhere used in John (as it is so often used by Luke) for ὁ Ἰησοῦς, except where it appears most appropriately in the post-resurrection narratives. Again, the use of καίτοιγε in iv. 2 is without parallel in the New Testament, whereas John's use of καί adversative is one of his marked characteristics. Apart from several unusual words, v. 4 is textually unsound; xii. 6 is queried, but not upon stylistic grounds.

The literary unity of the Fourth Gospel has been challenged upon the ground that a careful reading of the text reveals numerous seams and sutures. The force of this argument has been greatly reduced by the general recognition that several considerable displacements have taken place in the text.[1] Another factor that should be borne in mind, when confusion of order and even discordant conceptions are discovered, is that the Evangelist certainly makes use of Mark and Luke, and probably of the teaching and preaching of the Witness (the Beloved

[1] See the next chapter.

Disciple); it is more than possible that personal memories and other traditions have also entered in.

There are three snares into which the critical student of this Gospel may easily stumble. We may call them the fallacy of false analogy, the fallacy of anachronism, and the fallacy of subjectivity. (*a*) The great success achieved in the documentary analysis of many books in the Old Testament is no proof that the same method is valid here. Marked differences of vocabulary and phraseology consistently recur when documents have been combined which represent different stages of cultus, historical background, and thought, and may even be separated by centuries of development. Such conditions have played no part in the composition of the Fourth Gospel. If two or more hands have written the several parts which compose the Gospel they must have been, to all intents and purposes, contemporaries. Only the most careful literary examination of style could hope to prove a distinction of authorship. (*b*) It is a mistake to look for the logical consistency of a modern philosophical thinker or a rigidly consistent historian in a Christian writer of the first or early second century. No more weighty plea has been urged against the unity of these writings than the divergent strains with regard to the return of our Lord, and the last things. Yet it should be remembered that, if there is one book in the New Testament about whose unity of style there can be no question, it is the Epistle to the Hebrews. But in that book we find side by side, without any apparent sense of incongruity, the Judaic conception of the two ages, and the Platonic conception of the two worlds, the real and the phenomenal. In seeking to understand the inconsistencies of thought that are sometimes discernible in this Gospel we should not forget that it may represent a long growth in the writer's mind, that the sections may have been written at considerable intervals, under varying influences and in different moods.

(c) Not the least easy blunder to fall into is that of forming a conception of the kind of thinker who wrote the Gospel, and rejecting as impossible all that seems inconsistent with this mental image.

All this admonishes us to seek some objective test as a corrective to vague impressionism, on the one hand, or, on the other, a too exclusive reliance upon deductions drawn from unevenness of narrative or imperfect consistency in the presentation of ideas.

As we approach the question of style, a preliminary reminder may be useful. Unity of style is quite consistent with the use of various sources, oral and written. Lucan characteristics appear when the Third Evangelist is following Mark very closely, when he is writing from other sources than Mark or Q, and even in the Acts when he is far from the Palestinian background. It is possible to test John's fidelity to Mark and Luke in a few passages, and to note even in these sections how his own characteristics assert themselves. Three examples may be offered for comparison.

(a) In the Baptist's proclamation of the Coming One, words were used which are recorded by all four Evangelists, and in the Acts, in almost identical form. The most striking difference is that, whereas in Matthew, Mark, and Luke the adjective ἱκανός is used and is followed by the aorist infinitive, and in Acts ἄξιος is used, and is followed by the aorist infinitive, John uses ἄξιος followed by his favourite substitute for the infinitive, ἵνα with the subjunctive.

(b) In the narrative of the Anointing at Bethany in John xii., the verbal resemblances are so close that documentary dependence is beyond question. The one phrase μύρου νάρδου πιστικῆς πολυτίμου (-τελοῦς) would be enough to prove this. Yet a comparison of John xii. 7 with Mark xiv. 6, 8 shows how the same favourite Johannine construction reappears.

(c) A comparison of the story of the cure at Bethesda with the Marcan narrative of the healing of the paralytic at Capernaum shows remarkable verbal similarities ; but, however closely the words agree, Mark as usual subordinates the verb of previous action, whilst John co-ordinates. (Mark ii. 12 ; John v. 9.)[1]

It would be easy to offer other indications that, whilst the vocabulary of the Fourth Gospel is sometimes influenced by that of a written source which is being closely followed, the grammatical structure of the sentence, or the habitual Johannine locution, will not betray dependence on any source.

Canon Streeter has said, ' The three Epistles and the Gospel of John are so closely allied in diction, style, and general outlook that the burden of proof lies with the person who would deny their common authorship. . . . We are forced to conclude that all four documents are by the same hand. And few people, I would add, with any feeling for literary style or for the finer *nuance* of character and feeling, would hesitate to affirm this, but for the implications which seem to be involved.'[2] This is undoubtedly the general impression that is made upon the reader. The unity is felt even by the reader of the English version. It is still more strongly felt by the reader who is accustomed to the idioms, the turn of the sentence, the vocabulary, the constructions, which continually strike his attention in the Greek text. But we must go further, and ask, ' How far is this impression made by certain familiar parts of the Gospel and Epistles ? Will every part of the Gospel bear out this general impression? ' A complete linguistic investigation would be an enormous task, and we must not forget that this test of diction and style is only one factor of many that must be taken into account in determining the question of unity of authorship.

---

[1] See Appendix B for a linguistic comparison of these texts
[2] *The Four Gospels*, p. 460.

The table of parallels between the style and vocabulary of the Gospel and the Epistles, given by Dr. A. E. Brooke in his commentary on the Johannine Epistles (*I. C. C.*),[1] is enough to prove the general identity of authorship, and the late Archdeacon Charles's detailed examination of the minutiae of Johannine grammar in his monumental commentary on the Apocalpyse (*I. C. C.*)[2] not only confirms this judgement regarding the First Epistle, but shows that the linguistic affinities of the two shorter Epistles are definitely with the First Epistle, and not, as some scholars have affirmed, with the Apocalypse. For the more exact examination of the various theories of partition or redaction on a large scale, it seems desirable to collect a list of idioms and constructions which are either distinctively or predominantly Johannine, and then observe their distribution. As chap. xxi. is the key to Dr. Bacon's position, it is well to study the style of that section of the Gospel with special care. But, to avoid prejudice in considering the authorship of that chapter, our first list[3] contains those peculiarities of style which have most strongly gripped the writer's grammatical or lexical interest during a protracted study of the Greek text of John. This list should be enlarged and applied to the other passages marked R in the Baconian theory, as well as to such systems of differentiation as have already been mentioned. The next list to be prepared contains striking features in the language of chap. xxi., with such parallels as the remaining chapters furnish. The presence or absence of such idioms in the Johannine Epistles should be observed. The reader can then form his own conclusion as to the bearing of such indications of language upon the question of unity and integrity.

The following characteristics may be given as an

[1] pp. i.–xv.
[2] Vol. i., pp. xxxiv. ff.
[3] See Appendix B.

THE UNITY OF THE GOSPEL

instalment¹ of such a complete list as scientific thoroughness would require.

(a) *Preference for possessive adjectives rather than genitive of personal pronoun.* On closer examination this is reduced to a preference for the possessive in the first person singular. J. H. Moulton remarks: "Ἐμός occurs forty-one times in John, once each in 3 John and Revelation, and thirty-four times in the rest of the New Testament. It must be admitted that the other possessives do not tell the same story: the three together appear twelve times in John (Gospel and Epistles), twelve in Luke, and twenty-one in the rest of the New Testament.'² E. A. Abbott lays stress on the frequency of what he calls the 'vernacular possessive,' i.e. the unemphatic use of the genitive of the personal pronoun αὐτοῦ *before* the article. It occurs in John about eighteen times, and in all the Synoptists not more than eight. The same difference in a smaller degree is perceptible in the Johannine and the Synoptic use of μου, σου, ὑμῶν. If Abbott is right in finding a rising scale of pronominal emphasis thus (1) μου τὰ ῥήματα, (2) τὰ ῥήματά μου, (3) τὰ ἐμὰ ῥήματα, (4) τὰ ῥήματα τὰ ἐμά, a better test than the prevalence of the possessive adjective would be the use of the unemphatic genitive of the pronoun.³

(b) One of the most striking features of the syntax of the Johannine writings is the extraordinarily free use of the particle ἵνα with the subjunctive, where the idea of purpose is not even latent. The development of this surrogate for the infinitive was part of a widespread tendency in Hellenistic, as can be seen by the victorious exclusion of the infinitive in every dialect but one of Modern Greek. Some of its uses are shared with other writers of the New Testament, others were very common in the *Koine*, and

¹ See the tables given in Appendix B.
² *Grammar of New Testament Greek*, vol. i., p. 40, n. 1.
³ See table in *Johannine Grammar*, 2560 ff.

can be paralleled easily in Epictetus. But specially Johannine in the New Testament is the elliptical use in the phrase ἀλλ' ἵνα, its substitution for the explanatory (acc. and) infinitive after a demonstrative, its use as a temporal particle after a noun of time, and after combinations of ἐστίν with a substantive or an adjective.

(c) Πᾶς ὁ, c. pres. part., where the meaning is no more than 'he who,' is of course not peculiar to John, and is found five times in Matthew in the Sermon on the Mount, and five times in Luke. But its occurrence thirteen times in the Fourth Gospel, thirteen times in the First, and once in the Second Epistle, is significant.

(d) Akin to this is the *collective use of* πᾶν followed by ὁ three times in the Gospel, and once by τό in the First Epistle.

(e) The use of ἄν (for ἐάν), *if*, is peculiar to this Gospel in the New Testament (apart from the reading of D at Matt. xxviii. 14), and is found six times.

(f) The temporal use of ὡς οὖν, *now when*, six times, and in the reverse order three times, occurs nowhere else in the New Testament (Col. ii. 6 not being an exception, for ὡς there = *as*).

(g) Μέντοι comes five times in John, elsewhere in the New Testament only three times (2 Timothy, James, Jude). This is of special interest, as Wellhausen (followed by Bacon) says that the appearance of this word in xii. 42 is evidence of the Redactor's hand, for elsewhere this word is only found in late passages.

(h) Another point may be mentioned as an instance of Johannine usage, though it is rarely referred to in discussions on the unity of these writings. From time to time we find an *interchange of synonyms in the same sentence,* or the same context, in such a way as to raise, for any other writer, a wonder whether a distinction of meaning should not be enforced. Indeed, in the older commentaries great ingenuity was displayed over some of these Johannine passages. The two clearest instances are the interchange of αἰτέω and ἐρωτάω, and of φιλέω and ἀγαπάω. May we not add, of βόσκω and ποιμαίνω, and of ἀρνία and προβάτια? We should also include λαλέω and λέγω, as well as ποιέω and πράσσω.

A study of the tables given in Appendix B will impress different minds in different ways. It would be absurd to claim that they amount to a demonstration. We may, however, point out that there is a remarkable distribution of these characteristics through all parts of the Gospel, narrative and discourse, Galilean and Judaean. But the present writer, to his surprise, has been led by the study to change his former belief that the Appendix came from a different hand than that which wrote the rest of the Gospel. There are verses in the Appendix, such as 24 and 25 which may be a later attestation. The similarity of style between the Epistles and the Gospel is also strong enough to claim attention, although one observes a monotony in the First Epistle which is sometimes relieved in the Gospel by the habit of ringing changes in the vocabulary.

Those who think that the writer of the Epistles was the translator of the Gospel from Aramaic into Greek will account for stylistic resemblances in this way, and rule out such evidence as we have attempted to give as irrelevant to the question of authorship. We do not, however, believe that the case for regarding the Gospel as a translation from an Aramaic original has been made out.[1]

In spite of the very strong reasons for attributing the Epistles to the same author as the Gospel, some writers deny this on internal signs of discordant theological opinion. These scholars lay stress on the more primitive eschatology and soteriology of the Epistle, the less personal conception of the Spirit, the change of emphasis in the doctrine of God from the metaphysical to the ethical aspect, and in the conception of belief from the moral to

[1] See Moulton, *Grammar of N. T. Greek*, ii., pp. 483 f.

the intellectual.[1] Such contrasts lie before us as we compare the two writings. Some part of the difficulty is removed if we allow for the difference of treatment as between a pastoral letter dealing with the practical dangers of a definite community and a Gospel, in which both form and substance were determined in large measure by what the author regarded as the historical conditions of his story. It would be still easier to understand the dissonance if we could regard the Epistle as an earlier production, and the Gospel as the result of the same writer's maturest brooding over the reminiscences of the Beloved Disciple. For in the Gospel itself we find traces of more than one phase in the Evangelist's religious and Christian thought. Nowhere has this been more clearly seen and explained than by E. F. Scott. Amongst the very instances which he gives of the inconsistencies, real or apparent, within the Gospel are the selfsame contrasts which have been cited as arguments for dissociating the Epistle from the Gospel. 'An intellectual view of religion is combined with a strongly ethical view. The idea of an eternal life in the future stands side by side with that of a life realized here and now. . . . The Spirit is another name for the exalted Christ, and almost in the same verse a separate power. "Belief," which is sometimes hardly to be distinguished from the Pauline "faith," is elsewhere little more than an intellectual assent.'[2] Dr. Scott traces these frequent oppositions of thought to two main causes: the combination of an earlier type of Christian belief with another which arose later in a different world of thought, and the attempt to interpret a historical revelation given in terms of personal life by means of a philosophical doctrine. There is another consideration to which he bids us

[1] For literature on the whole question, see Appendix B.

[2] *The Fourth Gospel*, p. 12. E. F. Scott insists upon the integrity of the Gospel in his three more recent books, *The Ethical Teaching of Jesus*, pp. 5 f., *The First Age of Christianity*, pp. 217 ff., and *The Gospel and its Tributaries*, p. 179.

give heed, that the Fourth Gospel was written by a man of profoundly religious temperament, in whose living experience widely differing elements were fused without ever finding logical relationship in his mind.

The problem of the integrity of the Gospel is thus bound up closely with that of the unity of authorship of Gospel and First Epistle. It is with some satisfaction that we find a critic so far from the reproach of conservatism as Dr. Walter Bauer declaring at the close of his commentary[1] on the Gospel: ' One and the same man wrote the entire book ; not uninterruptedly, but as he brought himself repeatedly to his task.' After referring to the long series of works in Germany and England devoted to the analysis of the Gospel he continues : ' It has deepened the impression that we can only speak of the unity of the Gospel of John with great reserve. But quite as much, at least in me, the feeling has grown that certain results can be obtained giving a rather complete representation, but only on condition that very comprehensive and careful investigations are made, taking into account language as well as subject-matter, and bringing in the First Epistle.'

In spite of the attempts made by Bousset and Johannes Weiss to bring the Apocalypse into the circle of Johannine writings by supposing the Christian parts of Revelation to come from the pen of the author of the Gospel,[2] and notwithstanding Lohmeyer's cautious leaning towards identity of authorship,[3] the opinion of the majority of[*] modern scholars endorses the judgement of that remarkable higher critic of the third century, Dionysius of Alexandria. ' It is plainly to be seen that one and the same character marks the Gospel and the Epistle throughout. But the Apocalypse is different from these writings

---

[1] *Handb. z. N.T.*, ed. 2, pt. 6, pp. 229, 241.
[2] *Vide supra*, p. 66.
[3] *Handb. z. N.T.*, IV., iv., pp. 198 f.

and foreign to them; not touching, nor in the least bordering on them. Moreover, it can be shown that the diction of the Gospel and of the Epistle differs from that of the Apocalypse. For they were written, not only without error as regards the Greek language, but also most artistically in their expressions, in their reasonings, and in their arrangements of explanations. They are far indeed from betraying any barbarism or solecism, or any vulgarism whatever. For the writer had, as it seems, both the requisites of discourse—namely, the gift of knowledge and the gift of expression, as the Lord had bestowed both upon him. I do not deny that the other writer saw a revelation and received knowledge and prophecy. I perceive, however, that his dialect and language are not accurate Greek, but that he uses barbarous idioms, and, in some places, solecisms. It is unnecessary to point these out here, for I would not have any think that I have said these things in a spirit of ridicule—let no one think it—but only with the purpose of showing clearly the difference between the writings.'[1]

[1] Quoted by Eusebius, *Hist. Eccles.*, vii. 24 f. The whole passage from which this extract is taken is given in Greek, with an English translation, in G. Milligan, *The New Testament Documents*, pp. 262–5.

CHAPTER II

TEXTUAL DISLOCATIONS AND CHRONO-
LOGICAL ORDER

WHEN Tatian compiled his harmony of the four Gospels *
towards the close of the third quarter of the second century
he exercised some freedom in changing the order of material drawn from the Fourth Gospel. This, of course,
does not presume that he suspected the existing text of
the Gospel, still less that where his order differs from that
found in all our manuscripts he is a witness for the original
arrangement of the text. Tatian is a witness to the perplexity which from earliest times has assailed all who have
tried to adjust the chronology of this Gospel to the require-
ments of a coherent Life of Christ.

The discovery of the Sinaitic Syriac version of the
Gospels forty years ago, with its transpositions of the text
in the trial narrative in chap. xviii., seemed to bring startling corroboration to Spitta's recently published suggestions that textual dislocation had taken place at a very
early period in the history of the text of the Fourth Gospel.
But, whatever modifications Spitta may have since made
in his theories, and however many varieties of rearrangements have been proposed by different scholars, the
publication of Moffatt's *New Translation of the New Testament* brought the whole question within the range of
popular interest. If it is too much to say that Moffatt
has brought the subject from the study to the street,
we can at least say that he has helped it to pass from
the pulpit to the pew. With this most accessible

text-book open before us, we may follow the principal rearrangements, asking the reason for every such change, and then pass on to consider other transpositions that have been proposed. (*a*) iii. 22–30 is placed between ii. 12 and ii. 13, for in its usual context it interrupts the expository meditation which follows upon the conversation of Jesus with Nicodemus; whereas in its new position the paragraph describes the progress from Galilee to Jerusalem by way of Judaea. (*b*) vii. 15–24 is brought back to follow v. 47, for the assertion in vii. 19 that the Jews wished to kill Jesus is a clear reference to v. 18, and the defence in vii. 21–4 of doing good on the Sabbath seems an obvious allusion to the charge brought forward in v. 16. The sequence of thought runs on directly from vii. 14 to vii. 25. (*c*) x. 19–29 is transposed to follow immediately after the last verse of chap. ix. For x. 21, 'These are not a madman's words. Can a madman open the eyes of the blind?' is in place in the dispute that arose over the miracle of healing described in chap. ix.; it would be irrelevant, weeks afterwards, at the feast of the Dedication. On the other hand, the allegory of the Good Shepherd is a fitting sequel to x. 26–9. (*d*) In chap. xi. there are two minor transpositions, verse 5 being brought back to stand between verses 2 and 3, and verses 18, 19 being postponed to a place between verses 30 and 31. (*e*) In chap. xii., verses 44–50 are inserted in the middle of verse 36, to the great improvement of the sequence of thought. (*f*) It is generally admitted that the Farewell Discourse in the Upper Room cannot preserve the original order of thought and speech. The closing words of chap. xiv. are obviously out of place if two whole chapters have to intervene before the Master offers the high-priestly prayer for the standing disciples, and then leads them forth. Moreover, the statement in xvi. 5 sounds strange after xiii. 36 and xiv. 5. Dr. Moffatt meets these difficulties by inserting the whole of chaps. xv. and xvi.

in the middle of xiii. 31. (g) The order of chap. xviii. presents such difficulties that, at so early a date as that of the archetype of the Sinaitic Syriac, verse 24 had been inserted between verses 13 and 14, and verses 19–23 between verses 15 and 16. In this way the separate trial before Annas, peculiar to the Johannine story, is eliminated, and the account of Peter's denials runs on without a break. This is not quite the solution offered in Dr. Moffatt's translation, for he transfers verses 19–24 to a place between verses 14 and 15. According to this arrangement, the examination of Jesus took place before Annas, who then sent the prisoner to Caiaphas, and in the courtyard of his house the denials of Peter took place.

It is strange that Dr. Moffatt, when removing vii. 15–24 to follow chap. v., refrained from making the most obvious re-arrangement, one that has often been proposed, even by those[1] whose conservative attitude to the text is impatient of most conjectural alterations. In chap. v. the scene is laid in Jerusalem, where a cripple is healed, and a long discussion follows. This is continued in vii. 15–24. But chap. iv. closes with Jesus in Galilee, and chap. vi. begins with the words: 'After these things Jesus went away to the other side of the sea of Galilee.' It is quite obvious that this presupposes a Galilean context. Moreover, the section vii. 1–14 opens with the words: 'After these things Jesus walked in Galilee: for he would not walk in Judaea, because the Jews sought to kill him.' In the sequence now determined by Dr. Moffatt this follows the open suggestion that the life of Jesus is endangered in Jerusalem (vii. 19), and points to a journey from the city to the north. We may therefore add to those transpositions already noted in Moffatt's *New Testament* (h) the removal of chap. vi. to a place between chaps. iv. and v.

To these more or less obvious changes in the order of narrative or discourse we may add, with Warburton

[1] e.g. by Lagrange, *op. cit.*, p. cxx.

Lewis and J. M. Thompson, (*i*) the removal of viii. 12–20 to a new position before vii. 1–14. The reason given for this is that, with the removal of the interpolated *pericope de adultera* (vii. 53–viii. 11), viii. 12–20 seems out of place after chap. vii., which ends in a climax. This section, however, starts in the middle of an argument. Yet another proposed re-arrangement of chap. vii. may be mentioned. (*j*) E. D. Burton suggested that the sections in this chapter should stand thus: vii. 15–24, 1–14, 25–36, 45–52, 37–44. By this slightly different distribution of the sections the officers sent to arrest Jesus report the same day, and not some days later. A glance at the table of proposed re-arrangements in Appendix D will show what a large measure of agreement there is amongst those writers who are convinced that the present order of the sections in the Fourth Gospel does not agree with the intention of the Evangelist himself. With the minor divergences we are not now concerned.

The questions which arise in the mind of the student of the Gospel are these: (1) Do these discontinuities in narrative or discourse point to some primitive dislocation of the text, and is this suspicion supported by any objective test? (2) Is there any other probable explanation of the manifestly disordered state of the text? (3) What bearing will our answer have upon the further question of the worth of the chronological data provided in this Gospel?

(1) The first indication that the text of the Gospel has not been fixed and firm from the beginning is the fact that the *pericope de adultera* (vii. 53–viii. 11) found a place in many texts of the Gospel. But the absence of this section in the earliest uncials and versions (apart from the Codex Bezae and some fifth-century old Latin MSS. and Jerome's Vulgate), and the omission of any exposition of it in the earliest commentators, show that we must regard it as too late an intrusion to be much of a guide in the present inquiry. A more useful line of investigation follows the

measurement of space required. It was Spitta who first applied this test by counting the number of letters in the section vii. 15–24 in Tischendorf and in Tregelles, and then discovering that the length of each of the transposed passages is a multiple of the same unit. Mr. Warburton Lewis pursued this inquiry further, and found that this section occupies 18.5 lines in the small edition of the WH text, whereas chaps. xv.–xvi., which form another section for transposition, take 111 or 112 lines, or exactly six times this unit of length. However, a careful measurement of chap. v. shows that the length of this is not a multiple of 18.5 lines in WH, but it is of 9.3. Not long after this, Professor A. C. Clark[1] and Mr. Cronin,[2] working independently, came to the same conclusion, that our present text of John was copied from one which was written in lines of ten–twelve letters, with 167–8 letters forming a page unit. Mr. J. M. Thompson[3] works the problem out rather differently with substantially the same results. Finally, Dr. G. H. C. Macgregor set forth his conjectural rearrangement of chaps. vii. and viii. with numerical calculations. (A) vii. 15–24. (B) viii. 12–20. (C) vii. 1–14 plus vii. 25–36. (D) viii. 21–59. (E) vii. 45–52 plus vii. 37–44. [(F) vii. 53–viii 11].

(A) contains 18.5 lines and fills two pages, so does (B), so does (F). But as neither the divided portions of (C) nor the interchanged portions of (E) are multiples of the page unit, and so liable to accidental displacement, the transpositions here must be explained otherwise. The remarkable coincidence in numerical results gives plausibility to Spitta's theory that the leaves were originally pasted together, that they fell loose and were then put together in the wrong order. This points not to a papyrus

---

[1] *The Primitive Text of the Gospels and Acts* (1914), pp. vi., 68 ff., J. T. S., xvi. (1915), pp. 225 ff.
[2] J. T. S., xiii. (1912), pp. 563–71.
[3] *Expositor*, VIII., ix., pp. 421 ff.

roll so much as to a codex. Professor Clark even makes the startling suggestion that there was an archetype of the four Gospels in book form before the middle of the second century.[1] But it is hardly surprising that little headway has been made by a theory which seriously contends that 'such incongruous passages as the end of our Mark, or the *Pericope Adulterae*, are to be taken as composed for the places they now occupy, even if they did hold that place as early as A.D. 150.'[2] Of course the theory that there was an archetype of the Fourth Gospel in codex form is not at all dependent on the far-reaching speculations and conclusions of Professor A. C. Clark, although it was natural that endorsement by so eminent a specialist in another field of textual criticism should be hailed as valuable support. There is yet another consideration to bear in mind. It is quite possible to find a calculus which explains some of these disarrangements by accidental displacement. But, as we have seen from Dr. Macgregor's scheme, this will not account for all. His own proposal is that in various ways a copyist might try to reconnect contextually when some first disarrangement had taken place.

(2) General agreement that our present text of this Gospel is disordered in many places by no means involves agreement as to the cause. One of the most acute observations in B. W. Bacon's keen analysis is that at every point where dislocation is evident a Redactor can be traced. To quote his words exactly, ' In every case these displacements occur in conjunction with passages which by their direct connexion with the Appendix or otherwise give independent evidence of having been introduced by R.'[3] We may be sceptical about the existence of Dr. Bacon's ubiquitous Redactor, and may not agree to assign the section iii. 31–6 to this alien hand. But we shall

[1] *Op. cit.*, p. 70.   [2] J. H. Moulton, *C. R.*, xxix. (1915), p. 54.
[3] *Op. cit.*, p. 523.

see presently that there is a case for suspecting that the whole Nicodemus episode has been misplaced, and we must therefore take note of the very confused phraseology with which the next section begins. Dr. Bernard remarks about iv. 1, 2 : ' A passage which has been rewritten for the sake of clearness, but the style is not that of John.'[1] Another instance which Dr. Bacon offers is the story of Peter's denial, where he would make the Redactor responsible for the insertion of xviii. 14–18 and 24–7. Again we need not follow the ingenious arguments for attributing this and other passages which introduce the unnamed disciple as necessarily interpolations by a later hand, but, following Professor Bacon's clue, we notice again textual confusion at the very point at which a transposition has so often been recognized. Père Lagrange, in his note on xviii. 24, has shown that the connecting particle at the beginning of this verse varies in our different textual authorities, but, whilst οὖν fits perfectly in its present place, and no one would have thought of changing it, δέ, though out of place here, would fit perfectly after verse 13. Thus the latter reading would explain the various other readings[2] precisely on the theory of a displacement. Other examples might be given to show that, not only considerations of subject-matter, but slight disturbances in the text, suggest to us that some displacement has taken place. If the disarrangement is merely the result of accident, not only in the original separation of leaves, but in their fresh grouping, we should not expect these signs of editorial handiwork. If, however, we postulate an editor who carefully re-arranged the disturbed leaves we are left astonished at his singular ineptitude in leaving such an obvious misfit as the present position of chap. v. But this difficulty becomes all the greater if the

[1] *I. C. C.*, vol. i., p. xxxiii.
[2] Some groups read *et*, and in others there is no connecting particle at all.

disturbance of the text is due to the deliberate work of a systematic Redactor, who went right through the Gospel, inserting Synoptic material or considerable passages to suit his own ends in winning ecclesiastical sanction, either by rehabilitating Peter or by suggesting apostolic authorship. The blunderer whose faults have called down such strong condemnation could hardly be the careful literary craftsman which this theory requires. In that case he must have studied the style of the original work so closely that his imitation has deceived many who have come to the Gospel with ears trained in literary criticism or in the linguistic characteristics of Hellenistic Greek! Editorial glosses and comments here and there may be suspected, but that is a very different matter from extensive redaction.

If the data are too numerous and too complex to admit of explanation solely on the ground of chance disturbance of leaves, and if the reasons given for the creation of a Redactor are too subtle and far-fetched to be convincing, is there any alternative theory? There are many signs that the Gospel was not left in the form of a finished work. There are also indications that the writer went over his rough draft adding fresh incidents or meditations, inserting comments, elaborations, reconsiderations. It is in this way, probably, that we attain an understanding of the otherwise perplexing interruptions in the thought and rhythm of the Prologue, and the duplications and, as some have said, the inconsistencies of the Farewell Discourse. It has often been observed that the sequence of thought in the Prologue runs smoothly if the verses relating to John the Baptist are omitted (i. 6-8, 15). If these verses originally came immediately before verses 19 ff., they would form an opening for the Gospel not unlike the beginning of Mark. When the Prologue was written and prefixed to the rough draft of the Gospel these verses may well have been detached from their former position and inserted in the Prologue to emphasize the subordination of the Baptist, or to bring his witness into prominence. Later on, in the record of the Last Sayings, it is not improbable that the Evangelist wrote two meditations at different times upon the discourse in the Upper Room, * based upon the memories of the Beloved Disciple. There are stories that have been begun, but never finished, such as the visit of the Greeks in chap. xii. It is at least conceivable that we have the unfinished pages of the Gospel, almost as the Evangelist left them, in varying stages of revision, for the most part grouped according to the writer's chronological design, but imperfectly arranged, and awaiting his final revision. We can well understand that the reverence in which he was held in the Johannine circle, especially if he was regarded as preserving in large measure the message of the Beloved Disciple, would keep the disciple or disciples who published the work from tampering unduly with the order of the leaves, or from adding more than what were regarded as a few necessary touches.

(3) Such a theory assumes that the chronology of the Gospel is substantially that which was deliberately intended by the Evangelist, but that where internal evidence points to a slight disarrangement of adjacent leaves adjustments must be made. Inasmuch as chap. xii. brings Jesus to Jerusalem for the last week we need not at present enter into details such as the right arrangement of verses in chap. xviii. The question immediately before us is, What general outline of the ministry of Jesus is offered in the Fourth Gospel when we allow for the probable order of the leaves supposing that the Evangelist had published the Gospel in its final form ? That some sort of chronology is definitely in the writer's mind scarcely admits of dispute. As Mr. Warburton Lewis[1] was the first scholar in this country to work out the question of dislocations in its

[1] *Disarrangements in the Fourth Gospel* (1910).

bearing on chronology, we shall take the several sections of the first eleven chapters in his order,[1] finding out for ourselves what course of historical narrative is then disclosed. After that we shall turn again to Mr. Lewis's book to consider his findings and the proposals that he offers for a comparison of this chronology with that of Mark.

(*a*) i.–ii. 12.—After the Prologue, John is introduced, baptizing at Bethany beyond Jordan, where he hails Jesus as Lamb of God, and Son of God. Jesus calls a few disciples, then travels to Cana in Galilee. Afterwards He removes with His family and His disciples to Capernaum. (*b*) iii. 22–30.—Some time afterwards He journeys to Judaea, where He and His disciples baptize, attracting many. John hears of this at Aenon, and testifies again to the superiority of Jesus. (*c*) ii. 13–iii. 21. —Jesus goes up to Jerusalem for the Passover. The cleansing of the Temple follows, 'signs' lead to the belief of many, and Nicodemus visits Jesus by night. (*d*) iii. 31–6.— The conversation with Nicodemus is continued. (*e*) iv.— Jesus travels from Judaea to Galilee via Samaria, where He gains the faith of many. The Galileans welcome Him, having seen the works done at the feast in Jerusalem. At Cana He heals the son of the king's officer from Capernaum. (*f*) vi.—Jesus crosses the sea of Galilee, feeds the five thousand, joins the disciples as they are trying to make headway on the Lake against contrary winds, is beset by the crowds who have crossed the Lake and followed Him to Capernaum. The discourse on the bread of life, spoken in a synagogue there, leads to the secession of many disciples. Then follows Peter's confession, and the warning against the treachery of Judas. (*g*) v.—Jesus goes up to Jerusalem for ' a feast of the Jews.' By healing a cripple on the Sabbath He incurs the hostility of the Jews, who begin to ' persecute ' Him (verse 16). Jesus defends Himself

[1] See Appendix D, p. 303.

and counter-attacks His critics by showing that they stand condemned by the very Moses to whom they appeal. (*h*) vii. 15–24.—Amazement of the Jews at the knowledge of Jesus, who continues the argument by showing how they fail to keep the law of Moses, whilst He does the will of Him who sent Him. They themselves break the Sabbath law in order to preserve the ordinance of circumcision. (*i*) viii. 12–20.—Teaching of Jesus in the Temple. ' I am the light of the world.' (*j*) vii. 1–14.— Jesus returns to Galilee because the Jews are looking for an opportunity of killing Him. When the feast of Tabernacles comes round, Jesus does not at first go up with the pilgrims, because of Jewish hostility, but, going up secretly, He appears half-way through the festival and teaches in the Temple. (*k*) vii. 25–52.—Surprise of the Jerusalemites at the appearance of Jesus, knowing of the plot to slay Him. In spite of a renewed attempt to seize Jesus, He continues preaching, with the crowd divided in opinion. The servants of the Sanhedrin fail to arrest Him. Nicodemus protests against the condemnation of Jesus unheard. (*l*) viii. 21–59.—Further preaching of Jesus provokes the anger of His hearers by His claims, and by His denial that they are in the true spiritual lineage of Abraham. Jesus escapes from the attempts made to stone Him, and goes into concealment. (*m*) ix.— Cure of a man born blind, who suffers excommunication. Jesus seeks him out and instructs him, and rebukes the Pharisees among those who hear the conversation. (*n*) x. 19–29.—Further division among the Jews regarding this cure. Jesus is in Jerusalem for the feast of Dedication, when He is asked to relieve suspense by stating openly who He is. He replies that only His own sheep hear His voice. (*o*) x. 1–18.—Allegory of the Good Shepherd. (*p*) x. 30–42.—A declaration of unity with the Father leads to a renewed attempt to stone Jesus, who replies to the charge of blasphemy. A further attempt is made to capture

Him, but He escapes, crosses the Jordan to the place where John had formerly baptized, and here wins many to belief in Him. (*q*) xi.—After hearing of the illness of Lazarus at Bethany, Jesus crosses to Judaea. The raising of Lazarus leads many of the Jews to believe in Jesus, and as a result the Sanhedrin determines on His death. Jesus withdraws from Judaea to a district adjoining the desert, to a town named Ephraim. Meanwhile, those pilgrims who have come up to Jerusalem early for the Passover are curious to know whether Jesus will come up for the feast. (*r*) xii.—Jesus arrives a week before the Passover.

If we reduce this summary of the restored Johannine narrative of the ministry of Jesus to barest outline we have, as a sequel to the baptism, the call of some disciples, a Galilean ministry beginning at Cana and continued at Capernaum. Some time after follows a Judaean ministry parallel to the mission of the Baptist. During this period, Jesus visits Jerusalem for the Passover. Then comes a further Galilean ministry, leading to great popularity. Jesus does not go to Jerusalem for the next Passover, but about that time of the year His popularity reaches its zenith with the feeding of the multitude. Some time after, Jesus goes up to Jerusalem for a feast, where His action and teaching begin a long controversy with the Jerusalem Rabbis. There follows a retreat to Galilee, and a return visit to Jerusalem for the feast of Tabernacles. Three months later, Jesus is again in Jerusalem for the feast of Dedication. He then escapes to Trans-Jordania, whence He returns to Judaea and Bethany, then retreats immediately to Ephraim, coming back to Jerusalem for the last Passover. There are thus within the limits of the Johannine account of the ministry three Passovers, at two of which Jesus is in Jerusalem. There is an undefined period before the first Passover, part of which is spent in Galilee, part in Judaea. Some time after this first Passover a long Galilean ministry begins, which lasts until after the second Passover. Jerusalem is visited after this for another feast, probably Pentecost, for there is a return to Galilee until the feast of Tabernacles in the autumn. There does not seem to be any further Galilean ministry, but Jesus appears to spend the remaining months either on the further side of Jordan or north of Judaea until the third and last Passover.

If we now turn to Mr. Warburton Lewis's findings we discover a similar plan, but with two remarkably interesting suggestions. He shows that there is an unexpected harmony with the Marcan course of narrative, and that the early tradition embodied in Acts x. 37 is corroborative. It will be well to give the parallels for the general course of events. In details there are marked divergences, for, apart from the Marcan omission of any visits to Jerusalem until the last Passover, the minute record of the first week after the Baptism in the Johannine record leaves no room for the Temptation sojourn in the wilderness which Mark places immediately after the Baptism.

John i. 35 ff. Gathering of first disciples.
John ii. 1–11. Galilean ministry, beginning at Cana.
John ii. 12. Continuation of the ministry in Galilee after a short stay in Capernaum.

Mark i. 35–ii. 17 records the extension to the surrounding towns and villages. John iii. 22–30 tells of an active Judaean ministry 'after these things,' and of the anxious concern of John's disciples at the rapid growth of this movement. The opposition and the discussions recorded in Mark ii. 18–iii. 6 have many resemblances to this section. Mark iii. 7–8 tells of great crowds from the south and east. John iv. describes a journey through Samaria to Galilee, corresponding to the Marcan note that 'Jesus with His disciples withdrew to the sea' (Mark iii. 7). John vi. tells of a Galilean ministry which lasts until after the next Passover, and thus corresponds to Mark iii. 7–vi.

et seq. It is significant that John records no visit to Jerusalem between the Passover of the first year of the ministry until the Pentecost early in the last year. Then it is that the hostility of the Jews comes to a head, and Jesus returns to Galilee. But in the Marcan story ' we find that it was just at this time, viz. in the period following the Passover of A. D. 28, that Jesus (1) concluded His regular ministry in Galilee by (2) an irreparable breach with the Pharisees (Mark vii).' To this we may add the striking fact that at this very point Mark records : ' Now the Pharisees gathered to meet Him with some scribes *who had come from Jerusalem.*' To quote Mr. Warburton Lewis's own summary : ' This double breach is again followed by journeys in various directions, to Jerusalem (John v.), to the borders of Tyre and Sidon (Mark vii. 24), to Dalmanutha (Mark viii. 10), to the villages of Caesarea Philippi (Mark viii. 27, Luke ix. 18 f.), and then, after fixed resolution to leave Galilee (Luke ix. 51) for Jerusalem, by journeys to that city, the first since Pentecost being recorded in John vii. The chapters vi., v., vii., as re-arranged, follow in train along the line of the Evangelic history from the crisis of the Galilean ministry to the outbreak of the undisguised hostility evoked by the ministry in Judaea. It therefore appears that the only argument against the entire compatibility of the narratives of Mark and John at this period of the ministry is the argument from the silence of Mark about journeys to Jerusalem—an argument not allowable in the case of so incomplete a narrative.'[1] And, if the silence of Mark about these visits to Jerusalem appears a serious obstacle to regarding as historical the Johannine record of a Judaean ministry, we have still to account for the Marcan statement about the crowds who followed Jesus in the early Galilean days ' from Judaea and from Jerusalem and from Idumaea, and beyond Jordan.' When all

[1] *Op. cit.*, p. 13.

allowance has been made for rhetorical exuberance, the words point to a mission in the south and beyond Jordan. In addition to the strongly attested reading of Luke iv. 44, 'And He was preaching in the synagogues of Judaea,' there is the tradition preserved in Acts x. 36–7, 'You know the message He sent to the sons of Israel when He preached the gospel of peace by Jesus Christ (who is Lord of all) ; you know how it spread over the whole of Judaea, starting from Galilee after the baptism preached by John.' This is the order of the narrative as set forth above.

The main point to consider is that this result has not been brought about by juggling with the arrangement in order to suit any harmonistic scheme. The re-arrangement of the sections has been determined by purely internal evidence. It matters not for the question of chronological order of narrative whether we follow F. W. Lewis and J. M. Thompson in placing viii. 12–20 before vii. 1–14, or follow Moffatt and Bernard in leaving it in its place in the record of the feast of Tabernacles. For order of events, there is almost complete agreement, amongst those who allow any re-arrangement of the text, that chap. vi. was intended to precede chap. v. In that case it is of less importance to determine the feast referred to, but not named, in v. 1. Those who identify 'a feast of the Jews' with the Passover allow scarcely enough time between vi. 4 and v. 1, in view of the secession described in vi. 66. Pentecost seven weeks later admits time for the waning of a popularity which was at its height at the point described in vi. 15. But even if, with J. H. Bernard, we were to take this feast to be the Passover, we should not have to allow a year between v. 1 and vi. 4, but only a few weeks between vi. 4 and v. 1.

There is one other question of disarrangement which affects the chronological outline of the ministry. We have already seen that Moffatt, Warburton Lewis, and Bernard agree in placing iii. 31–6 immediately after iii. 21, thus making the passage part of the discourse with Nicodemus. But, whereas those intervening verses iii. 22–30 are brought by Warburton Lewis and Moffatt into position immediately after ii. 12, thus recording a successful Judaean ministry between the opening of a Galilean ministry and the first Passover visit to Jerusalem, Bernard places them after iii. 36, thus dating that Judaean ministry immediately after the first Passover, and finding an excellent connexion with iv. 1–3. Now Macgregor in this matter independently arrived at the same conclusion. But he makes an original suggestion that the sayings given in iii. 14–21 find their true setting in chap. xii. His arrangement of verses in that chapter is xii. 1–32, iii. 14–15, xii. 34, iii. 16–21, xii. 35–6a, 44–50, 36b–43. There is general agreement that dislocation has taken place in the section about Nicodemus. Macgregor would transpose some of these words to the occasion of the last Passover. But the Nicodemus section is closely bound up with the episode of the cleansing of the Temple, as Tatian clearly recognized. A bold suggestion has been tentatively offered by Mr. G. P. Lewis[1] that the sections relating to the cleansing of the Temple and to Nicodemus originally stood in the context of chap. xii., so that the remaining sections in chaps. ii., iii., iv. stand in the same relative positions in the proposed schemes of Warburton Lewis, Moffatt, Bernard, and Macgregor. But by bringing the Nicodemus interview into the last week we remove the difficulty raised by three statements in iii. 2. It is difficult to see why, at this stage in the ministry of Jesus, Nicodemus should desire secrecy in approaching Him, why the teaching should already have so deeply impressed Jerusalem, and what 'works' had yet been

[1] In an unpublished paper read before the Birmingham New Testament Seminar on April 23, 1929.

performed in the city to produce such faith in Him. It would be easier to understand all this if the two episodes were transposed to the feast of Tabernacles, as by Tatian, who places them after vii. 31 or to the final Passover, when the most serious chronological discrepancy between John and the Synoptics would be removed, for John would then give the same date as his predecessors for the cleansing of the Temple. The rather elaborate scheme proposed by Mr. G. P. Lewis must be studied in the Appendix,[1] but we may here note that it does not belong to the group of theories which seek a common explanation in the accidental displacement of leaves. A Redactor is called in, who transferred these episodes and the accompanying discourse material to chaps. ii. and iii., and then rewrote the awkward verses iv. 1–3 to improve the new connexion, afterwards compensating for the removal of these sections by inserting in chap. xii. a conglomeration of sayings duplicating the ideas contained in the discourse with Nicodemus.

It is a strong temptation to seize so plausible a remedy for what is usually regarded as the chief chronological flaw in the Gospel as it stands. But to do so would be to vitiate the argument which has been maintained so far, that without resort to adroit manipulations of the text for ulterior ends, but by allowing for the probability that in some cases the leaves of the rough draft of the Gospel were left imperfectly grouped, we can avail ourselves of internal evidence sufficient to give us a reasonably likely re-arrangement. This on the whole gives an impression that the Evangelist had the knowledge and intention to supply information about the ministry of Jesus which is not in serious conflict with the knowledge which we derive from the other Gospels. This question must now be studied more closely in the light of the relation of the Fourth Gospel to the Synoptic Gospels.

[1] See Appendix D.

CHAPTER III

*RELATION TO THE SYNOPTIC GOSPELS AND THE PROBLEM OF HISTORICITY

'THE Fourth Gospel is not a faithful historical account of the life and teaching of Jesus.' Such is the blunt verdict of M. Jean Réville at the close of his critical analysis.[1] Dr. P. W. Schmiedel dismisses the matter with a mere wave of the hand. ' A book which begins by declaring Jesus to be the *logos* of God and ends by representing a cohort of Roman soldiers as falling to the ground at the majesty of His appearance (xviii. 6), and by representing 100 pounds of ointment as having been used at His embalming (xix. 39), ought by these facts alone to be spared such a misunderstanding of its true character as would be implied in supposing that it meant to be an historical work.'[2]

A far more discriminating judgement is given by Professor C. H. Dodd. ' We may now say with confidence that for strictly historical material, with the minimum of subjective interpretation, we must not go to the Fourth Gospel. Its religious value stands beyond challenge, and it is the more fully appreciated when its contribution to our knowledge of the bare facts of the life of Jesus becomes a secondary interest. This is not to say that it makes no such contribution. But it is to the Synoptic Gospels that we must go if we wish to recover the oldest and purest tradition of the facts.'[3]

[1] *Le Quatrième Évangile*, p. 297.   [2] *Encyc. Bib.*, ii. 2542.
[3] *The Authority of the Bible*, p. 228.

Any attempt to estimate the historical value of the Johannine record must therefore start with a comparison between the Fourth Gospel and the Synoptics. For the present we shall limit ourselves to narrative, leaving over the question of the Johannine presentation of the teaching of Jesus for a later chapter.[1] This comparison furnishes data under four headings. (*a*) Episodes common to John and the Synoptics; (*b*) episodes peculiar to John; (*c*) Synoptic episodes omitted by John; (*d*) Synoptic episodes not recorded by John, which have yet left a trace in the Johannine narrative.

(*a*) Under the first head are to be placed the ministry of the Baptist and his testimony to Jesus, the call of the first disciples, the healing of the officer's son at Capernaum, the feeding of the five thousand, the walking on the sea, the triumphal entry, the cleansing of the Temple, the anointing at Bethany, the last supper, the warning of the betrayal, the warning of the denial, the betrayal and arrest, the resistance of Peter, the trial before the high priest, the trial before Pilate, the people's choice of Barabbas, the crucifixion and burial, the empty grave. In addition to these we should, perhaps, identify the story of the miraculous draught of fish given in John xxi. 1-13 with the similar story placed earlier in the ministry of Jesus in Luke v. 1-11. It is also worthy of remark that in the Fourth Gospel, as in the Synoptic Gospels, Peter's confession of faith follows the crisis in the Galilean ministry, being placed after the feeding of the multitude, the walking on the sea, the demand for a sign, and the close of the period of popularity.

(*b*) Of the episodes peculiar to this Gospel, the most remarkable are four miracles: turning water into wine at Cana, healing the impotent man at Bethesda, giving sight to the man born blind (at Siloam), and the raising of Lazarus. Amongst the others are the interviews with

[1] Part III., chap. iii., *vide infra*, p. 213 ff.

Nicodemus and with the woman of Samaria, the advice given to Jesus by His brothers to go up to Jerusalem to win disciples at the feast, and then, in the course of the narrative of the Passion, the visit of the Greeks, the feet-washing, the judicial appearance before Annas, with certain episodes in the post-resurrection story, more especially the visit of Peter and the other disciple to the sepulchre, and the conviction of Thomas.

(c) Synoptic episodes not represented in the Fourth Gospel are too numerous to be recorded in detail. The most significant omissions are the actual baptism of Jesus, the temptation in the wilderness, the cure of demoniacs and lepers, the association of Jesus with outcasts and sinners, the transfiguration, the institution of the Eucharist, the agony in Gethsemane, the cry of dereliction on the cross.

(d) Synoptic episodes which, while not related by John, have yet left a trace in the Fourth Gospel include the choosing of the Twelve (cf. John vi. 70), the imprisonment of the Baptist (iii. 24), the agony (John xii. 27, xviii. 11), and possibly the Eucharist (John vi. 53, 54).

Before we can settle the question, How and why does John modify the Synoptic material? there is the preliminary question to answer, Did John know and use any or all of the Synoptic Gospels? By general consent he made use of Mark. In addition to the verbal resemblances given in an earlier chapter,[1] it is enough to refer to the parallel narratives of the feeding of the multitude (John vi. 1-15; cf. Mark vi. 32-44, viii. 1-10). There is less complete agreement regarding John's use of Luke. Stanton[2] denies it, whilst Streeter[3] gives reasons for the opposite view. Some considerations in favour of the theory that the Fourth Evangelist knew Luke's Gospel are that in these Gospels alone Annas (Luke iii. 2; John xviii. 12, 24)

[1] *Vide supra*, p. 102. [2] *Op. cit.*, iii., p. 220. [3] *Op. cit.*, p. 401.

and Martha and Mary (Luke x. 38 ; John xi. 1 f., xii. 2 f.) are named. In both, the Jews ask if the Baptist is the Messiah, and are told by him that he is not (Luke iii. 15 ; John i. 19–20). In Luke vii. 38 the woman who was a sinner wiped the feet of Jesus with her hair after bedewing them with tears. This was a simple and natural action. But when we read in John xii. 3 that Mary acted thus after pouring precious ointment on the Master's feet, we are as much surprised at the unsuitability of the instrument as at the unbound tresses of the lady of the house. The only possible explanation is that the Evangelist, by association of ideas, has worked into his otherwise authentic account of the incident at Bethany a reminiscence of the familiar but distinct story told by Luke. In the Passion narrative the treachery of Judas is attributed by both to Satan's entrance into him (Luke xxiii. 3 ; John xiii. 27). The Mount of Olives is mentioned as a favourite resort of Jesus and His disciples (Luke xxii. 39 ; John xviii. 2). Peter's denial is foretold after, not during, supper (Luke xxii. 31–4 ; John xiii. 36–8). It was the right ear of the high priest's servant which Peter cut off (Luke xxii. 50 ; John xviii. 10). Pilate thrice declared Jesus to be innocent (Luke xxiii. 4, 14, 22 ; John xviii. 38, xix. 4, 6). The sepulchre in which Jesus was laid had never yet been used (Luke xxiii. 52 ; John xix. 41). Two angels appeared to the women at the empty tomb. To these Goguel[1] adds three striking points of agreement : the thought that the assumption of Jesus is regarded by both Evangelists as the end of the ministry of Jesus (Luke ix. 51 ; John xiii. 1), that Luke speaks (xxiv. 49) of the gift of the Spirit as of the promise of the Father in a way that recalls the Johannine doctrine of the Paraclete, and that the frequent escapes of Jesus from the hands of His enemies, in the Fourth Gospel (John viii. 59, x. 39, xii. 36.), are analogous to the story in Luke iv. 29. The first would be more

[1] *Introd. au N.T.*, ii., p. 225.

impressive if the Lucan term ἀνάλημψις had recurred in
* John, who employs the figure of μετάβασις.

Reasons have often been suggested for the Evangelist's choice, or rejection, of the material at his disposal. Thus of the many signs which Jesus wrought he selected, amongst others, four which serve to enhance the superhuman power of Jesus : the nature miracle at Cana in Galilee, the healing of a man who had been a cripple for thirty-eight years and of another man who had been blind from birth, and, above all, the raising of a man who had been four days in the tomb. On the other hand, it is easy to find plausible grounds for some of the omissions. Thus the divine dignity of our Lord might seem to be compromised by the story of the temptation, the agony in the garden, and the cry of abandonment on the cross. Polemical or apologetic aims may have led to silence regarding the submission of Jesus to baptism by John, and the institution of the Eucharist ; and, if Gnostic errors were as keenly present to the mind of the writer of the Gospel as when the First Epistle was written, we may, perhaps, bring the strange avoidance of any reference to demoniacs under the same head. Theological propriety may have led the Evangelist to suppress the story of the transfiguration, since he regarded the whole incarnate life of Jesus as a revelation of His glory (John i. 14, ii. 11, xi. 4, 40) which would be perfectly manifested only after His death (John vii. 39, xiii. 32, xvii. 1, 4, 5). It is not so easy to think that the Johannine Christ is deliberately brought into the deferential company of a Nicodemus as an offset to the humble companionship of publicans and sinners described in the Synoptics. The ' higher social *milieu* ' of which Windisch speaks[1] can be found in the earlier Gospels as well.

At the same time there are many touches in some of

[1] *Johannes und die Synoptiker*, pp. 112 f., ' Das proletarische Milieu der Synopt. ist fast ganz versunken.'

these narratives which suggest either that this Evangelist is dependent upon sources other than the Synoptics, or that he is taking them from an earlier source which he and the Synoptists are using in common. Thus the note appended to the witness of John to Jesus, 'These things took place in Bethany beyond Jordan, where John was baptizing' (John i. 28), has no theological value, and can hardly have been added to give topographical realism to a narrative, since it introduces perplexity into the story, for the only Bethany which is known is the village near Jerusalem. The same may be said of the note in John i. 44 that Bethsaida was the home of Andrew, Peter, and Philip. In the account of the cleansing of the Temple, whatever may be our judgement of the chronological position which this episode occupies in John, the discussion with the Jews (John ii. 18–20) is independent of the Synoptic record, but is most appropriate and gives a clue to the origin of the false witness brought against Jesus at His trial (Mark xiv. 58). In the story of the healing of the officer's son, the term used, βασιλικός, is more correct; for Galilee was at that time under the rule of Herod Antipas, not of the Roman procurator, and an officer in Herod's little military establishment suits the context far better than a subordinate officer in the Roman army. Either this Evangelist is correcting the story in its Matthew-Luke form, or else he is going back to an older tradition which has been inexactly modified in Q. Goguel[1] has acutely observed that in two episodes recorded in John vii. 1–13 and x. 40–2 there is a picture of Jesus waiting upon opportune circumstances which stands in sharp contradiction to the Evangelist's fundamental conception of the absolute opposition which clashed with the work of Jesus. There is therefore internal evidence that these two passages depend upon early tradition. In this, as in other cases of the use of

[1] *Introd. au N.T.*, ii., p. 430.

non-Synoptic information, we may think of written sources, or of an eyewitness whose memoirs have been taken down by the Evangelist.

It is when we come to the Passion narrative that we are most keenly alive to the presence of some other authority besides the Synoptic tradition behind the Fourth Evangelist. This subject has received very full attention in a monograph by Maurice Goguel,[1] who detects signs of an early tradition in the threefold indication that the Last
* Supper took place on the day before the Passover (John xiii. 1, xviii. 28, xix. 14), in the first announcement of Judas's treason (John xiii. 18–20), in the topographical detail in the description of the garden (xviii. 1), in the intervention of the cohort and the chiliarch in the arrest (xviii. 12), and of Nicodemus in the story of the burial (xix. 39). There is another story which might well be added to these episodes. M. Goguel treats the account of the feet-washing as an elaboration of the saying in Luke xxii. 27, ' For whether is greater, he that sitteth at meat, or he that serveth? is not he that sitteth at meat? but I am in the midst of you as he that serveth.' On the contrary it seems likely that the story preserved in the Johannine narrative of the Last Supper has left this one trace in the Third Gospel, and that there is an echo of that incident in the words used in 1 Pet. v. 5, ' Yea, all of you gird yourselves [ἐγκομβώσασθε] with humility [as with a slave's apron], to serve one another.'

The introduction of a Roman officer and a band of Roman soldiers into the story of the arrest is at first sight an improbable embellishment. On closer examination, however, it is not unlikely that, if the Sanhedrin, or its most active spirits, had resolved on delivering Jesus up to the Roman authority as a dangerous stirrer up of sedition, they would take the precaution of seeking some

[1] *Les Sources du récit johannique de la Passion.* See especially pp. 104 ff.

help from the officer whose special duty at the feast it was to prevent dangerous disorder from arising in the Temple court. Years after, another chiliarch, Claudius Lysias, took counsel with the Sanhedrin when the peace of the city seemed to be imperilled by another Jew, a follower of the same Jesus.[1] According to the Johannine account the Temple police went forward to arrest the man whom they wanted, and it was only when Peter's rash flourish with the sword threatened armed resistance that the soldiers took the lead. The picturesque exaggeration of xviii. 6 does not destroy the historical value of the tradition as a whole.

The relationship of the Fourth Gospel to the Synoptics is the subject of an exhaustive discussion by Professor Windisch,[2] who considers three possibilities, according to which the Johannine Gospel is supplementary to, independent of, or interpretative of, the Synoptics, and rejects all these in favour of a fourth attitude—namely, that it replaces them. This rigid differentiation of aims seems too artificial, and we see more reason to say that John often supplements and interprets the Gospels already in general favour, and that he sometimes even corrects them, than that he intends to supersede them. The statement (John iii. 24) that 'John was not yet cast into prison' loses any significance unless the writer presupposes his readers' knowledge of a period of activity in the life of Jesus which is definitely dated as falling after that event. Now, the Marcan narrative of the public ministry of our Lord begins with the clear statement, 'Now after that John was delivered up, Jesus came into Galilee, preaching the gospel of God' (Mark i. 14). The natural inference is that the Fourth Evangelist wishes to inform his readers that he is describing a stage in the ministry of Jesus before the period with which Mark's narrative opens. Whatever reason may have led him to leave out of the story of the Last Supper any account of

[1] Acts xxii. 30. [2] *Johannes und die Synoptiker.*

the institution of the Eucharist, it is incredible that he regarded this as unhistorical. The evidence of 1 Cor. xi. 23 ff. proves how very early was the Church's belief that its central rite went back to the night on which the Lord was betrayed. Silence assumes knowledge in this case, even though the transference of eucharistic teaching to the occasion when the crowd by the Galilean lake was miraculously fed may mark a correction of emphasis. Again, there are signs of severe compression in the description of the successive stages in the trial of Jesus. Even Windisch[1] remarks of the two brief allusions to Caiaphas (xviii. 24, 28) that this is the one place in John where the reader familiar with the Synoptic narrative is inclined to insert: 'For details, cf. Mark (or Matthew).' Whether we accept some re-arrangement of the text in John xviii. 12–28 as some[2] have proposed or leave the verses as they now stand, the story of the trial before Pilate presupposes some knowledge of the charge which the High Priest forwarded. The question put by Pilate to Jesus (xviii. 33), 'Art thou the king of the Jews?' is not based on the answer given by the Jewish representatives to his question, 'What charge do you bring against this man?' (verses 29–30). It is only intelligible to those who may be presumed to know the Synoptic account of the trial before Caiaphas, in which the claim to Messiahship is held as proved, so that what shocked the High Priest as blasphemy could be presented to the procurator as high treason (cf. Mark xiv. 61–4, xv. 9–10). Windisch[3] remarks that in the Synoptics the Messianic claims of Jesus are brought out first at the trial, whereas in John this 'trial' has taken place in several acts (v. 19 f., x. 29 ff.), the climax of which can be mentioned briefly in xviii. 24, 28, whilst the earlier process can be summed up in xviii. 30, xix. 7, 12. Nevertheless, the reader who has not the clue

---

[1] *Johannes und die Synoptiker*, p. 79.   [2] *Vide supra*, p. 113.
[3] *Op. cit.*, p. 82.

provided by the Synoptic record would hardly understand the Johannine story of the trial. But the final proof of the compression which the writer can safely use in reliance upon an earlier and well-known history is the sudden introduction of the name of Barabbas (John xviii. 40).

There are several indications in the Johannine account of the last week that the Fourth Evangelist is in possession of authoritative information enabling him to correct the Synoptic chronology of that week in certain important details. The story of the anointing at Bethany is introduced (xii. 1) with a precise indication of time which so obviously contradicts the Marcan (and Matthaean) tradition that it is impossible to put it down to an artificial appearance of accuracy on the part of an imaginative writer. The scene at Bethany is dated 'six days before the Passover,' and precedes the triumphal entry, whereas from Mark xiv. 1 (followed in Matt. xxvi. 1) we learn that it was 'two days' before the Passover, and some time after the triumphal entry. Still more striking is the clear evidence that the Fourth Evangelist dated the Last Supper on the night before the Passover, and the crucifixion of Jesus on the day of the Passover (John xiii. 1, 29, xviii. 28, xix. 14, 36). The Synoptists (Mark xiv. 16 ; Matt. xxvi. 19 ; Luke xxii. 13) all say that the disciples who were sent in advance 'made ready the Passover.' Yet Mark and Luke both have allusions which raise doubts about the correctness of their identification of the Supper with the Passover (Mark xiv. 2, 43, 47, 53, xv. 46 ; Luke xxii. 38, xxiii. 56). Moreover, the phraseology of Luke xxii. 15, 16, although rather ambiguous, probably implies that Jesus knew that He would not live to eat the Passover with His disciples.[1]

---

[1] See *J. T. S.*, ix., pp. 569–72, for two independently written essays, by Professors F. C. Burkitt and A. E. Brooke, interpreting these verses in the sense of unfulfilled desire.

In considering the date of the Supper and of the Crucifixion, as also in determining whether the cleansing of the Temple is correctly placed in the last week by the Synoptists or earlier in the ministry by John,[1] the first need is to rid ourselves of the assumption that there is a threefold witness against the Fourth Gospel. As regards narrative Matthew is little more than a mere repetition of Mark. Those who accept the Proto-Luke theory, advanced with such cogent arguments by Canon Streeter, discriminate between those portions of Luke which belong to the earlier strata and those which bear the sign of later introduction from Mark. Let the reader examine the text of this pre-Marcan form of the Gospel, and ask himself whether Luke regarded the Last Supper as the Passover meal. Let him also see what place is occupied by the cleansing of the Temple. The experiment may be tried by reading Dr. Vincent Taylor's *The First Draft of St. Luke's Gospel*, which was drawn up on the basis of his book, *Behind the Third Gospel*, and of Canon Streeter's *The Four Gospels*, without any reference to critical questions raised by the Fourth Gospel. The story of the cleansing of the Temple, which only occupies two short verses in Luke, is treated as a Marcan insertion. In both these important questions we have to choose between the Second and the Fourth Gospels. It is therefore a matter which must be decided by internal evidence. This has led many modern scholars to favour the Johannine departure from the Marcan date of the Supper and of the Crucifixion. Certainly the great authority of Gustaf Dalman can be cited for the Synoptic as against the Johannine presentation.[2] His explanation is that the Fourth Evangelist knew that the words

[1] The question now under discussion is whether the Evangelist has *misplaced* this incident. In the previous chapter (pp. 126 f.) the question of the accidental *displacement* of the pericope in our present text of the Gospel was examined and rejected.

[2] *Jesus-Jeschua*, pp. 80 ff. (English trans., *Jesus-Jeshua*, pp. 86 ff.).

recorded by the Synoptists in connexion with the distribution of the bread and of the wine were actually spoken, but that he suppressed them in his account of the events of the last evening, transferring them to the discourse in Capernaum. He did this for a double reason. He wished to emphasize 'that it is the *Person* of our Lord (whose Flesh and Blood are the organs of His Spirit) that is of the greatest value to humanity (perhaps in opposition to a nascent tendency to over-emphasize the importance of the sign as such).' He also feared that, as the disciples could not distinguish between spirit and flesh (John vi. 60–3), the words if recorded in their original form would give rise to more serious misunderstandings, which would put the teaching and behaviour of Christians in an unfavourable light. Having, then, transferred words which were originally spoken at the Last Supper as a Passover meal to another place, to show that what our Lord said to His disciples on that last night had nothing to do with this Jewish rite, he was compelled ' to push back this last evening for one day, so that the Passover meal would have taken place after the death of Jesus. To the author, to whom the spiritual possession of God's grace and truth in Jesus was central, this method did not seem wrong.' Dalman naturally observes with reference to the influence of motive upon narrative, ' If this be the case, it is a serious warning to us not to put too much weight upon the Johannine presentation of the outward order of events of the earthly life of our Lord.'[1]

We shall consider later on the significance of the narrative in John vi. and the discourse on the Bread of Life.[2] At the moment, our concern is with the correctness or incorrectness of the Johannine date of the Supper and the Crucifixion. We have seen that within the Synoptic

[1] *Jesus-Jeschua*, pp. 84, 85 (English trans., pp. 90, 91).
[2] *Vide infra*, p. 209 ff.

Gospels there are marks of confusion on this point, and Dalman's treatment of these marks is not convincing. But there is another witness whose evidence turns the scale in favour of the Fourth Gospel in this matter. Paul's metaphor of Christ as 'our Passover,' and his allusion to the Resurrection 'on the third day, according to the Scriptures,' point clearly to a very early tradition that the Crucifixion took place on the day appointed for the slaying of the paschal lamb, and the first appearance of the risen Lord took place on the morning when the sheaf of the firstfruits was lifted up and waved by the priest in the Temple. 'Purge out the old leaven, that ye may be a new lump, even as ye are unleavened. For our Passover also hath been sacrificed, even Christ: wherefore let us keep the feast, not with old leaven, neither with the leaven of malice and wickedness, but with the unleavened bread of sincerity and truth' (1 Cor. v. 7 f.). 'But now hath Christ been raised from the dead, the firstfruits of them that are asleep' (1 Cor. xv. 20). The language is metaphorical, but its symbolism depends for its appropriateness upon the historical tradition.[1] In support of this contention we must also refer to Canon Box's powerful arguments which show that the ritual of the Supper is to be identified with that of the Kiddush of Passover rather than the paschal meal itself.[2] The weight of the evidence seems, therefore, to show that in this matter the Fourth Evangelist is following information which he has good reason for

---

[1] See B. W. Bacon, *Expositor*, VIII. xxvi., pp. 432 ff., for the significance of 1 Cor. xv. 4.

[2] See G. H. Box, *J. T. S.*, iii. (1902), pp. 357 ff., F. C. Burkitt, *J. T. S.*, xvii. (1916), pp. 291 ff. Since writing this chapter I have met with Dr. Oesterley's important book, *The Jewish Background of the Christian Liturgy*. In chap. vi. (pp. 157 ff.) he discusses the Antecedents of the Eucharist, and in chap. vii. he gives further arguments in support of the identification of the Last Supper with the Kiddush. His learned reasoning powerfully confirms the conclusion at which I had already arrived with the help of the data provided by Professors Box and Bacon. Additional patristic support is adduced.

preferring to the definite statement of the Synoptists. Critical opinion is not so generally favourable to the Johannine dating of the cleansing of the Temple. This question is bound up with another—that is, the difficult problem of the raising of Lazarus. The Synoptic Gospels are silent upon this tremendous miracle and for them it was the cleansing of the Temple that provoked the bitter hostility of the high-priestly group. With John, the raising of Lazarus focuses the enmity of the authorities at Jerusalem. It cannot be denied that *Formgeschichte* has shaken somewhat the older confidence that the Marcan narrative provides a reliable chronological framework for the ministry of Jesus. Inasmuch as Mark records only one visit to Jerusalem, if that tradition describing the cleansing of the Temple had no time-context, the Evangelist had no option, but would inevitably place it during the final week. We have seen that the story was not in Proto-Luke, but was inserted with other Marcan matter in a sentence or two. If the raising of Lazarus is dismissed as unhistorical there is less doubt that Mark is right in bringing in the cleansing of the Temple as a decisive factor leading to the death of Christ during that last Passover visit. But if, however the story be accounted for, persistent rumours of some stupendous work of healing won for Jesus a royal welcome into the city, we have a sufficient cause for the determination to take swift and effective measures for silencing Him for ever. Some scholars still maintain the possibility that the dramatic act was repeated. But, whilst the older writers did so for harmonistic reasons, Dr. Vacher Burch finds a reason for the different time and position given to the expulsion of the vendors in this and the other Gospels in the repetition of the contrasts of Christ's revelation, as the successive Passovers presented the same features. The word of Jesus recorded by John as spoken in connexion with this incident (John ii. 19) was brought up as a charge against Him in the trial, and flung in His face as He hung upon the cross (Mark xiv. 58, xv. 29). Dr. Burch[1] interprets it as 'a clear-cut antithesis between the religion of the Temple and the revelation of the Revealer whom the tomb could not hold. . . . The teaching of Christ in its Passover context cuts at the roots of Jewish religion. What the Fourth Gospel underlines, by giving the Expulsion the place it holds in the text, is the vital antithesis of the Revealer over against a repudiated ritual.' If Dr. Burch is considered to have made out the case for a coincidence of literary structure and festal chronology, with its corollary that the acts and words of Jesus at each of the great feasts were signs primarily of 'Christ's attitude towards and religious valuation of the capital expressions of Hebrew religion,'[2] then our problem is greatly simplified. For, in that case, John's principle of selection was to avoid repeating those episodes at the festal periods which 'both the cycle of the festivals and the cardinal things in His teaching' would compel Jesus to repeat. If, on the other hand, the study of the Gospel is not held to sustain this ingenious theory, we are thrown back upon the choice between placing this incident at the beginning or at the end of the ministry. Accidental displacement seems out of the question. We have then to decide whether the Evangelist placed it at the beginning for doctrinal or dramatic reasons, or because he had good ground to trust the tradition on which he relied for the order of narrative material. In view of the sound tradition of which he avails himself in other places, and seeing that Synoptic evidence means here no more than Mark, who has only the final week in which to place any incidents belonging to Jerusalem, we feel strongly drawn to accepting the Johannine date. Our chief misgiving arises from the close connexion with the Nicodemus episode,

[1] *St. John's Gospel*, pp. 69 f.   [2] *Ibid.*, p. 205.

which might have fitted more naturally into a later stage of the Jewish hostility to Jesus. Archbishop Bernard definitely prefers the Marcan dating of the cleansing of the Temple, and attributes the Johannine position to 'some mistake which cannot now be explained.'[1]

There is one more striking chronological difference upon which a few words should be said. Luke records a story of a great haul of fish, followed by Simon's words of shame and the Master's commission to him as a 'catcher of men' (Luke v. 4-11). This stands as a detached episode in the Third Gospel, which has probably been placed where it is because Simon has been named towards the close of the preceding pericope. Simon's words, 'Depart from me, for I am a sinful man, O Lord,' have no relevance in their present context, but are full of meaning if we regard this as a variant form of the tradition of a post-resurrection appearance to Simon. He who had protested so passionately that he was ready to go both to prison and to death with his Master (Luke xxii. 33), that though all might be offended yet would not he (Mark xiv. 29), has now tasted the bitterness of failure and disgrace. This is the man whose self-humiliation has prepared the way for reinstatement and active service. Surely internal evidence here is on the side of the Fourth Gospel?

[1] *I. C. C.*, 'St. John,' i., pp. 86 ff. A very strong case for accepting the Johannine date is made by Professor C. J. Cadoux in *J. T. S.*, xx., pp. 311 ff. John ii. 20 (not likely to be a carefully calculated fiction) dates this episode as Passover A.D. 27—too early for the final Passover of the ministry. Mr. Warburton Lewis (*J. T. S.*, xxi., pp. 173 ff) meets our difficulty regarding Nicodemus by placing the incident in A.D. 27 *after* the first Galilean ministry.

Chapter IV

THE BACKGROUND OF THOUGHT IN ITS RELATION TO THE JOHANNINE MESSAGE

In the preceding chapter an attempt has been made to show that the Fourth Evangelist was by no means indifferent to historical reality, that he used sources of information which are sometimes not only equal in value to the sources used by the earlier Evangelists, but even superior to them. For all that it would be quite wrong to deny that, in the general presentation of his message, Jesus is seen through a medium of ideas which separates Him in many ways from the familiar figure of the Synoptic Gospels. The most obvious example is the theological term Logos, which dominates the Prologue, and raises the suspicion that the following story is to be related in the interest of some philosophical theory. But this is not the only sign that the Gospel is an interpretation as well as a historical narrative, and that the monologues and dialogues are flung against a background of thought which must be examined unless we are to miss much of the writer's meaning.

Two quotations from scholars of high repute will show how very differently the same book may be read by emphasizing different elements in that background. The first is from Professor Kirsopp Lake, who writes: 'After the Prologue the Logos does not seem to be mentioned again; Jesus appears as the supernatural Lord (though this word is not characteristic of the Gospel), who reveals the Father to men. He offers them

THE BACKGROUND OF THOUGHT 145

salvation by regeneration in baptism, and by eating His flesh and blood in the Eucharist. They become supernaturally the children of God. This is the teaching of the Hellenized Church, not of the historic Jesus. But running through the Gospel there is also another line of thought which regards salvation as due to knowledge rather than sacraments. What is the relation to each other of these two ways of regarding salvation?'[1]

A different view is taken by Professor Adolf Schlatter in his recent book.[2] ' It has been said that John Hellenized the message of Paul. Is it possible to make the thought and purpose Greek without the words becoming Greek? Then is the language of John Hellenized? John has been called a mystic. Was there ever mystical life without mystical language? He calls himself a disciple of Jesus who accompanied Jesus from the Jordan to the cross. If he was a Palestinian, who thought in two languages so widely separated from each other, only academic training could prevent his Greek from betraying its origin.'

Several explanations of the Johannine world of thought lie near the surface in these quotations. First, there is the theory that Greek philosophic thought, mediated through Alexandria by way of Philo, is the key to the true understanding of this Gospel. Secondly, Hellenistic mystery religions, with their stress upon union with divinity through sacramental acts, are said to have contributed ideas and phrases which have left a deep mark upon the Evangelist's mind. Thirdly, some of the peculiar features of the Gospel are believed to prove kinship with Gnosticism in several of its forms. Finally, there is a strong reaction already setting in against looking to the ends of the earth for influences which were at this time

[1] *Landmarks of Early Christianity*, pp. 124 ff.
[2] *Der Evangelist Johannes*, p. viii.

operating in various ways within the borders of Judaism.

(a) It was inevitable that the use of the term Logos in the Prologue should fasten the attention of many scholars upon the works of Philo, in whose writings the streams of Jewish religious speculation and Greek eclecticism mingled and flowed on as one river. The influence of his methods of symbolism and allegory, which can be traced in many parts of the Fourth Gospel, will be dealt with in a later chapter.[1] Philo used the term Logos, which had been current in Greek speculation about divine things from Heraclitus to the Stoics, to express that personified activity of God in creation and revelation which was represented in later Jewish thought by the conception of Wisdom. The thought had already found its way into the New Testament in the cosmic Christology of Colossians and in the exordium of the Epistle to the Hebrews. The word itself first appears in Christian literature in the Prologue. It is not necessary to suppose that the Evangelist was personally acquainted with the writings of Philo, but from the description which Luke gives of Apollos (Acts xviii. 24) it is easy to imagine how Philonic terms and conceptions made their way into the Church at Ephesus. By the time that this Gospel was written, the term Logos must have been as familiar in educated circles as 'evolution' was a generation ago, or as 'relativity' is to-day; whilst in the Jewish Diaspora its special implications in the Alexandrian theology must have played an increasing part in missionary propaganda. The most obvious resemblances to Philo's doctrine of the Logos in the Fourth Gospel[2] are to his conception of the Word as a mediator

[1] See Part III., chap. i., pp. 179 ff.
[2] The fullest list of Philonic parallels to John is given by Grill, *Untersuchungen*, i., pp. 106–39. The subject is treated in most commentaries and books on the Fourth Gospel. Of special value are Moffatt, *I. L. N. T.*, pp. 523 f.; Feine, *Theologie des N. T.*, pp. 346–56; Windisch, *Die Frömmigkeit Philos*, pp. 113–20; H. A. A. Kennedy, *Philo's Contribution to Religion*; articles, 'Logos,' *E. R. E.* (Inge) and *D. C. G.* (E. F. Scott).

between the transcendent God and the universe, as son of God before all creation and His image, reflecting the glory of the Father, the agent of divine activity in creation and revelation. Further resemblances may be traced in the philosophical dualism of Philo, to which the practical dualism of flesh and spirit corresponds in John, so that, in both, the true life is only created in men's souls by a divine act. Still more striking is Philo's identification of the divine Logos with manna (cf. John vi. 31–5) and with the Paraclete (cf. John xiv. 16 ; 1 John ii. 1). On the other hand, Philo's dominating interest is metaphysical, whereas John's is religious. With Philo the Logos is an immanent power bringing to the world a revelation of the unapproachable, transcendent God, whilst John represents the Logos as mediating fellowship between God and man, who thus attains eternal life. John dwells upon two ideas which are far beyond Philo's range of thought, when he gives personality to the Logos, and, above all when he brings forward the doctrine of the Incarnation. Thus, as it has been well said, ' though he borrows the conception, he does not borrow from it.'[1] Throughout the Gospel it is the Jesus of historical reality who is the subject of all the writer's thought. The majestic Figure whose deeds and words are expounded by the Evangelist, sometimes in a theological interest, owes nothing to Greek or Alexandrian philosophic thought. ' The picture of Jesus Himself has nothing in the least answering to it in Philo, and the very ideas which have most appearance of being derived have been brought under the transfiguring influence of an original and creative mind, and turned out stripped of their philosophical dress, and robed with a new spiritual beauty to captivate the world.'[2]

(*b*) In the second decade of this century the attention

[1] Denney, *Jesus and the Gospel,* p. 91 : ' He borrowed the Logos, because it lent itself to the convenient and intelligible expression of this independent Christian conviction.'
[2] J. Drummond, *Character and Authorship of Fourth Gospel,* p. 24.

of scholars was diverted from Hellenic philosophy to the Hellenistic mysteries as a determinative factor in the shaping of early Christian thought and worship. Others had explored this field in the history of religion, but the two men who did most to apply their results to the study of Christian origins were Richard Reitzenstein and Wilhelm Bousset, whose *Kyrios Christos* marked the beginning of a new stage in the religious-historical treatment of the New Testament. The Messiah, or Christ, was the name under which Jesus was preached to Jews, but, when the gospel was carried beyond Palestinian soil to the Gentile world, Messianic terms were meaningless. The missionaries of Christ, however, were greatly aided in their task of interpreting their message by the widespread influence of mystery-cults where some divinity was reverenced under the name ' Lord.' The original Palestinian Church already had this designation for Jesus, as is shown by the primitive prayer, '*Marana tha,*' preserved in this Aramaic form in the Pauline letter. Bousset attempted to show that, as soon as this transference of Christian faith and worship to Gentile soil was accomplished, Hellenistic ideas found their way into the Christology and the cultus of the Church, Paul and John being the great representatives of this new movement in the New Testament. He certainly does call attention[1] to the striking fact that the term ' Lord ' only appears in the Fourth Gospel after the Crucifixion, and acknowledges that this fact must not be pressed as evidence that the Evangelist kept this term for the exalted Lord of Christian faith, otherwise we have still to account for its entire absence from the Johannine Epistles. He also calls attention to the strange fact that John retains the primitive title, Son of Man, but divests it of its apocalyptic associations, though not entirely of its eschatological reference (John v. 27 ff.). The title Son of God characterizes a new

[1] *Kyrios Christos*, ed. 2, p. 155.

conception which this Gospel brings forward to supersede the older Palestinian Son of Man. We must not stay to discuss how far this term has its roots in an original Christian attitude to Christ, for it is the next point in Bousset's treatment of Johannine thought that has become the starting-point of the latest debate. While treating Pauline and Johannine piety as variants of the same type, he distinguishes John's Christ-mysticism from Paul's by tracing it to a God-mysticism which is most characteristic of Hellenistic piety. This is most clearly seen in 1 John iii. 2, which expresses the idea of deification through the vision of God, even though it stands here in an eschatological context.[1]

It is this distinction between Christ-mysticism and God-mysticism which Schweitzer has developed with such surprising results in his latest book.[2] As his earlier book, *Paul and his Interpreters*, clearly showed, Schweitzer is opposed to those, like Reitzenstein and Bousset, who regard Paul as the innovator who Hellenized Christianity. Schweitzer's thesis is that Paul did not Hellenize Christianity, but prepared the way for its Hellenization by his doctrine of union with Christ.[3] Paul never speaks of union with God or of 'being in God.' He asserts that believers are God's children, but this is not an immediate, mystical relationship to God, but an experience mediated and realized by means of the mystical fellowship with Christ. This 'being in Christ' is also represented as being freed from sin and law, possessed by the Spirit of Christ, with an assurance of the resurrection, and it begins by an experience of dying and rising with Christ. So much is clear, but Schweitzer goes on to claim that this Pauline

[1] *Kyrios Christos*, ed. 2, pp. 163 f.
[2] *Die Mystik des Apostels Paulus* (1930), E.T. by W. Montgomery, *The Mysticism of Paul the Apostle* (1931).
[3] *Ibid.*, p. ix: 'Paul was not the Hellenizer of Christianity. But in his eschatological mysticism of the Being-in-Christ he gave it a form in which it could be Hellenized.'

mysticism is also eschatologically conditioned[1] and continuous with the teaching of Jesus. The teaching of both was eschatological, but, whereas that of Jesus followed the teaching of Daniel and Enoch, that of Paul followed the lines begun in Baruch and 4 Ezra. The former type looked for only one crisis, the latter expected two crises, one ushering in the millennial interval which must be followed by the second resurrection, leading on to the eternal kingdom of righteousness. For Paul, the death and resurrection of Christ marked the end of the old order. This was the necessary difference between his teaching and that of the Master. 'Paul shares with Jesus the eschatological world-view and the eschatological expectation, with all that these imply. The only difference is the hour in the world-clock in the two cases. To use another figure, both are looking towards the same mountain range, but whereas Jesus sees it as lying before Him, Paul already stands upon it and its first slopes are already behind him.'[2] For him the Messianic period has already come, although it is hidden from all but the elect until the return of Jesus in glory, which may now take place at any moment. The first crisis has come and gone, unseen by the world, but leaving its evidence in the change manifest in the interior lives of the saints.

Such is Schweitzer's argument that Paul's eschatology is continuous with that of Jesus. He now goes further and attempts to show that the Pauline mysticism is a development of the teaching of Jesus Himself. The preaching of Jesus already contained a Christ-mysticism. This is shown in such phrases as Matt. v. 11-12; Mark viii. 35, 38. In this connexion we must consider the significance of the miraculous feeding of the multitude (Mark vi. 34-44). Such a saying as ' He that receiveth

[1] *The Mysticism of Paul the Apostle*, p. 112. Paul's mysticism is ' the eschatological conception of redemption looked at from within.'
[1] *Ibid.*, p. 113.

you receiveth Me, and he that receiveth Me receiveth Him that sent Me ' (Matt. x. 40) supports this view. In Matt. xxv. 31–46 the ethical holds its significance by means of the mystical. The least of the brethren of the Son of Man belongs to the community of the elect who are in fellowship with the Son of Man. Jesus thus taught a Christ-mysticism as it availed for the age in which the coming Messiah went about unrecognized in earthly form. Paul taught a Christ-mysticism as it availed for the age which followed the death and resurrection of Christ. Jesus had attained Messiahship through His death. He had won by His death forgiveness of sins for those who belong to Him. It is here that Paul's mysticism finds its central doctrine. The elect share with one another and with Christ in a bodily life which in a special way displays the powers of the death and resurrection of Jesus. The saints participate in the body of the risen Lord. They are now ready for the conditions of the resurrection life before the general resurrection has taken place. Then, by a simplification, to participate in the life of the risen body of Christ (the power of His resurrection) becomes participation in the ' Body of Christ.' At this point those who have read Schweitzer's earlier books will see how all this is linked up with his conception of the eschatological character of baptism in the Gospels and in Paul, as well as the significance of the Lord's Supper.

The great contrast between Pauline and Johannine mysticism, as we have already seen, is said to be that between God-mysticism and Christ-mysticism. Those responsible for Hellenizing Christianity are Ignatius, Justin, and, above all, the Johannine Theology. Although Schweitzer dates the Fourth Gospel at the beginning of the second century he places it at the end of this process of development.[1]

Hellenistic mysticism perceives the need of being able

[1] *The Mysticism of Paul the Apostle*, pp. 349–69.

to appeal to the teaching of Jesus. Hence the Fourth Gospel was written that Jesus might appear as the Logos-Christ, who proclaims the redemption to be obtained by the operation of the Spirit as a result of fellowship with Him. This redemption (like that developed in the Ignatian letters) depends on the attainment of immortality by being in Him who brings immortality. This condition is conceived as Rebirth. The ' being in Christ ' is also a ' being in God ' (cf. John xvii. 21). These two together make the fundamental distinction between the Hellenistic and the eschatological mysticism.[1]

There are expressions in the preaching of the Logos-Christ which sound as if redemption were gained simply through faith in Him (John iii. 36, viii. 51, xi. 25–6). In others the Logos-Christ refers in clearest terms to baptism and the Eucharist, affirming that rebirth, by water and Spirit, and eating and drinking the flesh and blood of the Son of Man are necessary to salvation. Schweitzer tries to combine these two conceptions of redemption by saying that the Logos-Christ requires faith in Himself, not only as the incarnate Word, but as the bringer of the sacraments. So long as the Logos-Christ is upon earth, all the power of the Logos-Spirit is concentrated in Him and works immediately from Him. After His glorification the Spirit, operating through baptism and the Eucharist, has the faculty of imparting immortal life to men. By correlating such passages as John vi. 56 and 1 John iv. 13, Schweitzer attempts to show that, where the Spirit is promised, the sacraments are also intended, and, conversely, where the sacraments are brought into view, the coming of the Spirit is also presupposed (John vii. 39, xvi. 7, xvi. 12–13). The idea of the mystical body of Christ is not maintained in the Hellenized mysticism of ' being in Christ,' for it is altogether eschatologically conditioned.

[1] *The Mysticism of Paul the Apostle*, pp. 350 f.

Schweitzer discovers hidden as well as open allusions to the sacraments everywhere. Water (with an allusion to baptism) has a place in almost all the miracles, e.g. John ii. 1–11, v. 2 ff., vi. 16–21, ix. 1–11 ! The same applies to such sayings as iv. 14, vii. 37–9. In John xix. 34–5 and 1 John v. 6–8, water and blood mean baptism and Eucharist. So also the Feet-washing is to be interpreted. As the Spirit could not be given until after the glorification of Jesus, He gave His disciples their baptism in two stages : the water in this rite on that last night and the Spirit after the Resurrection (John xiii. 7–8, xx. 21–3). Similarly the Eucharist is traced, not only in John vi. 1–13, but in such surprising places as iv. 34–8, xii. 23–4. ' The sacramental stands for so much, in the Johannine mysticism of union with Christ, that the main significance of the death of Jesus is, according to it, the provision of the sacraments.'[1]

The Synoptic account of the Last Supper is omitted because of the Evangelist's belief that Jesus could not thus have administered the bread and wine as His flesh and blood, since the Spirit who works this change does so by reason of the death and resurrection of Christ. Therefore John undertakes to annul the story of the institution as an erroneous tradition. On the other hand, because the Logos-Christ is conscious of coming into the world and meeting death in order that the resurrection may be mediated through the sacraments, He intimates to His hearers that they shall see still greater works than those which He performs during His earthly life (John v. 20 f., xiv. 12). Thus Paul and John both attribute greater powers to the glorified than to the incarnate Christ. Yet in the Johannine thought the supernatural is already present with the appearance of the Logos-Christ, whereas this begins in Paul's scheme after the death and resurrection of Jesus. Similarly the Law is not a problem to

[1] *The Mysticism of Paul the Apostle*, p. 364.

John as it was to Paul, for the Law became meaningless from the moment that the Logos-Christ appeared. His coming marked the beginning of the redemption and the judgement. As bringer of immortality He wrought a division amongst men. The separation to life or to death is a judgement fulfilled in the sacraments. Christ's return as Spirit, working in the sacraments, is thus already His return for judgement. The Fourth Evangelist purposely makes Jesus in His farewell discourse speak in such a way that His words are to be understood sometimes of the return in the Spirit and sometimes of the end of history. It is not easy to say how much living eschatological expectation remains in the Fourth Gospel, but there is certainly an expectation of the visible parousia of the Son of Man, and a general resurrection to judgement.

Schweitzer lays great stress on the freedom of Paul's mysticism from Hellenizing influences, and attributes the Johannine mysticism largely to the play of these contemporary forces. He therefore rejects Deissmann's dictum,[1] 'The greatest monument of the most genuine understanding of Paul's mysticism is the Gospel and Epistles of John,' and adds, 'One might as well say that Beethoven was the best interpreter of J. S. Bach!'[2]

This exposition has been given at considerable length, not only because of the great interest that attaches to all that Schweitzer writes, but also because his recent book is the fullest attempt that has yet been made to relate the Pauline mysticism to the eschatology of the Gospels and at the same time to differentiate the Johannine mysticism from that of Paul.[3] There is much that is valuable in the

[1] *Paul*, English trans., ed. 2, p. 155.
[2] *The Mysticism of Paul the Apostle*, p. 372.
[3] [Dr. Howard apologized for this 'tedious summary of Schweitzer's argument', but regarded it as necessary because there was no English translation of Schweitzer's book. A translation is now available, and references to it have been inserted, but it seemed worth while to retain Dr. Howard's exposition. C. K. B.]

argument for continuity between the teaching of Jesus and that of Paul. The continuity between the teaching of Jesus and that of the Fourth Gospel, however, can also be argued. In the Synoptic Gospels the apocalyptic view of the Kingdom of God is not the only one expressed in the teaching of Jesus. The two conceptions are found side by side, as they also are in the Fourth Gospel. The experience of the risen Lord and the manifest presence of the Spirit in the Church has brought a new factor of interpretation into the thought of the coming of Christ. In both Gospel and First Epistle there is a forward look to the perfected manifestation of Christ. Though eternal life is already a present experience, and judgement is already at work in the world, yet all that is now going on in silent process is to be revealed in some future climax of judgement. In exaggerating the Hellenism of the Fourth Gospel Schweitzer omits such unmistakably Jewish conceptions as the Lamb of God,[1] and puts an impossible strain on the one text, John xvii. 21 ff., to show that God-mysticism rather than Christ-mysticism is the mark of distinction between the doctrine of the living union in Paul and that taught by John. Allusions to the sacraments, especially to baptism, are found in places where nothing but uncontrolled fancy could discover anything of the sort. Faith is not given the place which it occupies in the teaching both of Paul and John, yet it is just in connexion with the gift of eternal life that faith comes into strongest relief. We have already noticed how Schweitzer overlooks the relation between the Synoptic (and Pauline) term ' Kingdom of God' and the Johannine term 'eternal life.' But by bringing the latter exclusively into the sacramental context he suggests an association with the Hellenistic conception of

[1] On this and many other points, see the searching criticism of Schweitzer's book in a valuable article, ' Das Johannesevangelium und die Hellenisierung des Christentums,' by Professor Wilhelm Michaelis, of Bern, in *Kirchenblatt für die reformierte Schweiz*, lxxxvi. (August 14, 1930), pp. 257–64.

deification,[1] which is entirely absent from the Johannine writings, though the first beginnings may be traced in a well-known phrase of Ignatius,[2] and its full acceptance by Christian Fathers took place before the end of the second century.[3] Indeed the mere fact that Schweitzer can commit the glaring anachronism of placing the Johannine theology at the end of the sequence, Ignatius–Justin–John, raises doubts as to the validity of his method, both historical and exegetical. We shall have to examine the nature of the sacramentalism, as of the mysticism, of John in a later chapter, but at this point we must observe that the distinction between the conception of 'new creation' in Paul and 'new birth' (or 'birth from above') in John is magnified, the more so if we accept Ephesians as Pauline, whatever view may be taken as to the authorship of Titus.[4] It is most probable that Hellenistic mystery-terms were already coming into the Christian vocabulary when this Gospel was written, and that in some quarters the influence went beyond the loan of words. Nevertheless, the emphasis put upon faith and on the ethical demands of the new commandment, in the very passages where the mystical union with Christ is most prominent, leaves an impression on the mind of the reader that we are far removed from the outlook of Hellenistic mysticism.

(c) Other scholars, while recognizing resemblances, in the Prologue, to the language of Philo, and also feeling that there are points of contact with the religion of the mysteries, look rather in the direction of Egyptian Gnosticism for some parallels to the thought and language of the Fourth Gospel. Loisy writes[5]: 'The conception, religious

---

[1] Rohde, *Psyche*, ed. 7, ii., p. 2 : 'Wer unter Griechen unsterblich sagt, sagt Gott : das sind Wechselbegriffe.'
[2] Ignatius, *Ad Eph.*, xx. 2 : 'breaking one bread, which is the medicine of immortality, the antidote that we should not die, but live for ever in Jesus Christ.'
[3] See Inge, *Christian Mysticism*, pp. 356 ff.
[4] Cf. Eph. v. 26 ; Titus iii. 5.
[5] *Le Quatrième Évangile*, ed. 2, p. 89.

and mystical, of our Logos is much more strictly and directly related to Egyptian theosophy, which, using on one side the assimilation of the Logos to Hermes in the Stoic preaching, and on the other identifying Hermes with the god Thoth, saw in Thoth-Hermes, not only the Logos organ of the creation, but the mediator of the divine revelation and of regeneration for immortality, and worked, like our Gospel, with the mystic terms of " truth," " light," " life." It is with this mystery-doctrine that the Johannine conception, a theory of the Christian mystery, has affinity, without our being able to affirm, otherwise, that there is direct dependence.' In the same way, Professor C. H. Dodd[1] finds its affinity ' with that peculiar kind of Platonic thought, modified by oriental influences, which is otherwise best represented for us by the Hermetic literature of the second and third centuries. This Gospel is in fact one of the most remarkable examples, in all the literature of the period, of the profound interpenetration of Greek and Semitic thought.' It is needless to rehearse the examples, given in an earlier chapter,[2] of the way in which parallels have been brought out from other Gnostic sources which are traced to Syrian provenance. Probably none of them provides any evidence of sources from which the Fourth Evangelist drew. Harnack[3] looked upon ' the discovery of the Odes of Solomon as epoch-making for the historical elucidation of the Gospel of John,' but opinion now inclines to a date considerably later than that of the Gospel.[4] In the same way the eagerness with which the Mandaean writings were hailed, as showing how many of the conceptions and not a little of the language of the Fourth Gospel came from contemporary Gnosticism, has been checked by the evidence which Professors F. C. Burkitt[5] and Hans Lietzmann[6] have brought forward to

---

[1] *The Authority of the Bible*, p. 200.   [2] Part I., chap. iv. See pp. 77 ff.
[3] *Ein Psalmbuch aus dem* 1. *Jahrhundert*, p. 119.
[4] Goguel, *Introd. au N.T.*, ii., pp. 524 f.
[5] *J. T. S.*, xxix., pp. 225–35.   [6] *Ein Beitrag zur Mandäerfrage* (1930)

show that Mandaism is a late development of Marcionite Gnosticism, mingled with the astrological theosophy of Bardaisan, with Christian elements mediated through Nestorian channels, and biblical allusions borrowed from the Peshitta. It is, of course, possible that some of the Gnostic elements go back through oral tradition to Marcion and his contemporaries, and to that extent are typical of the syncretism which was so widespread in the second century. The closer examination of the Mandaean documents, however, as Lietzmann reminds us, will enable us to study the 'christianizing of an oriental Gnosis, not the Gnostic background of early Christianity.'[1]

(d) There are signs that the next important concentration of effort will be to work out the connexion between the teaching of Jesus as given in this Gospel and the more mystical element in early Jewish religious thought. For nearly thirty years, Professor Schlatter has been at work to show from second-century rabbinic commentaries on the Old Testament how the phraseology of the Fourth Gospel can be illustrated as thoroughly Jewish. Dr. Burney brought out some rabbinic parallels of thought, although his main interest was to establish the Aramaic cast of the Johannine sentence-structure.[2] Quite recently the well-known rabbinic scholar, Paul Fiebig, has dealt with two Johannine passages in two articles.[3] In one he shows what close rabbinic illustrations can be adduced for 'the Good Shepherd' and 'the Door' in John x. 11, 7. In the other he expounds the Feet-washing, with special reference to John xiii. 8–10, to dismiss the interpretation which Bauer has given whereby Jesus alludes here to baptism and the Supper. But the most complete application of the study of rabbinic thought to the interpretation of this Gospel is Dr. Odeberg's exposition of chaps. i.–xii.

---

[1] *Ein Beitrag zur Mandäerfrage*, p. 15.
[2] *Aramaic Origin of Fourth Gospel*, pp. 132, 133.
[3] ΑΓΓΕΛΟΣ, i., pp. 57 ff., iii., pp. 121 ff.

He has been struck by a remarkable parallel between the Fourth Gospel and early Jewish mysticism. In the latter there is a correspondence with certain strata in the Mandaean literature, including an identity of technical terms and expressions. Living within the environment of rabbinic Judaism and using its language and general phraseology, yet with respect to certain central tenets this mystical Judaism stands with Mandaism against Rabbinism. In the same way the Fourth Gospel has many passages with a terminology almost identical with the rabbinic, and yet these very passages 'put us in touch with a sphere of conceptions and ideas wholly removed from rabbinic ones.' The whole purpose of his commentary on the sayings in the Fourth Gospel is to show that there were in contemporary Judaism many different currents of thought by the side of Rabbinism. We have here a needed corrective to the tendency to treat the Johannine Gospel as the Gospel of Hellenism. At the same time, we must watch the reaction lest it should try to prove too much. If one example may serve, we notice that Paul Fiebig breathes a caution when Schlatter quotes rabbinic parallels to John iv. 42. The examples illustrate the word 'Saviour.' He cannot parallel 'the Saviour of the world.'[1] We thus come back to that admirable characterization of the Gospel by Dr. C. H. Dodd and complete the quotation. 'Some critics, approaching it from the side of Judaism, have pronounced it the most Jewish of the Gospels, while others, approaching it from the other side, see in it a thoroughly Hellenistic book. Nowhere more evidently than here does early Christianity take its place as the natural leader in new ways of thought, uniting in itself the main tendencies of the time, yet exercising authority over them by virtue of the creative impulse proceeding from its Founder.'[2]

[1] *Th. L. Z.*, lvi. (1931), 203.   [2] *Op. cit.*, pp. 200 f.

Summary

In the Second Part, four aspects of the complex Johannine problem have been viewed. Two of them are concerned with internal structure, and two with external relationship, but they are all vitally connected with the important question whether the Fourth Gospel has any title to be taken seriously into account as a representation of the outward course of the ministry of Jesus.

From time to time the integrity of the Gospel has been called in question. On the most diverse grounds, and in a considerable variety of ways, attempts have been made, either to show how an original *Grundschrift* has been overlaid with incongruous material from another document, or to claim that redaction on a large scale can be traced throughout the book. Many of these analytical schemes are very attractive until one finds that they are mutually destructive. Stylistic considerations leave a strong impression of substantial literary unity throughout the Gospel, and, in spite of some differences that can be pointed out, the recurrence of some of the characteristic marks throughout the Johannine Epistles strengthens the impression made by the general resemblance in subject-matter that they come from the same pen as the Gospel. The Apocalypse must be attributed to a different hand.

In several places internal evidence raises a strong suspicion that sections of the Gospel are not in their right order. A growing weight of opinion finds the explanation in a theory of displacement of leaves. Some attribute this to an accident which befell the manuscript after the writer's death, and the carelessness of the editor who regrouped the scattered leaves. Others, with greater probability, think that the writer left his manuscript imperfectly arranged, and the reverence in which he was held by his disciple prevented any change in the manuscript as it had been left, beyond a few words here and there. The discovery that, in several of the passages where re-arrangement is required on internal grounds, the displaced sections are, as regards length, multiples of a fixed unit has done much to remove this hypothesis from the class of capricious and subjective speculation which mars so many theories regarding this Gospel.

The consequent re-arrangement of the sections gives us a text of the Gospel which may now be examined to see how the ministry of Jesus in the Fourth Gospel compares with the data provided by the Synoptics. With one notable exception, there is no reason why the Synoptic account of the Galilean ministry, with journeys through Samaria and into the North, should not fall within the time-limits marked clearly in this Johannine outline of the life of Jesus from the Baptism to the Cross. John shows an intimate knowledge of visits to Jerusalem of which there are faint hints in Luke at least. In John there are indications of superior sources of information regarding the last days in Jerusalem, and in the matter of the Last Supper and the date of the Crucifixion there is a strong tendency to-day to accept the superiority of John to Mark. In one respect the general verdict goes against John. The narrative of the cleansing of the Temple is usually regarded as an example of Johannine *misplacement*, though a few scholars argue for accidental *displacement*, and think that this episode and the closely related section about Nicodemus originally came in chap. xii. Others think that in his source the Evangelist found it placed in the events of the last week as it stands in Mark, and that for dogmatic reasons he transferred it to the opening of the ministry. Recognizing that the choice is not between John and the Synoptics, but simply between John and Mark, and feeling how impossible certainty is in such a matter, we strongly incline to the opinion that the Fourth Evangelist is right in putting this episode at the first Passover. In that case, Jesus, after the first Galilean ministry and a ministry in Judaea parallel to that of the Baptist, came up to the Holy City at the Passover of A.D. 27, and there flung down His challenge to the false ideas of worship and religion at the very centre of Judaism. The main result of this part of our examination is that in certain respects the Fourth Gospel is a valuable source for our knowledge of the course of the ministry of Jesus, supplying information where the Marcan narrative fails us, especially about the visits to the capital for the festivals, and the conflicts that there arose.

The closing chapter of this part of the book considers how far the general outlook of the Gospel is determined by religious forces which belong to a period much later than the lifetime of Jesus, and to a *milieu* remote from Palestinian Judaism. In this connexion a lengthy examination was given to Schweitzer's theory that Paul's mysticism is Palestinian eschatological mysticism, definitely related to that of Jesus, whereas John's is a Hellenistic mysticism, quite unrelated to that of Jesus and Paul. While agreeing that the Fourth Evangelist is influenced by a strain of religious thought that is found in other manifestations in Syria and in Egypt, and later on in other syncretistic forms of Gnosticism, we are led to the conclusion that this was not the creative and dominant element in the thought of the Gospel. The historical Jesus is the central force behind the Gospel, drawing to Himself all the best thought in the world contemporary with the Evangelist.

This leads us on by a natural transition to the Third Part, in which we shall consider the interpretation of the

Gospel. The place which symbolism and allegory must take in our method of reading the narrative or the discourses; the temperament of the Evangelist, and the extent to which his mysticism influences his imagination as a writer; the attitude of the Gospel to the sacraments, and their current use or abuse in the Church,—these are waiting to be investigated in the light of the closing chapter of this Part.

Most important of all is the next question and its sequel, whether, beneath the unmistakable accent of the Fourth Gospel, we can hear the message of Jesus as He spoke in Palestine, and, further, whether we can assure ourselves that this Evangelist brings us a revelation from the Jesus who is the same yesterday, to-day, and for ever.

CHAPTER V

CRITICISM OF THE FOURTH GOSPEL
1931–1953[1]

THE outstanding events in this period have been the publication of two ancient papyri, both ascribed by palaeographers to a date not later, and possibly several decades earlier, than A.D. 150. Of these papyri, one is a fragment of a MS. of the Fourth Gospel itself, and the other contains part of a Gospel hitherto unknown but evidently related to the Fourth Gospel.

Rylands Papyrus 457, published in 1935 by Mr. C. H. Roberts, contains only John xviii. 31–3, 37, 38, but was originally part of a codex; whether the codex contained John only, or the four Gospels, or other parts of the New Testament or other books remains of course unknown. Its official designation in the New Testament apparatus is P^{52}; its main textual interest is that it shows no striking variant from the texts now commonly used.

Egerton Papyrus 2, also published in 1935, by Dr. H. I. Bell and Mr. T. C. Skeat, presents many more problems. In form it might well represent a couple of pages from our New Testament Gospels, and in substance also it is closely related to the canonical literature. In particular, there are very close parallels to John v. 39, 45; vii. 30, 32, 44; viii. 59; ix. 29; x. 25, 31, 39. To account for these parallels three hypotheses may be formulated. (*a*) John was a source of the 'new' Gospel. (*b*) The 'new' Gospel was a source of John. (*c*) The writers of the two

[1] In this chapter, where bibliographical details are not supplied reference should be made to the Bibliography (pp. 312-16).

Gospels drew independently upon the same traditional material. The verbal resemblance is so close as to make (c) improbable, though it cannot be excluded as impossible.[1] Professor C. H. Dodd[2] has argued very cogently in favour of (a), and if his views are accepted the writing of the Fourth Gospel must be pushed back to a date earlier than that of the papyrus, and we can say with some probability (though not with complete certainty) that John wrote not later than the earliest years of the second century.

This MS. evidence of the early use of the Gospel becomes the more interesting and important if it is held, with Mr. J. N. Sanders, that neither Ignatius nor any other of the Apostolic Fathers can be shown to have known it. Even Justin (according to Mr. Sanders) shows only the first tentative use of the Gospel by an orthodox Christian. The gnostic heretics indeed had used the Gospel earlier; and this early gnostic use, and early orthodox disuse, together constitute one of the major problems in the early history of the Gospel. The data also lead Mr. Sanders to the conclusion that the Gospel was written not (as the tradition maintains) in Ephesus, but in Alexandria. In support of this view he uses the following arguments: (a) The two papyri prove that the Gospel was in use in Alexandria before A.D. 150, and if it is not certain that Ignatius knew the Gospel this is the earliest evidence for its existence. (b) The Alexandrian gnostics are known to have used the Gospel. (c) Internal evidence points in the same direction. Alexandria, the home of Philo and of the authors of the *Corpus Hermeticum*, was a likely place for the development of a Christian Logos-doctrine, and forms a suitable background for the simultaneous anti-docetic and anti-Judaic polemic of the Gospel. (d) The heretical reputation of the Alexandrian Church would account for

---

[1] It is accepted by Dr. Mayeda.
[2] *Bulletin of the John Rylands Library*, xx (1936), pp. 56-92.

the slow reception of the Gospel by orthodox Christians.

The relation between Ignatius and the Fourth Gospel is undoubtedly of cardinal importance, and it must be noted that a view different from that of Mr. Sanders is taken by Dr. Christian Maurer, who believes that Ignatius knew the Gospel and quoted it, though somewhat loosely. Ignatius thus reproduces some of John's words, but he uses them in a new sense. Words such as 'Logos' were used by John in a biblical sense, but by Ignatius were filled with a gnostic content, so that though his epistles bear a superficial resemblance to the Fourth Gospel the Johannine and Ignatian theologies are essentially different.

A debated question on which unanimity still seems far distant is that of the original order and structure of the Gospel. The succession of those who have believed that displacements and redactional glosses can be detected has been continued, most notably by Mr. F. R. Hoare and Dr. Rudolf Bultmann. Mr. Hoare, like others before him, bases his reconstruction upon a division of the Gospel into sections of equal length, which he believes to have suffered disarrangement. Some of his most important suggestions are the reversal of ii. 1–iv. 3a and iv. 3b–43; the placing of vii. 15–24 between v. 47 and vi. 1; the rearrangement (after chapter ix), x. 19–xi. 33, xii. 23b–33, xi. 34–xii. 23a, x. 1–18; and the re-ordering of the Last Discourses as follows: xiii. 1–19, xv. 17–xvi. 4a, xiii. 20–xiv. 14, xvi. 15b–23, xiv. 15–24a, xvi. 4b–15a, xiv. 24b–xv. 16, xvi. 24–xvii. After chapter xvi Mr. Hoare makes no further rearrangements in the text of the Gospel. Dr. Bultmann's proposals are much more radical, and far too complicated to be given in detail here. He believes that the Gospel was constructed in the first instance on the basis of sources, to which he gives the names '*Offenbarungsrede*' (revelatory discourse) and '$\sigma\eta\mu\epsilon\hat{\iota}\alpha$-*Quelle*' (signs-source). Along with this source-material he finds in the Gospel numerous editorial and redactional glosses and comments; and the whole must at some time have been subjected to some disturbing and disruptive force, the result of which has been to leave it in a state of serious disorder. The evidence on which this last conclusion rests is primarily the detection of incongruities of thought. It is doubtful whether any displacement and redaction theory has been worked out so completely and consistently as Dr. Bultmann's, and it is its very completeness which makes it impossible for a brief summary to do justice to it. It is however hardly unfair to say that the author never succeeds in giving a completely satisfying account of *how* the disruption took place, and, though his work is a monument of learning and acuteness, perhaps the most enduring lesson to be learnt from it is that such modest theories as those of Mr. Hoare and many of his predecessors are ultimately unsatisfying: we must either rearrange (with Dr. Bultmann) a good deal more—or else a good deal less.[1]

Several outstanding English students of the Fourth Gospel have recently declared against displacement theories. This movement of thought is no return to a pre-critical handling of the Gospels, but is due primarily to two causes. In the first place, it has been recognized that chronological sequence and smoothness of itinerary were not the Evangelist's aim. He was not a historian (in the narrower sense), but a theologian. Consequently, to improve the chronology, or to smooth out an itinerary, is not necessarily to come nearer to the original form of his book. In the second place, a serious attempt has been made to expound the Evangelist's thought as it is developed through the Gospel, and the result has been the conviction that the book makes very good sense as it stands, and that though to rearrange it may improve

[1] Dr. Eduard Schweizer, on the basis of a detailed examination of Johannine style, decides that the stylistic uniformity of the Gospel renders it impossible to detect sources within it.

some thought-sequences it spoils others. If this conviction is justified there is no case for rearrangement.

One of the first scholars to express this view was Dr. R. H. Strachan, whose opinion carried the greater weight because in earlier writings he had himself maintained a theory of redaction. Others are E. C. Hoskyns and Professor C. H. Dodd, both of whom expound the Gospel in its traditional order, and can in general show good theological grounds for the present arrangement of the material. Professor Dodd writes as follows: 'It is . . . impossible to deny that the work may have suffered dislocation, and plausible grounds may be alleged for lifting certain passages out of their setting, where there seems to be some *prima facie* breach of continuity. Unfortunately, when once the Gospel has been taken to pieces, its reassemblage is liable to be affected by individual preferences, preconceptions and even prejudices. Meanwhile the work lies before us in an order which (apart from insignificant details) does not vary in the textual tradition, traceable to an early period. I conceive it to be the duty of an interpreter at least to see what can be done with the document as it has come down to us before attempting to improve upon it. This is what I shall try to do. I shall assume as a provisional working hypothesis that the present order is not fortuitous, but deliberately devised by somebody—even if he were only a scribe doing his best—and that the person in question (whether the author or another) had some design in mind, and was not necessarily irresponsible or unintelligent. If the attempt to discover any intelligible thread of argument should fail, then we may be compelled to confess that we do not know how the work was originally intended to run. If on the other hand it should appear that the structure of the Gospel as we have it has been shaped in most of its details by the ideas which seem to dominate the author's thought, then it would appear not improbable that we have his work before us substantially in the form which he designed' (pp. 289 f.). The latter alternative is, of course, that which Professor Dodd himself accepts.

Another disputed question is that of the relation between John and the Synoptic Gospels. On p. 130 of this book Dr. Howard wrote of John: 'By general consent he made use of Mark... There is less complete agreement regarding John's use of Luke.' This was in 1931 an accurate statement; but in 1938 Mr. P. Gardner-Smith published a strong argument that John wrote in complete independence of the Synoptic Gospels. He complains, not without justice, that critics who have discussed the relation between John and the Synoptic Gospels have tended to ignore the important part played in the first century by oral tradition, and to concentrate upon the comparatively small measure of agreement between John and the Synoptic Gospels, and neglect the much greater and no less significant differences. He proceeds to examine both the resemblances and the differences, and though he leaves the reader to weigh them, the one against the other, he makes clear his own belief that the latter outweigh the former. The resemblances can usually be accounted for as due to the use of common, or similar, traditions; the differences are often inexplicable on the assumption of direct literary relationship. Finally, Mr. Gardner-Smith points out that if his contention is accepted the questions of the date and independent historical value of the Fourth Gospel are reopened. His arguments have won some acceptance; they were in substance admitted by Dr. Howard,[1] and Professor Dodd, referring to Mr. Gardner-Smith's book, writes (p. 449): 'Definite evidence pointing to documentary relations between John and the Synoptics is seen to be singularly sparse, when once the presumption in favour of such relations is abandoned. The *prima facie* impression is that John is, in large

[1] See the second note on p. 173 below.

measure at any rate, working independently of other written Gospels.' For Hoskyns's discussion of the relation between John and the Synoptic material see pp. 174, 246 f.

Why did the Fourth Evangelist write as he did? Why did he write at all? These questions evidently touch upon the problem of interpretation, dealt with on pp. 243–66, below. But they also bear upon the problems of authorship and setting and must for that reason be mentioned here.

Most modern writers are agreed that there exists a connexion of some kind between the Fourth Gospel and Gnosticism. This seems to be affirmed both by the contents of the Gospel, and by its external history, in which it was first used by the gnostic heretics themselves, and subsequently adopted as a major weapon in the armoury of those who, like Irenaeus and Hippolytus, fought the Gnostics and drove them out of the Church, and though it was denied outright by W. Temple that the Gospel was anything but 'Hebraic' it becomes increasingly difficult to deny that John was aware of the terms of gnostic thought. It remains of course possible that his relation to this kind of thought was negative—that is, he knew it, but disliked, rejected and opposed it.

The thesis has been maintained by Dr. W. Oehler that the Gospel was written as a piece of missionary propaganda. Dr. Oehler considers the various points of resemblance which have been detected between John and the gnostic systems, and contends that the resemblance must mean one of two things. Either it is a fundamental resemblance of substance, in which case the Gospel is a fundamentally heathen book and has no true place in the New Testament; or it is only a superficial resemblance due to the employment by the Evangelist of current terminology with a missionary purpose in view.[1]

---

[1] Dr. Oehler believes that chapters xv-xvii were a sermon addressed to Christians, which has been inserted into a missionary tract.

A view in outline similar to Dr. Oehler's is taken by Professor C. H. Dodd, who writes: 'This in itself [the occurrence of non-Christian religious symbolism] suggests that the Evangelist has in view a non-Christian public to which he wishes to appeal. . . . The Gospel could be read intelligently by a person who started with no knowledge of Christianity beyond the minimum that a reasonably well-informed member of the public interested in religion might be supposed to have by the close of the first century, and Christian ideas are instilled step by step until the whole mystery can be divulged. If he was then led to associate himself with the Church and to participate in its fellowship, its tradition and its sacraments, he would be able to re-read the book and find in it vastly more than had been obvious at a first reading. . . . It seems therefore that we are to think of the work as addressed to a wide public consisting primarily of devout and thoughtful persons . . . in the varied and cosmopolitan society of a great Hellenistic city such as Ephesus under the Roman Empire ' (pp. 8 f.). It is right to add that Professor Dodd seems to allow to non-Christian factors a larger share in shaping the Evangelist's thought (as well as its expression) than does Dr. Oehler.

Maximum weight is given to non-Christian, and in particular to gnostic, factors by Dr. W. Bauer and Dr. R. Bultmann. For some account of their views see pp. 78–82. Since the first edition of this book was written, Dr. Bultmann's commentary on the Gospel has been published and it should here be noted that he believes the '*Offenbarungsreden*' (p. 166, *supra*) which were used by the Evangelist to have been Gnostic documents which John 'Christianized' and 'historicized' by combining them with the '$\sigma\eta\mu\epsilon\tilde{\iota}\alpha$-*Quelle*' in his account of Jesus. John himself, like this source-material, was at home within the sphere of Gnosticism, and in expressing the Christian faith (and in his polemic against the followers of John the Baptist) naturally employed the concepts and symbols with which he was familiar. He had in mind no particular circle of readers, but of himself produced a Gnostic-Christian Gospel.

An opposite position to that of Dr. Bauer and Dr. Bultmann is taken by F. Büchsel and Dr. E. Percy of Lund. The latter in particular examines, with great learning, the teaching of the gnostic sources on Dualism, the Redeemer and Redemption, and tests the relation of the Fourth Gospel to this teaching. His conclusion is negative: John's book, and his purpose in writing it, have nothing to do with Gnosticism. A very balanced account of, and contribution to, the discussion is made by Dr. E. Schweizer.

It is characteristic of the work of the late Sir Edwyn Hoskyns that in interpreting the Fourth Gospel he took his stand firmly within the biblical and Christian tradition. Were his not a posthumous and admittedly incomplete work there would perhaps be legitimate ground for the complaint that he omitted consideration of the non-Christian parallel material without justifying his omission. This however must not be allowed to obscure the importance of the positive contribution he made to the understanding of the Gospel (see pp. 244–50, *infra*). For him, John is primarily a theologian and churchman, confronted with a disorderly historical tradition, and an equally disorderly church life, in which Judaism and Docetism, arising out of a riot of uncontrolled religious ' experience ', were perhaps the chief dangers. Similar problems confronted Ignatius, who, in dealing with them, insisted bluntly upon the historical reality of the flesh of Jesus, and upon the threefold structure of the Church's ministry of bishops, elders, and deacons. The latter point was no concern of John's, and the former he handled with much greater profundity, working up the earlier historical tradition in theological form.

ADDITIONAL NOTES TO PART II

Page

100 Line 5. In *The Fourth Gospel, its Significance and Environment* (3rd edn, revised and rewritten; London, 1941) Dr. Strachan withdrew his theory of redaction; see especially p. 81, note 2. He also finds unconvincing the theory of dislocations.

103 Line 6. Here, and elsewhere (see especially pp. 128–43), it is assumed that John used Mark as a source. The truth of this assumption was called in question by Mr. P. Gardner-Smith in *St. John and the Synoptic Gospels* (Cambridge, 1938). On this book Dr. Howard wrote (*Christianity according to St. John*, p. 17, note 2): ' With one proviso, I am almost persuaded by the cumulative weight of the arguments. The qualification which I should make is, that before the Gospel was published there was some verbal assimilation to a few of the Marcan and Lucan narratives (such as the Anointing, and the Feeding of the Multitude) by the hand of the Editor.'

105 Line 2. For a fuller study of Johannine *characteristica* see E. Schweizer, *EGO EIMI* ... (Göttingen, 1939).

107 Line 15. The opposite point of view has been strongly pressed, for example by Dr. R. Bultmann in his commentary (especially pp. 542 f.).
Line 23. On this question see now especially M. Black, *An Aramaic Approach to the Gospels and Acts* (Oxford, 1946).

109 Line 28. In the first edition (1943) of his book (*L'Évangile de Jean d'après les recherches récentes*; Neuchâtel and Paris) Dr. P. H. Menoud wrote that the once unpopular view that the Gospel and Apocalypse were written by the same author was ' *en passe de devenir l'opinion commune* ' (p. 65). In the second (1947) he noted a further change of opinion. The conviction that the two works sprang from the same author ' *est loin d'être unanime ... toutes les opinions sont aujourdhui représentées, la discussion n'est pas close* ' (p. 74).

111 Line 1. Recent work on the Gospel suggests that there has been either much more or much less disturbance of the original order of the Gospel than the modest amount discussed in this chapter. On the one hand, Dr. Bultmann proposes a very extensive and radical rearrangement; on the other, E. C. Hoskyns, Dr. Strachan and Dr. Dodd interpret the Gospel as it stands. See pp. 166 f.

116 Line 2. This suggestion does not seem so startling now. It is known that papyrus codices existed at an early date. See F. G. Kenyon, *Books and Readers in Ancient Greece and Rome* (Oxford, 1932), and especially C. H. Roberts, 'The Christian Book and the Greek Papyri', in *J.T.S.*, old series l (1949), pp. 155–68.

117 Footnote 2. The short reading (with no connecting particle) shows characteristically Johannine asyndeton, and may very well be correct.

119 Line 5. This view rests in part on the observation (see p. 112) that the last words of ch. xiv. appear to form the end of the discourse. A fresh interpretation of these words is given by Dr. Dodd (*op. cit.*, pp. 406–9), who proposes 'some such translation as this: "The Ruler of this world is coming. He has no claim upon me; but to show the world that I love the Father, and do exactly as He commands,—up, let us march to meet him!"' (p. 409).

128 Chapter III. On this subject see especially P. Gardner-Smith, *op. cit.*, and E. C. Hoskyns, *The Fourth Gospel* (ed. 2, 1947), pp. 58–85. The latter has a particularly important discussion of the material classified in this chapter under (d) 'Synoptic episodes which, while not related by John, have yet left a trace in the Fourth Gospel'.

132 Line 2. μεταβαίνειν is used at v. 24, vii. 3, xiii. 1, but only the last passage refers to the departure of Christ from this world (cf. 1 John iii. 14). ἀναβαίνειν is used in John sixteen times, and used of the ascent of Jesus to the Father at iii. 13, vi. 62, xx. 17 (*bis*).

134 Line 10. The question of the divergence between John and the Synoptic Gospels with regard to the date of the Last Supper and Crucifixion is most fully treated in J. Jeremias, *Die Abendmahlsworte Jesu* (2nd edn., Göttingen, 1949), who gives a very full bibliography, and concludes that the synoptic tradition is correct. See, however, the reply to this argument in Vincent Taylor, *The Gospel according to St. Mark* (London, 1952), Additional Note K, pp. 664–7.

137 Line 33. See the note on p. 134. The verse is ambiguous, but it is important to notice that Luke himself did not regard it as expressing an unfulfilled desire, since he represents the Last Supper as the passover meal.

ADDITIONAL NOTES

140   Line 22. The argument is two-edged. The theological interpretation of the death of Jesus may have reacted upon the historical narrative.
Line 26 and footnote 2. The argument regarding the Kiddush seems to be incorrect. See. J. Jeremias, *op. cit.*, pp. 23–6.

143   Line 5. See further R. H. Lightfoot, *The Gospel Message of St. Mark* (Oxford, 1950), pp. 60–79.

148   Line 26. The statement is misleading. The word κύριος occurs in John i.–xv. (curiously, it is not used in chapters xvi.–xix.) no fewer than 37 (34) times, and of these the majority refer to Jesus.

153   Line 2. In this Dr. Schweitzer is followed by Dr. O. Cullmann, in *Les Sacrements dans l'Évangile johannique* (Paris, 1951).

PART III: PROBLEMS OF INTERPRETATION

CHAPTER I. SYMBOLISM AND ALLEGORY

CHAPTER II. MYSTICISM AND SACRAMENTALISM

CHAPTER III. THE TEACHING OF JESUS IN THE JOHANNINE IDIOM

CHAPTER IV. THE FOURTH EVANGELIST: HIS MESSAGE AND ITS ABIDING VALUE

CHAPTER V. INTERPRETATION OF THE FOURTH GOSPEL 1931-1953

CHAPTER I

SYMBOLISM AND ALLEGORY

THE four chapters in Part II. have entirely failed in their purpose if they have not made it quite clear that there is a strong element of history in the Fourth Gospel, and that the Evangelist believed that he was making use of reliable sources in tracing the story of our Lord's appeal to Judaism and His rejection by the religious authorities of His own people. In presenting his conception of Jesus to the Church and the world of his time he availed himself of the contemporary religious vocabulary, but was conscious of no departure from fidelity to the Palestinian situation in which the supreme revelation was given. Nevertheless, the reader who comes to the study of this Gospel after steeping himself in the language of the Synoptic story is instantly aware of a subtle change in the outlook. The atmospheric medium through which events are seen is not the same. The individuality and temperament of the writer are an important factor in the problem of interpretation.

One example of this difficulty occurs to every reader's mind. In the story of the Crucifixion it is written: ' Howbeit one of the soldiers with a spear pierced His side, and straightway there came out blood and water. And he that hath seen hath borne witness, and his witness is true: and he knoweth that he saith true, that ye also may believe. For these things came to pass, that the scripture might be fulfilled, A bone of him shall not be broken. And again another scripture saith, They shall look on him whom they pierced' (John xix. 34–7). The three statements in this passage are (*a*) that the death of Jesus was accompanied by an extraordinary incident ; (*b*) that this incident has been most solemnly attested as true, and is therefore significant for faith ; (*c*) that it is a fulfilment of Scripture. We need not inquire into the scientific explanations or discussions to which the statement (*a*) has given rise. It may be accepted that the writer believed that his account was correct, whatever the actual physiological details may have been that lie behind the tradition. Nor need we linger over the third statement (*c*), for this is merely an example of the apologetic use of *Testimonia*, or Old Testament parallels to events in the life of Jesus. It is not even necessary to decide about the personal reference in the pronoun (ἐκεῖνος): ' and *he* knoweth that he saith true.' For our present inquiry the important point is why this circumstance attending the death of Christ should be significant for faith. There are at least three important attempts to answer this question. (1) Professor Burkitt[1] brings in 1 John v. 6–8 to show that the writer was refuting the docetic heresy which denied the true humanity of our Lord and the reality of His experience of death. ' The living personality has in it three elements, viz. spirit, water, blood. From the "water" we are begotten, by the "blood" we are sustained, and the "spirit," or breath, is the immaterial element that enters at birth and leaves at death. The spirit quitted Jesus when He died (John xix. 30), leaving behind the water and blood of a human body, the existence of which was demonstrated to the onlookers by the spearthrust of the soldier.' If this interpretation should be accepted, the passage before us is not in the true sense symbolical. It is a fragment of psycho-physiology attesting a historic fact in a theological interest. (2) Others[2]

[1] *Gospel History and its Transmission*, p. 233, n.1.
[2] e.g. A. E. Brooke, *Peake's Commentary*, p. 763*b*; cf. *I. C. C.*, 'Johannine Epistles,' pp. 132 ff.

connect the passages in Gospel and Epistle, and find in the former an emblematic corroboration of the truth stated symbolically in the latter, 'that the Passion as well as the Baptism was an essential note of His Messianic work.' In this case the 'water' represents the baptism of our Lord as the inauguration of His ministry, and the 'blood' represents the death in which that sacrificial life came to its inevitable end. (3) Others, again, find in these words an allusion to the two sacraments of baptism and the Eucharist, around which revolved the instruction of the early Church about the life and teaching of Jesus. As Dr. B. W. Bacon puts it[1] : 'The sacraments came first, the literature came afterward. It grew up around the sacraments, interpreting and enforcing their lessons. The first disciples did not appeal, as we do, to two witnesses, the Spirit and the Word, but to three : the Spirit outpoured from heaven ; and the water ; and the blood.'

Far-fetched and unnatural as much of the patristic exegesis of these passages may be, a sound instinct has told readers in every generation that Johannine language lends itself readily to religious symbolism. The Christian worshipper who sings Toplady's great hymn knows that he is giving a symbolical value to the text in St. John[2] :

> Let the water and the blood,
> From Thy riven side which flowed,
> Be of sin the double cure,
> Cleanse me from its guilt and power.

[1] *Jesus and Paul*, pp. 9 ff.

[2] Toplady's hymn was published in 1776. As a foot-note on the history of the popular symbolism of the Johannine text it is interesting to observe that he probably drew some hints from Dr. Brevint's *The Christian Sacrament and Sacrifice*, prefixed to J. and C. Wesley's *Hymns on the Lord's Supper*, 1745. 'O Rock of Israel, Rock of Salvation, Rock struck and cleft for me, let those two streams of blood and water which once gushed out of Thy side bring down pardon and holiness into my soul ; and let me thirst after them now, as if I stood upon the mountain whence sprung this water, and near the cleft of that rock, the wounds of my Lord, whence gushed this sacred blood.' See J. Telford, *The Methodist Hymn-Book Illustrated*, p. 256.

This is the most conspicuous example in the Gospel of the writer's fondness for discovering a deeper meaning in an incident or event. Sometimes this interest seems to find play in minute details. Sometimes an entire episode raises a doubt whether we are not in the region of allegory.

(*a*) Many writers have been impressed by the mystical value of numbers[1] in this Gospel. To some it seems evident that the structure of the Gospel as a whole is determined by the numbers three and seven. This is certainly not obvious, and it is only when the fact is pointed out[2] that we are aware that there are journeys which Jesus made three times, or that there are words which He spoke seven times. There may be some significance in these numerical totals, but the effect is not self-evident to any reader as is the case with the fivefold division of Matthew, or the sevenfold grouping of the parables in Matt. xiii. Still less is a comparison possible with the repeated emphasis upon the number seven in the Apocalypse. To other writers the detailed use of numbers is evidence of Philonic influence. Thus the thirty-eight years which the cripple waited at Bethesda correspond to the thirty-eight years which elapsed before Israel crossed the brook Zared. Unfortunately we are not told that this man had been waiting at Bethesda for all those years, and it is not easy to see why the Evangelist should suppose his readers would think of Deut. ii. 14 rather than of the period of forty years by which the wanderings of the Israelites in the wilderness were usually recalled (cf. Ps. xcv. 10). The five porches of Bethesda, again, have suggested to some imaginative readers the five senses of unredeemed humanity, and are thus a symbol for the unregenerate passions. The story of the conversation with the Samaritan woman in chap. iv. has provided rich material for this allegorical treatment. The woman's five husbands have been taken on Philonic principles to stand for the 'five seducers,'

[1] See Appendix G.   [2] See E. F. Scott, *The Fourth Gospel*, pp. 21 f.

which lead the soul away from God. The precariousness of this method appears when we find many commentators declaring with equal confidence that the reference is really to the five deities worshipped by the five nations who were settled in Samaria from Babylon after the destruction of the Northern Kingdom by the Assyrians (2 Kings xvii. 24–34; Josephus *Ant.*, IX., xiv. 3).[1] Perhaps the best word on this has been written by Dr. Peake: ' The woman of Samaria is, of course, the half-heathen Samaritan community. She has had five husbands, that means the five heathen gods mentioned in 2 Kings xvii. 31, 32 as worshipped by the Samaritans. Her present irregular lover is Yahweh, whom she illegitimately worships. It is a pity for this interpretation that these gods were seven and not five; that they were worshipped simultaneously and not successively; and it is hardly likely that idolatry should be represented as marriage, when its usual symbol is adultery, or that the author should have represented Yahweh under so offensive a figure.'[2] The last chapter of the Gospel is even richer in opportunities for the allegorist. Simon Peter swam two hundred cubits, and that number (according to Philo *ap.* Gen. v. 22) signifies repentance. If the Evangelist meant this he was unfortunate in his expression, for he merely says that Simon Peter cast himself into the sea, and adds that the other disciples came in the little boat, ' for they were about two hundred cubits away from the land.' It was not then Peter, but the other disciples of whom the remark is made. Perhaps we should be suspected of a hypercritical attitude if

---

[1] Nestle, *Z. N. T. W.*, v. (1904), pp. 166 f., traces this interpretation back to a thirteenth-century copyist who entered in the margin of the passage in Josephus a gloss which linked it with John iv. 18. From the time of D. F. Strauss this interpretation has been a commonplace with critical commentators. For a rather different form of this allegorical reading see Odeberg, *op. cit.*, pp. 179 ff.

[2] *Crit. Intr. to N.T.*, pp. 205 f. See also Appendix G, note (b).

we observed that on these principles the repentance of these disciples was only approximate, and that the significance of the 'little boat' is still left unexplained. It would be impossible to enumerate all the symbolical values which have been discovered in the number of the fish caught on that occasion. Two stand out as more plausible than the rest. Jerome[1] alludes to the learned poet Oppian of Cilicia, and says that Latin and Greek writers on the nature and properties of animals declare that there are a hundred and fifty-three species of fish. The statement is not to be found in Oppian, who merely says that he does not think that the species of fish in the sea are less numerous than the classes of animals on land. As Père Lagrange says, 'If this opinion was really widespread, it would explain our case: each fish represents a species and symbolizes a nation or human category.' But, until some more reliable evidence than Jerome's vague statement is forthcoming, we can hardly make use of this interpretation, and it would be well to leave Oppian's name out of the question. Augustine gives another explanation which is quite in the strain of Philo. The number 153 is the fulfilment of the potentiality[2] of 17. But 17 is the sum of 10 (that is, the Law, represented by the Ten Commandments) and 7 (that is, the Spirit; cf. Rev. i. 4, iii. 1), so that the number 153 signifies all those who are included in the saving operation of divine grace, which makes reconciliation with the Law. One more example must suffice. In the story of the miracle at Cana attention is called to the six water-pots 'set there after the Jews' manner of purification.' The question has been asked: If there is any significance in the number to the writer who

---

[1] Jerome *ap*. Ezek., 47. See *Patr. Lat.* xxv. c. 474. Oppian (*c.* A.D. 180), i. 89. See Lagrange *in loc.*

[2] The 'potentiality' of a number is the sum of the series of numbers of which it is the final term. Thus the potentiality of 4 is $1+2+3+4 =10$. So 153 is the realized potentiality of 17, $(1+2+3+4+ \ldots 17)$.

records 'this beginning of His signs which Jesus did in Cana of Galilee,' may it not be that there is a subtle allusion to the week-days preparing for the perfect dispensation of the Sabbath, the Law preparing for the Gospel, of which the wedding-feast is the type?

We cannot dismiss the possibility that the symbolism of numbers sometimes entered into the consciousness of the Evangelist, on the ground that it is remote from our modern ways of thought. Before we can determine whether the least fantastic of these interpretations ought to be allowed a place in the understanding of the Fourth Gospel we must consider some aspects of the Evangelist's style. It is a great advantage here to be able to follow the guidance of a scholar who writes with expert knowledge on all that relates to Philo.

(b) Dr. H. A. A. Kennedy[1] thinks that Philo's relation to the Old Testament as history shows one or two directions in which his method sheds some light on the Fourth Gospel, but adds that 'it is necessary, on the whole, to distinguish between Philo's allegorizing and that symbolic element in the Fourth Gospel which comes more fully to light the more exhaustively its material is investigated.' The points which deserve notice are: (1) The Evangelist's description of the typical miracles which he selects as 'signs.' (2) His deliberate association of these with elaborate discussions which aim at a spiritual interpretation of them. (3) His predilection for mysterious sayings which admit of divergent explanations (e.g. ii. 19–21, iii. 14–15, iii. 29, iv. 18, iv. 35, vi. 53 f., vii. 38, xii. 24, xiii. 8–10). (4) His use of expressions which have a twofold meaning (e.g. i. 30, iii. 3, 8, iii. 14, iv. 10, v. 25, xi. 11, xii. 32). (5) His symbolic explanations of localities (e.g. ix. 7). (6) The inner allusiveness of such passages as i. 46–51, iv. 15–26. (7) His reticence regarding 'the disciple whom Jesus loved.' All these

[1] *Philo's Contribution to Religion*, pp. 46 ff.

features in the Evangelist's style, as Dr. Kennedy rightly insists, ' impart a certain esoteric flavour to the Gospel throughout. That forms an essential element in the author's symbolism. And it involves an elusiveness which marks the contrast with Philo.'

(c) It is important to observe this fundamental distinction between the Philonic and the Johannine method. When we come to consider the discourses of Jesus in this Gospel the resemblance will be far more close. In the stories of the Old Testament, Philo had material before him which he could not treat at the same time as both historical and religious. He preserved the religious value by sacrificing the history upon the altar of allegory. Renan[1] has said the best word upon this subject. ' Philo sees allegories in the old texts ; he does not create allegorical texts. A sacred and ancient book exists ; the plain interpretation of this text is embarrassing or unsatisfactory ; hidden, mysterious meanings are looked for. Illustrations of this are to be found in abundance. But that any one should write a long historical narrative with the after-thought of hiding symbolical subtleties in it, which could only be discovered seventeen centuries later, that is something which is hardly conceivable. There are supporters of the allegorical explanation who, in this case, play the rôle of the Alexandrians. Perplexed by the Fourth Gospel, they treat it as Philo treated Genesis, and as the entire Jewish and Christian tradition has treated the Song of Songs.'

(d) We therefore distinguish between the allegorizing method which treats the story as a mere transparency through which we can see the real meaning, and the method of the Fourth Evangelist who describes what he believes to be veritable fact, but with a keen eye to the deeper revelation which the story may contain. No

[1] *Vie de Jésus*, ed. 17 (1882), p. 509.

reader can miss the dramatic instinct which leads the Evangelist to set forth the life of the incarnate Word as a supreme conflict between light and darkness. There are dramatic touches throughout the story, but more especially in the narrative of the Passion, which reveal the writer's sense of the significance of the apparently trivial. Sometimes this approaches tragic irony, as when Caiaphas, in enunciating the principle of ecclesiastical expediency, bore unconscious witness to the virtue of vicarious suffering, or as when Pilate, exhibiting the scourged prisoner arrayed in the mocking trappings of royalty, exclaimed, ' *Ecce Homo!* ' There are those three places (xi. 49, 51, xviii. 13) where the crafty Caiaphas is alluded to as being ' High Priest in that year,' which some pedantic or obtuse commentators have fastened upon as proof that the author was ignorant of such an elementary matter of Jewish usage as that this office was normally held for life. Apart from the frequent transference of the dignity from one member of the family of Annas to another, of which the writer was doubtless familiar, there is an ironical intention in the words. This was the astute opportunist who held the highest religious responsibility in the land in that fateful year, when the incarnate Logos ' came to His own place, and His own folk did not receive Him ' ! As E. A. Abbott well says, ' Luke dates the coming of " the word of God " about Jesus from (*inter alia*) " Annas and Caiaphas." John dates Caiaphas from Jesus.'[1] Again, when Judas leaves the Upper Room after taking the sop, the Evangelist adds the terse comment : ' And it was night.' Yet the paschal moon was shining at the full. He was thinking of the dark night of the soul. All these are instances of tragic moments of sharp contrast, when opportunity and destiny were balanced in the scales, and human souls were waiting on their doom. By an easy

[1] *The Fourfold Gospel*, (i.) Introduction, p. 135.

transition we pass from these dramatic symbols to the mysterious sayings and constant ambiguities of which Dr. Kennedy has reminded us.[1] The writer tells the story in his own way, and it is not the way of any other Evangelist, but the story is one which he has heard or read.

(e) A question of crucial importance remains. Is it legitimate to trace this tendency further, and to interpret as Johannine allegories some of the more perplexing stories of miraculous display of power over nature?

This is not the desire of a minimizing Christology, which is prepared to reduce Jesus Christ to the proportions of ordinary humanity. Neither is it a relic of the obsolete materialism of sixty years ago which jauntily proclaimed that 'Miracles do not happen.' Much of the older discussion about miracles becomes obsolete when clearer definition of terms is achieved. Some of it is due to a failure, on one side, to distinguish between physical portent and spiritual value, and, on the other, to recognize that a supremely noble Personality could exercise powers latent in human nature which are beyond the imagination of the ordinary man. This is not the place to discuss miracle in general.[2] We have to do with certain miraculous stories in the Fourth Gospel. At an earlier stage[3] we met with the assertion that in this Gospel it is the writer's habit to enhance the miraculous element. In one instance at least we believe that the reverse is the case, and that if we had only the Johannine account of the 'walking on the sea,' we should probably infer that

---

[1] *Vide supra*, p. 185.
[2] On the larger question see Johannes Wendland, *Miracles and Christianity* (trans. by H. R. Mackintosh, 1911), F. R. Tennant, *Miracle and its Philosophical Presuppositions* (1925), A. E. Taylor, *David Hume and the Miraculous* (1927), C. J. Wright, *Miracle in History and in Modern Thought* (1930), and an essay, 'The Theory of Miracle,' in Henry Bett, *Studies in Religion* (1929).
[3] *Vide supra*, p. 132.

Jesus was walking *by* the sea,[1] or in the surf, and that the disciples were far nearer the shore than they imagined in the uncertain light.

The two narratives which give greatest perplexity as they stand are that of the turning water into wine and the account of the raising of Lazarus.

In both we have to depend upon the narrative in John without corroboration or correction from Synoptic sources. In the case of the raising of Lazarus it is exceedingly difficult to explain the entire silence of the other Gospels upon an event of such tremendous significance. Even if there should be good reasons for Mark's omission, it is impossible to understand Luke's silence, for he shows knowledge of the home of Martha and Mary, and relies upon a special source other than Mark for the narrative of the Passion. There is the added difficulty that Jesus is represented as deliberately waiting for Lazarus to die in order to have the opportunity of bringing faith to His disciples by raising the dead (John xi. 15), and as asking the Father in this way to convince the crowd that He had sent Him (verse 42). The earlier story (in chap. ii.) lacks the sublimity of the eleventh chapter, with its glimpse into the sorrow of Jesus beside the tomb of His friend, the anguish that shook His soul, the serene faith that triumphed over death. There is something incongruous in the thought of displaying supernatural power to relieve the embarrassment of a host and to furnish an additional supply of wine to wedding-guests who have exhausted the provision already made for their needs. In both narratives we seem to have a violation of principles which Jesus accepted as the outcome of the Temptation in the wilderness—that He would not make use of His reserve of power for personal ends or for coercing the minds of men into an attitude of belief in Him. It has sometimes been urged

[1] ἐπὶ τῆς θαλάσσης, vi. 19, may mean ' by the sea ' as in xxi. 1. But in Mark vi. 48, 49, it can only mean ' on the sea.'

that, whereas exemption from the pains of natural want was contrary to the will of God, altruistic sympathy for the distress of others led to the miraculous creation of wine at Cana. The occasion, however, seems almost trivial for such a ' manifestation of His glory ' that ' His disciples believed on Him.' Unless the Synoptic Gospels have misled us, the governing principle of Jesus was to arouse faith in Himself by spiritual appeal, not by overwhelming the reason of men. When a moral principle collides with a miracle we feel, by every Christian instinct, that it is the miracle that must go to the wall.[1] It is not surprising, therefore, that many explain this story as pure allegory. Thus for Heitmüller [2] the water-pots and water represent the Mosaic law, with its ritual for cleansing, and the Old Covenant. Wine, as in the world of Greek thought, signifies prophetic inspiration. Christianity is the religion of the Spirit. John could only baptize with water; Christ was to baptize with the Holy Spirit. The changing of water into wine marks the transformation of the legal religion of Judaism into the spiritual religion which Christ brought. More than that: in the Eucharist the wine represents the greatest of God's gifts in Christ, the blood of Christ ' which cleanses from all sin.' Finally, the Mother of Jesus represents the Old Testament theocracy out of which Jesus sprang, and between the old and the new dispensations Jesus set a sharp line of distinction; they were to have nothing to do with one another. It is further pointed out that there is a remarkable parallel to this story in the cult of the Greek god of prophetic

---

[1] Cf. J. B. Mozley, *Lectures on the Old Testament*, p. 34 : ' The rule of Scripture in substance is that no great moral or religious principle or law of conduct of which we are practically, upon general antecedent grounds, certain can be upset even by a real miracle ; but that, when the two come into collision as evidence, the miracle must give way and the moral conviction stand ; that no miracle, in short, can outweigh a plain duty.' (I owe this reference to my friend the Rev. T. Hilton Pollitt, who first called my attention to it many years ago.)

[2] *Die Schriften des N.T.*, ed. 3, iv., pp. 58 ff.

enthusiasm. At the feast of Dionysus in his temple at Elis empty water-pots became filled during the night with wine, whilst at Andros in the temple of Dionysus, on January 5, wine instead of water gushed out of a spring.[1] Heitmüller remarks that it is significant that later, on the feast of Epiphany (celebrated on January 5 or 6), it was the miracle at Cana that played a rôle as evidence of the theophany. The suggestion, of course, is that in popular tradition a legend, influenced by contemporary pagan cults and myths, grew up within Christian circles and reached the Fourth Evangelist, who saw its allegorical possibilities and thus embodied it in his Gospel.[2] On the other hand, not only the simplicity of the Johannine narrative, but the way in which Cana is referred to later on (iv. 46) as the place ' where He had made the water wine,' seems to show that to the Evangelist this was an actual occurrence. It is easy to conjecture how the story first arose. Can we not trace its origin in the artless narrative? We see the anxiety of Mary when she found that the servants were concerned that the wine was running short, and her appeal to that Son whose resourcefulness she had learned to rely upon throughout the silent years. When the servants turn to Him for counsel He bids them pour water from the now filled water-pots into the diminishing supplies of wine, for the guests have already feasted well. The real miracle is that under the influence of Jesus, and stimulated by the royal wine of His heavenly discourse, their joy exceeded all the festal mirth of the earlier time, each guest rose above his ordinary level of thought and speech, his conversation sparkled with a brighter wit, and, when the feast was over, it was

---

[1] Pausanias, VI., xxvi. 1 ; Pliny, *Hist. Nat.*, ii. 231, xxxi. 16.

[2] E. A. Abbott (*Encyc. Bib.* ii. 1800) and W. Bauer (*Hdb.* in loc.) cite passages in which Philo writes of Melchizedek as representing the divine Logos offering wine instead of water, and speaks of the Logos as the divine οἰνοχόος τοῦ θεοῦ καὶ συμποσίαρχος. (*Leg. Alleg.*, iii. § 82, *De Somn* ii. § 249. Mangey, i. pp. 103, 691.)

remarked that the best wine had been kept to the end. Such may well have been the actual occurrence out of which the servants' tale, told in all good faith, grew into the legend of the water turned to wine. Then, when at last it reached the Evangelist, he saw the deeper meaning illustrated by the story which he accepted as historically true. The contrast between water and wine was too obvious a symbol to be lost on one whose mind ran so readily in that direction. It may be said that he recorded the story for the sake of its allegorical meaning, but it has every appearance of being regarded by the writer as a genuine occurrence in the early ministry of Jesus.

The raising of Lazarus has given such perplexity to many minds which are sincere without being habitually sceptical, that it is not surprising that some have examined the text of the Gospel closely in order to find marks of later redaction. One of the best attempts to deal with the story in this fashion is that of Dr. R. H. Strachan,[1] who thinks that 'the material of the Lazarus story has been chosen by the original Evangelist out of the traditions available to him, not for its historical value but for its dramatic significance.' At the same time he finds indications of editorial revision in three difficulties, viz. the publicity of the event, the apparent inconsistency in the explanation of the delay referred to in verse 6, and the ambiguity in the description of the relationship between Lazarus and the two sisters. 'Beneath and behind the picture there lies some story of raising from the dead, like the Jairus story; but, as even the most conservative critics to-day would admit, all the effects are dramatically heightened, and the interaction of events is dramatically presented.'[2] Others[3] have offered here the most tempting hypothesis of creative allegorization that this Gospel affords. In Luke's Gospel we have a story of two sisters,

---

[1] *The Fourth Evangelist*, pp. 225 ff.   [2] *Ibid.*, p. 236.
[3] e.g. E. F. Scott, *Fourth Gospel*, p. 37 f.

SYMBOLISM AND ALLEGORY

Martha and Mary, and a parable of the rich man and Lazarus, which ends with the words, 'If they hear not Moses and the prophets, neither will they be persuaded if one rise from the dead.' Has not the Evangelist himself composed this story as an allegory to show that, even though a convincing demonstration were wrought, men's hearts would only be hardened against truth and love unless they had first yielded to the moral suasion of a spiritual appeal? There is much that deserves consideration in this theory, for it is very strange that the name Lazarus should only occur in the New Testament in that parable, apart from the eleventh chapter of John and its immediate sequel. For some years that seemed to the present writer the only solution of the problem; but it is not easy to see just where the marks of allegory come in. Dr. Garvie declares his conviction that the witness is not romancing: 'if he is, he is one of the most consummate realists in fiction, for so vivid is the impression he makes of reality.' Mr. Edward Grubb[1] has attempted to conserve the historicity of the story by advancing a theory that Lazarus was restored from a prolonged trance. Dr. Bernard admits the possibility of such an explanation. 'We conclude, then, that the narrative of chap. xi. describes a remarkable incident in the ministry of Jesus. It may be that the details are not reproduced by John with such precision as a modern historian would desiderate. In that case, there is room for the hypothesis that Lazarus was raised from a deathlike trance by an extraordinary effort of will, and exercise of spiritual power, by Jesus. Those who do not accept "miracle" in any form may be inclined to adopt some such hypothesis. But that Jesus could literally recall the dead to life is not impossible of credence by any one who believes that He Himself "rose from the dead."'[2] The most convincing reason for

[1] *Expository Times*, xxxiii. pp. 404 ff.
[2] *I. C. C.*, 'St. John,' vol. i., pp. clxxxv. f.

rejecting the theory of pure allegorizing on the part of the Evangelist is that advanced by Dr. Walter Lock,[1] who protests that the anti-gnostic purpose of the writer all through the Gospel must have made it impossible for him to guarantee spiritual truths by tales which he had himself built up out of hints supplied by the Synoptic tradition. The historical problem remains unsolved, for the silence of the earlier Gospels has never yet been explained. We can only presume that the Beloved Disciple had described some restoration to life of one whose friends had given him up for dead, and that the Evangelist, connecting it with the closing months of our Lord's ministry, and with the deepening hostility of the chief priests, retold the story with all his energy of dramatic insight, to illustrate the theme : ' I am the resurrection and the life.'[2]

[1] *J. T. S.*, ix., p. 445.
[2] Cf. P. Gardner, *Eph. Gospel*, p. 284 : 'We must be content to say that the story is probably a transposition into a higher key of something which really happened, but which probably did not take the great place in the imagination of the people of Jerusalem which the Evangelist supposes.'

CHAPTER II

MYSTICISM AND SACRAMENTALISM

'THE Gospel of St. John—the "spiritual Gospel," as Clement already calls it—is the charter of Christian Mysticism.'[1] So wrote the present Dean of St. Paul's in his Bampton Lectures, and went on to describe Johannine Christianity as identical with Christian Mysticism, or, at any rate, as the ideal which the Christian mystic sets before himself. It is generally agreed that a strain of mysticism runs through the Johannine writings, but the term is used with such wide variations of meaning that some attempt must now be made to define more exactly the different senses in which the Evangelist has been regarded as a mystic.

(a) There is the speculative mysticism of the Alexandrian type, according to which the Gospel history was only one striking manifestation of a universal law, or little more than a dramatization of the normal psychological experience. The Fourth Gospel, unlike this, lays the utmost stress on the necessity of remembering that the Christian revelation was conveyed to mankind by a series of historical events (John i. 14), whilst the First Epistle not only restates the reality of the Incarnation (1 John i. 1–3), but makes the confession that Jesus Christ has come in the flesh the test that separates the spirit of truth from the spirit of antichrist or of error (1 John iv. 1–6). We have already observed[2] that the fundamental distinction between the Logos doctrine of Philo and that of the

[1] W. R. Inge, *Christian Mysticism*, p. 44.   [2] *Vide supra*, p. 147.

Johannine writings is that a speculative idea has been replaced by a personal identification of the pre-existent Logos with the incarnate life of Jesus.

(b) Another view regards the mystic as the ecstatic subject of visions, which he accepts as belonging to the same order of evidential value as those events which are certified by the senses. This has been applied to the Fourth Gospel and its author, with a wealth of illustrative material from the writings of the ecstatic mystics, by Miss Evelyn Underhill. This writer, largely influenced by Réville and Loisy (in his earlier phase), by Holtzmann and Jülicher, starts from the assumption, so common at the beginning of the century amongst critical scholars, that this Gospel ' is in no sense a historical, but a poetic and devotional book.'[1] The difficulty which such a view encounters is that it leaves the intensely objective character of much of the narrative quite unexplained. ' It is not the memory of the disciple—even the " beloved " disciple whose reminiscences, if he be not a purely symbolic figure, may well have coloured the Ephesian traditions of Jesus' death—but the vivid first-hand knowledge, the immovable certitude of the mystic " in union " with the Object of his adoration, which supplies material for this unearthly picture of the earthly life of Jesus.'[2] ' It is the fruit of his own vision and meditation, his own first-hand experience of the divine which he pours into the evangelical mould.'[3] In other words, the temporal background of the historic life receives the projection of the author's spiritual experiences. ' He selected, from the huge and quickly growing Christian legend, those events which seemed to him like the types, the dramatic representations, of the great wonders and changes which had been wrought within his soul.'[4] This, however, would not by itself carry the weight of such a stubborn declaration

---

[1] *The Mystic Way*, p. 217.
[2] *Ibid.*, p. 229.
[3] *Ibid.*, p. 225.
[4] *Ibid.*, p. 234.

as 'And he that hath seen hath borne witness, and his witness is true : and he knoweth that he saith true, that ye also may believe.' Neither does it give any reason for the wealth of detail in descriptive narration where no allegorical motive can possibly be alleged. At this point, Miss Underhill brings forward parallels from the writings of the mystics to show how scenes in the Saviour's life have come with extraordinary vividness before the eyes of the ecstatic. Not only did St. Bernard receive through eye and ear the Virgin's account of her life ; not only did such mystics as Angela of Foligno and Julian of Norwich behold the Passion of Christ, as though they had been pilgrims in Jerusalem during that fateful week ; not only did St. Teresa see her Lord as He was on the morning of the Resurrection,—but there is the authentic record of the marvellously vivid experiences in which the poor German nun—Anne Catherine Emmerich—saw re-enacted many incidents in the earthly life of Jesus. If these visions have all the appearance of the records of a singularly observant spectator of actual events in the earthly life of Jesus, what is there to prevent us from attributing that minuteness of description which so often impresses us in the Fourth Gospel to the same cause ? It is hardly surprising that Canon Streeter, whose interest in the psychology of mysticism was deepened by his own examination of the mystic experiences of the Sadhu Sundar Singh, has given a qualified approval to this alternative to the theory of conscious literary invention. It does not bulk largely in his treatment of this Gospel,[1] for his masterly study of the relation between John and the Synoptics has brought to light much that lies altogether beyond the range of visions and auditions. The fact is, that it was easier to regard the Evangelist as an ecstatic when the Réville-Loisy theory of the nature and origin of the Fourth Gospel was in the ascendant. To-day, as we have

[1] *The Four Gospels*, pp. 390–2.

tried to show in an earlier chapter, a more patient study of the Gospel disallows such an assertion as that the Evangelist was 'absolutely uncritical in his use of material.'[1] Not one of the Evangelists was a critical historian in our modern sense of the term. Nevertheless, not even the writer of the Fourth Gospel can be dismissed quite so summarily. The true principle, which is richly illustrated in the three exquisitely beautiful and illuminating chapters which Miss Underhill gives to 'The Johannine Mystic,' is this: the events described by John 'had been the material of his meditation before they became the material of his gospel,'[2] and this 'still and brooding attentiveness of mind' had won from them a treasure of significance and beauty.

(c) Dr. Inge defines the Johannine mysticism as 'that *centripetal* tendency in thought and feeling which always strives to see unity in difference, the one in the many.'[3] He finds the climax of the doctrinal teaching in chap. xvii., where Christ prays for His disciples that they may be 'made perfect in one,' and that they 'may be one, as we are' (John xvii. 22, 23). 'Mutual inhabitation' displaces 'spatial externality.' At the same time, this mystical union of the souls that are in ethical harmony with God stands over against a sharp moral dualism. The Prologue speaks of a universal influence of the Logos in creation and more especially through the Incarnation. 'Without Him was not anything made that was made. . . . This is the true light which lighteth every man by its coming into the world' (John i. 3, 9). There is no room here for a Gnostic dualism which divides mankind into two classes, the pneumatic and the psychic; still less have we anything approaching a metaphysical dualism such as Manichaean speculation evolved. None the less, Jesus is set forth in this Gospel as one who tests the true

---

[1] E. Underhill, *op. cit.*, p. 225. [2] *Ibid.*, p. 225.
[3] *Cambridge Biblical Essays*, p. 259; see also *D. C. G.*, i., pp. 889 f.

character of men. His presence in their midst brings them into judgement. ' But as many as received Him, to them gave He the right to become children of God ' (John i. 12). ' My sheep hear My voice, and I know them, and they follow Me, and I give them eternal life, and they shall never die ' (John x. 27 f.). Those who show moral affinity with Jesus by faith and obedience, those who keep His commandments, abide in Him and He abides in them.

(d) The great name of Deissmann[1] is specially associated with the view that the very essence of the Pauline religion is fellowship-mysticism (as distinguished from absorption-mysticism) which finds its formula in the phrase, ' in Christ,' and that the great exponent of the Pauline mystical experience is the Fourth Evangelist. Deissmann discriminates between two types of mysticism, the acting and the reacting types, mysticism of performance and mysticism of grace. The Judaic Paul belonged, without success, to the former class. Paul the Christian had abandoned the striving mysticism and had received that immediate communion with God in Christ which is the divine gift. Deissmann is fond of quoting[2] Harnack's witty saying that, in the second century, only one man understood Paul; that was Marcion, and he misunderstood him. But he goes on to claim that there was an earlier and sympathetic interpreter of the Pauline mysticism, and that his interpretation is to be found in the Johannine writings. In spite of Schweitzer's sharp denial[3] of this relationship, there is enough in common between the allegory of the Vine and the branches, in John xv., and the Pauline doctrine of the living union of the believer with Christ for us to recognize the underlying identity of thought and experience. For, while such a *locus classicus* as Gal. ii. 20 emphasizes the individual and personal nature of this mystical experience of oneness with Christ,

---

[1] *Paul*, English trans., ed. 2, pp. 149 ff. [2] e.g. *ibid.*, p. 155.
[3] *Vide supra*, p. 154.

the complementary idea of the corporate unity of believers as fellow members in the mystical Body of Christ, which reaches its loftiest expression in Ephesians, has its analogue in the Johannine allegory. This is ' a parable of an organic union of God and men, an interrelation by which believers live in God and God expresses Himself through them—the Divine Life circulating through all who are incorporate with the Central Stock.'[1]

(e) Quite a different conception of the Johannine mysticism is that which Baron von Hügel unfolds. ' The Church and the sacraments, still predominantly implicit in the Synoptists, and the subjects of costly conflict and organization in the Pauline writings, here underlie, as already fully operative facts, practically the entire profound work. The great dialogue with Nicodemus concerns baptism ; the great discourse in the synagogue at Capernaum, the Holy Eucharist—in both cases, the strict need of these sacraments. And from the side of the dead Jesus flow blood and water, as these two great sacraments flow from the ever-living Christ ; whilst at the Cross's foot He leaves His seamless coat, symbol of the Church's indivisible unity.'[2] This passage is quoted at length to show how entirely this great Catholic authority on mystical religion seems to identify the mysticism of the Fourth Gospel with sacramentalism. Indeed, it is also represented as ecclesiastical ; for, after speaking of the deeply ethical and social character of the Knowing and the Truth on which such stress is laid in the conflict with Gnosticism, von Hügel continues, ' " He who doeth the truth cometh to the light " (iii. 21) ; and Christ has a fold, and other sheep not of this fold—them also He must bring, there will be one fold, one Shepherd ; indeed, ministerial gradations exist in this one Church (so in xiii. 5-10; xx. 3-5; xxi. 7-19). And the Mysticism

---
[1] Rufus M. Jones, *Studies in Mystical Religion*, p. 19.
[2] *Essays and Addresses*, i., p. 84 ; cf. *Encyc. Brit.*, ed. 11, xv., p. 456.

here is but an emotional intuitive apprehension of the great historical figure of Jesus, and of . . . God, the Prevenient Love (1 John iv. 10, 19; John vi. 44, iv. 14, vi. 35).'

Ecclesiastical spectacles have so coloured this reading of the Gospel that ' flock ' is mistranslated ' fold,' and a Petrine pre-eminence is discovered where most readers have found a definite subordination of Peter to John. The passages just cited give slender authority for ' ministerial gradations,' though there is more to be said for the possibility that the unbroken net and the seamless robe may stand for a mystical doctrine of the Church.

(f) Dr. Rufus Jones admits that no other New Testament writer has done so much to spread the principles of mystical religion as has the Fourth Evangelist. No other has coined so many expressions for the currency in use among groups of mystics. But Dr. Jones denies that John is so true a mystic as Paul. With Paul it is inward experience all the time. With John his own first-hand experience is objective (John i. 14, 1 John i. 1–2). And yet there are certain ideas in John which are truly mystical because they express ' a direct and immediate experience by which the soul partakes of God.'[1] He tells of ' a divine birth within, and the permanent presence of the Divine Spirit, imparting Himself to the human spirit.' The Johannine use of ' life ' is an example of this conception. The most characteristic term, however, is ' seed,' for, though it actually occurs but once (1 John iii. 9), yet the thought of a divine germ, a new life-principle expanding and becoming the very life of the person who receives it, is found under various figures. Whether the metaphor is ' water ' (John iv. 14) or ' bread ' (John vi. 35, 58), ' we are dealing with a process by which the believer takes into himself the Divine Life, and by an inward change makes it his own, so that he actually has

[1] *Studies in Mystical Religion*, p. 17.

"God abiding in him." ' We must continue the quotation[1] to show how Quaker as well as Roman Catholic finds a deeply mystical doctrine in the great discourse of chap. vi., whilst denying the kind of sacramental teaching which the other reads into it. 'This Lord's Supper calls for no visible elements, no consecrated priest. It calls only for a human heart, conscious of its needs, and ready to eat the Bread of God on the one momentous condition of willing and loving what Christ wills and loves. . . . "As the living Father sent Me, and I live because of the Father, so he that eateth Me, he also shall live because of Me."' In one other respect, Quaker and Catholic meet in their appreciation of the mysticism of this Gospel, though poles asunder in their practical embodiment of the conception. Mystical union in a divine society is needful for him who is to enjoy the privileges of personality. 'The divine-human conjunct Life is illustrated in the figure of the Vine and its branches.'

(g) Professor H. Weinel, of Jena,[2] finds in the Johannine piety three elements side by side, mysticism, faith-religion, and sacramentalism. The mysticism shows itself in the writer's attempts to express what he has felt in the depths of his inner life where he knows that the powers of language fail. Such passages as iii. 8, iv. 14, vii. 37 f. and, above all, iii. 11 testify to the sense of the mysterious processes of the divine working within the soul that can only be hinted at in picture-words. Even the faith-religion is so suffused by this mystical experience on the Evangelist's part that its contents are different from what we find in the other writers of the New Testament. (Cf. John iii. 16 ff., xi. 25 f., xii. 44 ff., vii. 38, i. 12 ; 1 John v. 1, v. 5, iii. 23.) The depth of this new form of Christianity is disclosed to us by the characteristic metaphors of water and spirit, of light and life, the

---

[1] *Studies in Mystical Religion*, p. 18.
[2] *Biblische Theologie des N.T.*, pp. 581–612.

anticipation of the heavenly blessings of the resurrection and the life, and the deepening of the conceptions of judgement and salvation. Although some of the characteristic phrases of the Pauline piety, such as 'in Christ' are absent, the Johannine religion is a 'Christ-mysticism,' and it is the risen Christ who will abide in His disciples (John xiv. 19 f.). Yet the ethical teaching of the historic Jesus will be fulfilled in those who abide in Christ (John xiv. 21 ff., xv. 7, 10, 1 John ii. 5, iii. 6). Thus the mystical union with the spiritual Christ is continuous with the historical revelation. Weinel lays stress on the distinction which Bousset (and, more recently Schweitzer[1]) has made between Christ-mysticism and God-mysticism. Here and there in Paul we have traces (1 Thess. i. 1, 2 Thess. i. 1, Col. iii. 3) of a God-mysticism, a conception of union with God, whilst that is essential to the Johannine religion. Fellowship with Christ leads up to union with God (John xiv. 20, xvii. 21). Sacramental doctrine is found in John, though, just as in Paul, it is not closely related to the mysticism. In both the third and the sixth chapters the sacramental reference is almost parenthetic, but it is not on that account unimportant. John has no intention of eliminating the sacrament or treating it as superfluous for the mystic. The fact remains that a man believes *and* is baptized, he verifies the words of Christ *and* partakes of the sacrament. So we find that 'he that is bathed' has part with the Son (John xiii. 8), the word of Jesus cleanses (xv. 3), and the 'truth' sanctifies (xvii. 17). Thus 'sacramental religion is a third way of salvation together with mysticism and the religion of faith.'[2]

In an earlier chapter[3] we saw how Schweitzer, with the aid of his eschatological theory, developed the views of Bousset and Weinel regarding the factor which distinguishes the Pauline from the Johannine mysticism, and

[1] *Vide supra*, p. 149. [2] Weinel, *op. cit.*, p. 609. [3] *Vide supra*, pp. 149 ff.

tried to prove that Paul's sacramentalism was rooted in his eschatology, whilst John's was conditioned by his Hellenistic environment.

The time has now come to examine the Johannine attitude to the sacraments. Baptism is referred to once (John iii. 5), with a possible allusion in another passage (xiii. 10). Probably there is a symbolical allusion to the two sacraments in the Epistle (1 John v. 8). The crucial instance is in the conversation with Nicodemus. If these words are taken as representing in substance an actual saying of Jesus to a Jewish Rabbi, there are three possible ways of understanding the condition, ' Except a man be born of water and the Spirit, he cannot enter into the Kingdom of God.' (*a*) The reference may be to John's baptism, and the national mission of repentance and hope out of which the movement led by Jesus took its rise historically. (*b*) The proselyte's bath of initiation may provide the illustration, for there was a rabbinic saying, quoted by Rabbi Jose ben Halafta, ' A proselyte who embraces Judaism is like a new-born child.'[1] (*c*) It is conceivable, though hardly probable, that Jesus was referring to the baptism which His disciples practised (John iv. 2). There are scholars who canvass the view that the words ' of water and ' are a later addition to the text under the influence of ecclesiastical usage. Professor Kirsopp Lake[2] has shown that the only other passages in the Gospels where baptism is enjoined by Jesus are Matt. xxviii. 19, where the evidence of Eusebius makes it extremely probable that the mention of baptism and of the Trinitarian formula are not a genuine part of the text, and Mark xvi. 16, which of course occurs in the later ending to the Gospel. With such signs of the tendency on the part of editors of the text to bring in references to

[1] See G. F. Moore, *Judaism*, i., p. 335.
[2] *The Influence of Textual Criticism on the Exegesis of the N.T.*, pp. 13–20.

baptism, Dr. Lake looks round for indications that interpolation may have taken place here also. He points out that there is nothing about water, and therefore about baptism, either in the original saying in verse 3 or in the final expansion in verse 8, so that the passage would yield a more consistent sense if it simply read : ' Except a man be born of the Spirit, he cannot enter the Kingdom of God.' In the next place, he shows how baptismal usage has affected the citation of this very verse in the Apostolic Constitutions (vi. 15, 3), and the baptismal formula has also been intruded when it is quoted in the Clementine Homilies (xi. 26). In very old authorities the suspected words have also crept into verse 8. Finally, he contends that Justin Martyr (*Apol.*, i. 61) in urging the necessity and fact of regeneration says, ' For Christ said, Except ye be born again, ye shall not enter into the Kingdom of Heaven.' In any case the words are loosely cited, but, as Justin was associating regeneration with baptism in the name of the Trinity, it is incredible that he should have omitted the reference to water if it was in his text of John, and should have appealed to Isa. i. 16–20 for the act of baptism as cleansing away sin.

Nevertheless, there is no manuscript evidence for the omission of the suspected words, so we must accept them provisionally as part of the text, and consider how they accord with the Johannine outlook as a whole. The sacramental tone of chap. vi. predisposes us to recognize sacramental symbolism here. Moreover, even though we have seen reason[1] to suspect editorial touches in iv. 1–3, it is quite possible that this embodies a belief derived from the Evangelist himself that baptism was sanctioned by Jesus. Assuming, then, that the words form part of the original text, but are to be interpreted as Johannine, rather than as *ipsissima verba* of Jesus, John iii. 5 may be taken in various ways. (*a*) We may take it as a

[1] *Vide supra*, p. 117.

Johannine gloss 'to bring the saying of Jesus [in verse 3] into harmony with the belief and practice of a later generation.'[1] (b) The Evangelist may be assuming the outward rite, with the associations of thought that have become inseparable from it (cf. Eph. v. 26, Titus iii. 5), while laying ' all stress upon the spiritual attitude to God through Christ which lends value and meaning to it.'[2] (c) Dr. Odeberg[3] has advanced the theory, supported by numerous passages from Jewish mysticism and from Gnostic writings, that the phrase under discussion belongs to a range of conceptions according to which ' water ' is used as a term for celestial ' seed,' viewed as an efflux from above, from God. So, then, ' to be begotten of water and spirit ' is identical with ' to be begotten from above,' and ' from water and spirit ' means ' from a spiritual seed,' in contrast to earthly, or fleshly (' sarcical ') seed. The similarity in thought to 1 John iii. 9 is immediately evident : ' Whosoever is begotten of God doeth no sin because his seed abideth in him : and he cannot sin, because he is begotten of God.' Dr. Odeberg denies that this expression ' of water ' contains any essential allusion to baptism, but it calls up a whole world of ideas, such as ' water as divine efflux—celestial waters—waters from above—life-giving, living water—the divine gift coming down from on high—waters of eternal life—waters of eternal truth.'[4]

The moral regeneration which Jesus demanded, according to the Synoptic record (Matt. xviii. 3), is here translated into another region of thought, of which we catch fugitive glimpses in the Pauline writings. ' Flesh and blood cannot inherit the Kingdom of God, neither can corruption inherit incorruption.' ' There are bodies celestial and bodies terrestrial . . . If there is a natural

---

[1] So Bernard, *I. C. C.*, in loc.
[2] Moffatt, *Theology of the Gospels*, p. 197.
[3] *The Fourth Gospel*, pp. 48 ff.   [4] *Ibid.*, p. 67.

body, there is also a spiritual body' (1 Cor. xv. 50, 40, 44). In this famous passage Paul is strongly under the dominance of his eschatological hope. In 2 Cor. v. 1-4 the eschatology has already undergone some transmutation. Paul is thinking of the believer's transition at the moment of death from life in this terrestrial body to life in the spiritual body. But in this very matter we have the 'earnest,' the partial anticipation, of the Spirit. Now what Paul here hints at—that already in this present life we have a partial experience of life in the supra-terrestrial body—is analogous to the Johannine idea that we have already in this present age 'passed out of death into life.' If this change is marked by unmistakable ethical results, 'because we love the brethren' (1 John iii. 14), so also to Paul love in the domestic realm is the result of a like transformation, by which, through 'the washing of water with the word,' those who have confessed their faith in Christ are cleansed and brought into the mystical body of Christ (Eph. v. 22 ff.).

Remembering how often the Fourth Evangelist uses a religious term with a subtle ambiguity, so that some readers will follow the more obvious meaning while others will discern the esoteric significance, we are disposed to regard the three interpretations just given, not as mutually exclusive, but as together conveying the truth. There is a reference in the Evangelist's mind to current usage, so that spiritual renewal is linked up with the impressive rite by which men abjured the old way of life and became as little children in the Kingdom of Heaven. There is a conscious stress on the spiritual change, without which no rite, however sacred, can avail to save the soul of man. There is also to the initiated, who understand these mystic thoughts of divine regeneration, the suggestion of a new life in a spiritual body, so that eternal life has already begun for them, even in this evil age.

The relation of the Fourth Gospel to the other sacrament of the Church turns upon two remarkable features in the narrative: the entire absence of any account of the institution of the Eucharist in the story of the Last Supper, and the discourse in chap. vi., which must to the first readers of the Gospel have inevitably suggested eucharistic language and meaning.

The omission of the story of the institution is involved in considerations that affect the early conceptions of the Eucharist. As Dr. Moffatt has reminded us,[1] there were three elements in the primitive theology of the Lord's Supper. It was regarded as (a) a feast of commemoration of the sacrificial death of Jesus, which inaugurated the new order of things for the Church, and looked forward to the Parousia (1 Cor. xi. 26); (b) a medium of spiritual union between the risen Lord and His people.[2] (1 Cor. x. 16, 17); (c) a bond of brotherhood which closely knit together the members in the mystical body of which Christ the Lord was head (1 Cor. xi. 29). It is with the second of these elements in the eucharistic doctrine of early Christianity that the Fourth Evangelist was in closest sympathy. It is possible that his reaction from the more tense apocalyptic expectation of the primitive Church is partly responsible for his severance of the eucharistic teaching from the Last Supper. It is also possible that, in recording the allegory of the true Vine and the long discourse upon the fellowship of the disciples with their Lord and with one another, he did not wish to identify this communion exclusively with any external rite. Strong and sacred as were the associations of that ever-to-be-remembered meal in the Upper Room, the Evangelist may have desired 'to detach the higher Christian teaching from mere occasion of history, and

[1] *Theology of the Gospels*, p. 198.
[2] C. Anderson Scott, *Christianity According to St. Paul*, pp. 182 ff.

instead to attach it to the eternal realities of the spiritual world.'[1]

There are two circumstances which make it almost certain that the long sermon on the Bread of Life is eucharistic in its reference. (a) It closes with the announcement of the treason of Judas Iscariot, which in the Synoptic narrative was made during the Last Supper (Mark xiv. 18 ff.; Matt. xxvi. 21 ff.; Luke xxii. 21 ff.), where it is also recorded by John (John vi. 70, 71, xiii. 21 ff.). (b) The miraculous feeding of the multitude, which provides the occasion of the discourse, is described in significant language. There are two accounts in Mark of such a miraculous supply of food for the crowd. In the first (Mark vi. 41; so also in Matt. xiv. 19 and Luke ix. 16) the central act is thus recorded : ' And He took the five loaves and the two fishes, and, looking up to heaven, He blessed (εὐλόγησεν), and brake the loaves; and He gave to His disciples to set before them; and the two fishes divided He among them all.' In the second account, that of the feeding of the four thousand, which is often regarded as a doublet of the earlier story, there is a significant change: ' And He took the seven loaves, and, *having given thanks*, He brake, and gave to His disciples, to set before them ' (Mark viii. 6). Here the word is εὐχαριστήσας, but in the following clause, εὐλογήσας is again the word used for ' blessing ' the ' few small fishes.' Now John records only the feeding of the five thousand, but he follows in one important respect the second narrative in Mark. ' Jesus therefore took the loaves; and, *having given thanks*, he distributed to them that were set down ' (John vi. 11). Still more remarkable is the way in which this incident is recalled in John vi. 23: ' Howbeit there came boats from Tiberias nigh unto the place where they ate the bread *after the Lord had given thanks*.' It is difficult to avoid seeing a

[1] P. Gardner, *The Ephesian Gospel*, p. 204.

subtle connexion with the technical term for the Lord's Supper, as we find it, for instance, in the Didache: 'And concerning the Eucharist, hold Eucharist thus' (ix. 1); 'On the Lord's Day of the Lord come together, break bread, and hold Eucharist' (xiv. 1).[1]

The discourse (said to have been given in a synagogue at Capernaum) which follows in the Johannine narrative begins with the claim of Jesus upon the faith of His hearers as the one sent by God. To this they replied with a demand for a sign, such as the manna which their fathers ate in the wilderness. This was a current expectation of the Messianic age. In that product of Pharisaic Judaism of the latter half of the first century called the Apocalypse of Baruch, we read of the time when the Messiah shall begin to be revealed: 'And it shall come to pass at that selfsame time that the treasury of manna shall again descend from on high, and they will eat of it in those years, because these are they who have come to the consummation of the time' (2 Baruch xxix. 8).[2] Then it was that Jesus claimed to be the bread of life that had come down from heaven to give life to the world. 'I am the bread of life: he that cometh to Me shall not hunger, and he that believeth on Me shall never thirst.' This is surely an echo of the words of Wisdom: 'They that eat me shall yet be hungry; and they that drink me shall yet be thirsty' (Ecclus. xxiv. 21). The parallel is closer in the words that follow a little later: 'If any man eat of this bread, he shall live for ever: yea, and the bread which I will give is My flesh, for the life of the world.' Then come the words about eating the flesh and drinking the blood of the Son of man which constitute the real problem of this chapter. In the familiar words of institution in 1 Cor. xi. 24 (cf. Mark xiv.

[1] Περὶ δὲ τῆς εὐχαριστίας, οὕτως εὐχαριστήσατε. Κατὰ κυριακὴν δὲ κυρίου συναχθέντες κλάσατε ἄρτον καὶ εὐχαριστήσατε.

[2] See Charles, *Apocr. and Pseudepigr. of O.T.*, Vol. II., p. 498.

22) the word 'body' (σῶμα) is used, not 'flesh' (σάρξ), and at first sight the Johannine use of the word 'flesh' might seem to disprove any connexion between John vi. and the Last Supper. But in Ignatius and Justin Martyr,[1] the writers who seem to represent the type of eucharistic doctrine most conspicuously in the thought of the Fourth Evangelist, it is this term 'flesh' which always occurs in connexion with the Eucharist. The sacramental associations of the words are therefore almost beyond dispute. However, the climax of the discourse is reached in verses 62, 63: 'What, then, if ye should behold the Son of man ascending where He was before? It is the spirit that quickeneth; the flesh profiteth nothing: the words that I have spoken unto you are spirit, and are life.' Merely eating the 'flesh,' or partaking of the sacrament of Eucharist, will not avail to gain eternal life. Jesus had already said: 'My meat is to do the will of Him that sent Me.' So His disciples will find that the spirit of the risen Christ will give them life as they do His will. It is His words as they fall into the hearts of His followers who believe in Him, and spring up and fructify, that alone can bring them into spiritual fellowship with God, and into the enjoyment of eternal life.

Why, then, does the Evangelist transfer this discourse from the Upper Room to the synagogue at Capernaum, and from the night of the betrayal to the period of public disputation in Galilee? We have already[2] noticed Dr. Stanton's suggestion that the writer placed the whole of this discourse-matter, after the miracle of the feeding, 'from his having been accustomed to use that miracle in his instruction of Christian assemblies as a text for setting forth Jesus as the living bread.' We accept this, and hazard a reason for the preacher's custom. A sacramental mystic himself, who found the

[1] See Appendix E.   [2] *Vide supra*, pp. 39 f.

real presence of the risen Saviour specially near to him in that central act of Christian worship with all its associations of the Redeemer's last night with His disciples before suffering the death upon the cross, he yet saw the perils of a crude literalism in the language which had come to be used about that sacrament.[1] But the Upper Room was no place for doctrinal polemic. The synagogue, where Jesus expounded the Scriptures and disputed with his adversaries about erroneous views of religion, was a more suitable scene for a correction of wrong views about the living bread. There, no doubt, he was aware that questions were asked and answered about the manna of the Messianic reign. So in this context he was accustomed to set his teaching concerning the Bread of Life, on whom believers feed in their hearts by faith with thanksgiving. When later in his Gospel he came to the Last Supper, the voice of controversy is hushed. There is one subtle hint only of the danger that haunts us even in the most sacred acts of the religious life: 'And after the sop then Satan entered into him.' But in that *sanctum sanctorum* of the Fourth Gospel service and communion are the lessons to which alone we listen. 'I have given you an example, that ye also should do as I have done to you.' 'I made known unto them Thy name, and will make it known; that the love wherewith Thou lovedst Me may be in them, and I in them.'

---

[1] See C. Anderson Scott, *op. cit.*, p. 121: 'Faith, especially the faith of uninstructed converts, is apt to look anxiously round for some " solid " foundation or justification of what is really a spiritual experience. And there is an inevitable tendency to transfer to the rite the efficacy which belongs to the faith which it expresses and confirms. The Fourth Gospel is not without indications of a tacit protest against such a development.' Is not the Evangelist's silence about the Lord's Supper in chap. xiii. a signal instance?

Chapter III

THE TEACHING OF JESUS IN THE JOHANNINE IDIOM

It has often been observed that the Jesus of the Fourth Gospel speaks quite differently from the Jesus of the Synoptics. Matthew Arnold conceded this much to the Tübingen criticism, which was his *bête noire*: ' Jesus never can have delivered the long connected harangues, or entered into the formal development of His own nature and dignity, or made the endless repetitions, which are in the Fourth Gospel attributed to Him. All this is so absolutely contrary to His manner, which we know both from His sayings in the Synoptics and from express testimony, that every rule of criticism bids us suspect it.'[1]

So sound a writer as Johannes Weiss remarks upon the unity of style in the speeches of the Gospel, which recalls the style in which the First Epistle is written. There is the same colour in the Prologue and in the words of the Baptist. ' It is evident that at least the words of Jesus passed through the author's way of thinking and are recast in his style. In contrast with the wealth of the Synoptic discourses in expression and in imagery, this style is poor and monotonous. Not only do we meet with the same expressions (light, life, believing, witnessing, glorifying, truth and falsehood, the hour is coming, or is not yet come), but even the same stylistic locutions constantly recur. The monotony is increased by the

[1] *God and the Bible*, p. 188.

fact that, instead of terse sayings, or groups of sayings rounded off, one theme is meditated upon in a long discourse, continually approached from fresh sides, without achieving any logical advance.'[1] Every reader has experienced a difficulty in saying where a discourse ends in this Gospel and where the Evangelist's commentary begins. Thus the passage John iii. 31-36 in our text of the Gospel forms part of the testimony of the Baptist. In the rearrangement of the text adopted above,[2] it becomes part of the conversation with Nicodemus. As regards style, we can only say that it is Johannine. Subject-matter alone determines whether the words were originally intended to be taken as an utterance of Jesus or of John the Baptist, or whether they are to be regarded as a comment by the Evangelist.

Nevertheless, the common objection that the Sayings of Jesus in the Synoptics are in the form either of parables or of maxims, whilst in John we have only elaborate discourses, requires modification in at least two directions.

(a) James Drummond[3] has selected from this Gospel sixty short and pregnant sayings, which easily stand by themselves, and imprint themselves on the memory. He concludes that it is not true that the Johannine Christ speaks like a Sophist, and abstains from using brief and concise sayings. Matthew Arnold, in the passage alluded to above, had quoted Justin Martyr's famous sentence: 'Short and concise are the sayings that came from Him, for He was no Sophist, but His word was power divine '[4]; and had shown that there are *logia* peculiar to the Fourth Gospel, which entirely suit the character and habit of Jesus as they are known to us from the Synoptics. He could not conceive how any one could deny this unless

---

[1] *R. G. G.*, ed. 1, iii. 2201.   [2] *Vide supra*, p. 120.
[3] *Character and Authorship of the Fourth Gospel*, pp. 18 ff.
[4] Justin Martyr, *Ap.* i. 14. 5.

he were constrained to denial by some thesis which he had to sustain. He gave as instances, 'My kingdom is not of this world'; 'In My Father's house are many mansions'; 'The good shepherd giveth his life for the sheep'; 'Other men laboured, and ye are entered into their labours'; 'The night cometh, when no man can work'; 'The servant abideth not in the house for ever; the son abideth for ever'; 'A woman when she is in travail hath sorrow because her hour is come; but as soon as she is delivered of the child she remembereth no more her anguish, for joy that a man is born into the world.'[1] The imposing list offered by Principal Drummond, which is not complete, is proof enough that John has by no means neglected this gnomic, or maxim-like, aspect of the teaching of Jesus.[2]

(b) C. F. Burney has shown, from the ease with which sayings of Jesus in Matthew can be retranslated into Aramaic poetic forms, that Jesus must have often adopted that style of exalted utterance, which could the more easily lodge in the memory of His hearers. He has also shown that the Fourth Gospel contains many such sayings, exhibiting, when retranslated into Aramaic, the accepted poetic features of parallelism, rhythm, and even, in some cases, rhyme. It is also true that the Prologue yields to the same method of treatment, and can be shown to 'take the form of a hymn, written in eleven parallel couplets, with comments added here and there by the writer.'[3] We must not, therefore, claim too confidently that the structure of the discourses, when they conform to the conditions of Semitic poetry, is in itself proof that these are authentic sayings of Jesus. What we are bound to recognize is the fact that much of the teaching of Jesus in this Gospel comes to us in a form which closely

---

[1] John xviii. 36, xiv. 2, x. 11, iv. 38, ix. 4, viii. 35, xvi. 21.
[2] The list of references is given below, Appendix F.
[3] Burney, *Aramaic Origin of the Fourth Gospel*, p. 40.

resembles that in which many of the sayings reach us in the Synoptics.[1]

When we turn from the question of form to that of subject-matter, the first requirement is to find what sayings of Jesus in the Fourth Gospel have direct or indirect parallels in the Synoptic tradition. Exact agreement is almost non-existent, and where we find it, as in such words as 'Arise, take up thy bed and walk' (John v. 8; cf. Mark ii. 11) or 'Arise, let us go hence' (John xiv. 31; cf. Mark xiv. 42), the occasion is not quite the same. Virtual identity may be recognized in several passages. Thus, 'Destroy this temple, and in three days I will raise it up' (John ii. 19) is authenticated by Mark xiv. 58. 'A prophet has no honour in his own country' (John iv. 44) recalls Luke iv. 24. 'He that loveth his life loseth it; and he that hateth his life in this world shall keep it unto life eternal' (John xii. 25) has a number of parallels (Mark viii. 35; Matt. x. 39., xvi. 25; Luke ix. 24, xvii. 33). 'He that believeth on Me, believeth not on Me, but on Him that sent Me' (John xii. 44) and 'He that receiveth whomsoever I send receiveth Me; and he that receiveth Me receiveth Him that sent Me' (John xiii. 20) are substantially the same declaration which is found in all three Synoptics (Mark ix. 37; Matt. x. 40, xviii. 5; Luke ix. 48, x. 16). 'A servant is not greater than his lord, neither one that is sent greater than he that sent him' (John xiii. 16, xv. 20) is obviously the saying which two other Gospels preserve (Matt. x. 24; Luke vi. 40). A considerable number of Synoptic parallels to Johannine *logia* can be supplied,[2] but in most of them the Johannine idiom covers a very real similarity of thought. Of course, it must be remembered that in rendering an Aramaic saying into Greek there is a double translation. A literal rendering of the words is only half the translation.

[1] For examples of Burney's evidence see Appendix F.
[2] See Appendix F.

A change of idiom is often involved if the meaning of a phrase is to be conveyed to those whose forms of thought are altogether different. All three Synoptists record the acted parable of the child set in the midst of the disciples. In Mark x. 15 and Luke xviii. 17 the saying of Jesus is given in precisely the same words: 'Verily I say unto you, Whosoever shall not receive the Kingdom of God as a little child, he shall in no wise enter therein.' In Matt. xvii. 3, 4 it appears in a slightly different form, 'Verily I say unto you, Except ye turn, and become as little children, ye shall in no wise enter into the Kingdom of Heaven. Whosoever therefore shall humble himself as this little child, the same is the greatest in the Kingdom of Heaven.' In another context, the Fourth Evangelist puts the same thought into different phraseology as suitable to conversation between Jesus and a Rabbi. 'Except a man be born anew, he cannot see the Kingdom of God. . . . Except a man be born of water and the Spirit, he cannot enter into the Kingdom of God.' We have already seen[1] that there is nothing in these words which lies outside the range of rabbinical discussion. To 'see the Kingdom of God' reminds us of the phrase used twice in the most Jewish part of the Gospel according to Luke: to 'look for the consolation of Israel' (Luke ii. 25), and to 'look for the redemption of Jerusalem' (Luke ii. 38). It seems that the metaphor of a new creation of man, whether by the healing of his infirmities or the forgiveness of his sins, was a favourite use with rabbinical teachers. But this new creation 'from above' had not the ethical signification which the new birth has in the New Testament. The Rabbis looked to the future alone for the fulfilment of the promise to give a new spirit, or a new heart.[2] It is very likely that the precise

[1] *Vide supra*, pp. 204 ff.
[2] Strack-Billerbeck, ii., pp. 420 ff. They point out that ἄνωθεν must go back to an Aramaic word meaning 'from above,' as there is no corresponding temporal adverb, 'again,' 'anew.'

form which the saying has assumed in John iii. 3–8 is determined by the phraseology current in the Greek-speaking religious world at the time when the Fourth Gospel was written.[1] The language of Paul (Rom. vi. 4) must have prepared the way for a more technical employment of such figures of speech. Later we meet with 'the laver of regeneration' (Titus iii. 5). The Epistle of Barnabas shows that baptism and the experience of the new creation were regarded as synchronous. 'We go down into the water full of sins and foulness, and we come up bearing the fruit of fear in our hearts, and having hope on Jesus in the Spirit.' 'When we received the remission of sins, and put our hope on the Name, we became new, being created again from the beginning[2]; wherefore God truly dwells in us, in the habitation which we are' (*Ep. Barn.* xi. 11, xvi. 8). We are justified then in saying that we have probably here a genuine saying of Jesus which in its Johannine form has a *nuance* and an application to contemporary needs that is the mark of the Evangelist.

It is commonly said that one of the links between the language of the Fourth Gospel and the Iranian redemption mystery is the constant use of the term 'sent' with reference to Jesus. The actual introduction of the explanatory comment on the (supposed) meaning of Siloam (John ix. 7) is often regarded as an esoteric indication of this mystical use of the word. Yet the word was used by Jesus of His mission from the Father, as the Synoptics clearly show (e.g. Mark ix. 37 and parallels). Moreover, Paul carried on this tradition (Rom. viii. 3; Gal. iv. 4). The fact that impresses the student of the Fourth Gospel is that this genuine thought of the mission of Jesus receives a prominence in the Johannine discourses through continual repetition, until 'He whom God has sent' has the force

---

[1] For references see Bauer, H. N. T., ed 2, *in loc.*
[2] ἐγενόμεθα καινοί, πάλιν ἐξ ἀρχῆς κτιζόμενοι.

JESUS IN THE JOHANNINE IDIOM 219

of a technical term.'[1] 'The Fourth Gospel,' writes Professor C. H. Dodd, 'lays special emphasis on the "sending" of Jesus, no doubt under the influence of a particular theological development, but surely not without reference to the more primitive idea of a prophetic calling.'[2]

It is the Evangelist's manner to take a saying of Jesus and render it into an idiom that is rich in meaning for his own contemporaries. He also harps on a word or thought of the Master until it rings through the Gospel. But even more distinctive of the Johannine mind is the way in which he receives a deep saying which has only just found isolated expression in the earlier Gospels, and develops it throughout the Gospel. The famous saying which is recorded in Matt. xi. 25-27 and Luke x. 21-22 has often been described as thoroughly Johannine. But there can be no reasonable doubt that it was a traditional word of Jesus which had been conserved in that early collection of sayings from which the writers of the First and Third Gospels drew so much of their material.[3] In the Matthaean form it reads: 'I thank Thee, O Father, Lord of heaven and earth, that Thou didst hide these things from the wise and understanding, and didst reveal them unto babes: yea, Father, for so it was well pleasing in Thy sight. All things have been delivered unto Me of My Father: and no one knoweth the Son save the Father; neither doth any know the Father save the Son, and he to whomsoever the Son willeth to reveal Him.' Even though this saying is almost without a parallel in the Synoptics, its presence in that early stratum of Gospel tradition should warn us against assuming too readily

---

[1] See iii. 17, 34, iv. 31, v. 24, 30, 36, 37, 38, vi. 29, 38, 39, 44, 57, vii. 16, 18, 28, 29, 33, viii. 16, 18, 26, 29, 42, ix. 4, x. 36, xi. 42, xii. 44 f., 49, xiii. 20, xiv. 24, xv. 21, xvi. 5, xvii. 3, 8, 18, 21, 23, 25, xx. 21.

[2] *Mysterium Christi*, p. 63 n. ('Jesus as Teacher and Prophet.')

[3] For a full survey of recent discussion respecting this *logion*, see Rawlinson, *The New Testament Doctrine of the Christ*, pp. 252 ff.

that the mystical teaching of the Fourth Gospel is foreign to the historical situation when placed upon the lips of Jesus.¹ The saying itself is not given in the Fourth Gospel, but the thoughts contained in it are expressed in various parts. The delivery of divine functions into the hands of the Son is claimed in John v. 22, 27, xiv. 13, xvi. 15, xvii. 2. The self-designation of Jesus as 'the Son' occurs fourteen times (John v. 19-26, vi. 40, viii. 35 f., xiv. 13, xvii. 1). The deep inter-communion of the Father and the Son resulting from reciprocal knowledge is represented in another fashion in John x. 15, 30, 38, xvii. 21, 25. The revelation of the Father through the Son is set forth by Jesus again and again (John vi. 45 f., viii. 19, 38, xiv. 6-11, xv. 15).²

So far we have been concerned with the underlying identity of substance in the teaching of Jesus as presented by the Fourth Evangelist compared with its earlier presentation. There are, however, some aspects of the Johannine discourses of Jesus which have caused grave perplexity to many readers. We have already quoted Professor Burkitt's vehement protest against the argumentativeness and mystification which to him is so 'repellent' in the report of our Lord's discussions with the Jews.³ His conclusion is that 'it is quite inconceivable that the historical Jesus of the Synoptic Gospels could have argued and quibbled with opponents as He is represented to have done in the Fourth Gospel.'

Before we accept this sweeping assertion without qualification, it would be well to bear in mind a few considerations. (a) Dr. Eisler has recently protested against 'the Neo-Marcionite subjectivism of certain

---

¹ K. L. Schmidt has given a timely warning against exaggerating the contrast between eschatology and mysticism in early Christian thought. For not only does eschatology survive in the latest book of the New Testament (2 Pet. iii. 13), but both types are found in the teaching of Jesus. *Z. N. T. W.*, xxi., pp. 277 ff. (esp. p. 288).
² On this subject see Stanton, *op. cit.*, iii., pp. 270 f.
³ *Vide supra*, p. 25.

critics, who claim for themselves the right to disregard any evidence in the Gospels which conflicts with their own preconceived picture of Jesus . . . to reject from among the documentary materials this or that statement as "unworthy" of Jesus' personality and His mission.'[1] There is, of course, a general and unitary impression left on the mind of the reader of the Gospels which acts as a criterion for him in testing the genuineness of what may seem to be incongruous with the whole portrait. But we must be on our guard against judging historical probability in a report of a first-century Palestinian discussion by modern standards of philosophical argument. (b) On the wider question of the fidelity of the Fourth Evangelist to conditions contemporary with the events described, the twice-told evidence of that great rabbinic scholar, the late Dr. Israel Abrahams, is of special importance. 'Most remarkable has been the cumulative strength of the arguments adduced by Jewish writers favourable to the authenticity of the discourses in the Fourth Gospel, especially in relation to the circumstances under which they are reported to have been spoken.'[2] And again he wrote: 'My own general impression, without asserting an early date for the Fourth Gospel, is that that Gospel enshrines a genuine tradition of an aspect of Jesus' teaching which has not found a place in the Synoptics.'[3] (c) Although the Synoptists report some discussions between Jesus and scribes of the Pharisees in Galilee, the only debates with the leaders in Jerusalem (who were responsible for His rejection) which they record belong to the last week. Yet in these few instances of the argumentative method adopted by Jesus we find some examples of the *argumentum ad hominem*—in other words it seems that Jesus met His opponents on

---

[1] *The Messiah Jesus and John the Baptist*, p. viii.
[2] *Cambridge Biblical Essays*, p. 181.
[3] *Studies in Pharisaism and the Gospels*, i., p. 12.

their own ground. Thus, when He was challenged to show His authority for the things He was doing, according to Mark xi. 30, Jesus countered with another question : ' The baptism of John, was it from heaven or from men ? ' (d) We have already seen in other connexions that the Evangelist is given to mingling his own commentary with words of Jesus, and it is often hard to draw the line which separates text from commentary. (e) The main examples of rabbinical debate given in this Gospel are John vii. 15–24, viii. 12–20, 21–59, x. 24–38. As Dr. Bernard has well said[1] : ' The kind of argument against the Pharisees reproduced ' in these passages ' is included by the Evangelist to bring out the profundity of the thoughts of Jesus, who, even while He had to dispute with the Rabbis as to the validity of His claims, knew that nothing could really be set against the tremendous pronouncement, " I am He that beareth witness of Myself " ' (viii. 18).

Bearing in mind these considerations, which show the extreme difficulty of deciding dogmatically how much is authentic tradition of words of Christ and just how much must be set down to the Evangelist, we pass on to the more vital question, What do such discussions tell us of the fundamental teaching of Jesus ?

The passage John v., vii. 15–24 (which, as already shown, is really one continuous section) has been acclaimed by Dr. Abrahams as an example of the Fourth Gospel's close acquaintance with Hebraic traditions.[2] Professor Burkitt has brought out most effectively its authentic revelation of the mind of Jesus on the questions raised by the healing of the cripple on the Sabbath. The doctrine of the incarnation of the eternal Son is here discussed against the background of definite historical conditions—that is, of a real Jewish dispute. The line on which Jesus

---

[1] *I. C. C.*, ' St. John,' i., pp. cxiii. f.
[2] *Studies in Pharisaism and the Gospels*, i., p. 135.

defended His action was expressed in the words, ' My Father worketh even until now, and I work.' ' Surely this means that the laws of Nature and of Right and Wrong do not observe the Sabbath. The same Father whom Jesus saw making His sun to shine on the evil and on the good, made His sun shine equally on the Sabbath and on the week-day. If all things were delivered unto Jesus by the Father, then all things told Him of the Father, things secular as well as things conventionally sacred.'[1] Well might Dr. Burkitt add his judgement that this way of thinking about the Sabbath came to the Evangelist from without rather than from within, by memory or tradition rather than by imagination.

In a similar way, Dr. E. A. Abbott[2] brings out the deeper meaning of the crucial saying in the polemical discourse viii. 21-58, ' Before Abraham was, I am' (verse 58). Just as Mark and Matthew represent Jesus, when questioned about Moses and divorce, as going back to that which was before Moses (Mark x. 5, 6) ; just as John represents Jesus, when censured for healing on the Sabbath, as again going back in thought to the beginning ; so here, ' Before Abraham was ' ' seems part of a Johannine exposition of Christ's habit of going back to " the beginning "—back to the intention of the Creator.' Nor is it fanciful to connect the words with the cry of Wisdom in Prov. viii. 22-36, for there is evidence in the Synoptic Gospels that Jesus identified Himself with the Wisdom of the Sapiential books.[3] Then the closing part of the discourse amounts to this : ' The Wisdom of God, the Spirit that is in Me, is not a Spirit that finds its delight in the winds that are God's angels, or in the flames that are His ministers, or in the beauties and glories of the inhabitable world. It is a Spirit like that of Abraham, who was pre-eminently the lover of man. But it is also the

[1] *Gospel History*, p. 241.   [2] *Son of Man*, pp. 729 ff.
[3] See J. R. Harris, *Prol. to St. John's Gospel*, pp. 57 ff.

Spirit in which God created man in His own image, long before Abraham was born. " Before Abraham was, I am." '[1]

It is evident that the Evangelist has preserved more than the mere substance of some of the controversies which took place in Jerusalem between Jesus and the official leaders of the national religion. The scene lives before his eyes, and he knows both the setting and the atmosphere. Some striking word or turn in the argument has been remembered, and here we have the easily recognized touch of Jesus. But there are mannerisms, such as repetitions of the same thought in a slightly different form, or peculiar turns of phrase which we mark as Johannine. Dr. H. A. A. Kennedy has called attention to the way in which Philo, who regarded the Pentateuch as inspired in every detail, expands discourses, such as God's instructions to Moses to warn Pharaoh, or Moses' injunctions to the spies. He takes the original words as his basis, and constructs upon them a composition which embodies some of the leading ideas, but supplements them in every direction. ' This process illustrates the usage of the Fourth Evangelist, for whom some saying or thought of Jesus forms the text of a carefully articulated discourse. It appears to him in no sense arbitrary to draw out on these lines the significance of a message which he regarded as wholly divine.'[2]

This method of treating a sacred text was an established part of Jewish religious instruction in the worship of the Synagogue during the last few centuries B.C. The public reading of the Hebrew Scriptures was accompanied by an oral translation into the vernacular, which was often a very free rendering mingled with interpretation.[3] From the word which meant ' interpretation ' or ' translation '

---
[1] E. A. Abbott, *ibid.*, p. 733.
[2] *Philo's Contribution to Religion*, pp. 50 f.
[3] The custom was believed to go back to the time of Ezra (Neh. viii. 7).

we have taken over the term, in its anglicized form, Targum. This term is applied by Dr. E. A. Abbott to the Johannine manner of recording sayings of Jesus. 'The Fourth Gospel asserts that all Christ's sayings, while He lived, were in need, so to speak, of a Targum. They were "proverbs," requiring the interpretation that would be given to them after His death by the Holy Spirit, in order to apply them to practice. Such an interpretation is a very different thing from our ordinary conception of a Targum. To us it seems a contradiction in terms to speak of an "inspired Targum." Yet that is what the Fourth Gospel is.'[1] The word 'proverb,' used here, occurs three times in the Gospel (John x. 6, xvi. 25, 29). In the margin of the Revised Version, 'parable' is given as an alternative meaning. In the first passage it refers to the allegory of the Shepherd, in the two later verses the reference is to the figurative and allusive teaching of the relationship between Jesus and the Father. This dark, mysterious mode of speaking is contrasted with plain and open speech. It is interesting to observe that the term is used in the two discourses where the reader is most eager to find the immediate presence of Jesus as speaker. If there is any part of the Gospel where the testimony of the centuries seems to show that we hear the living voice of Christ, it is in the allegory of the Good Shepherd who lays down His life for the sheep, and in the farewell words spoken after the Last Supper. But here it is that the Evangelist drops hints of baffled disciples, and the need of further explanation, of truths beyond their present range of understanding, and of the promise of the Spirit of truth who will bring to remembrance half-forgotten words, and will interpret and instruct.

No one would seriously contend that the five long chapters (xiii.–xvii.) contain a verbatim report of the conversation and prayer of Jesus in the Upper Room.

[1] *The Son of Man*, p. 411.

There are many sayings, short and aphoristic, which have every mark of authenticity. But there is also much repetition, and it is by no means easy to find a sequence of thought throughout. In particular, the five groups of sayings about the Paraclete seem to interrupt the flow of ideas. This is specially evident in the latter part of chap. xv. Dr. Bacon[1] sees in xv. 18–xvi. 2 a Johannine elaboration of discourse material found also in Matt. x. 17–22. Not a sentence in the warning of the world's antagonism is incongruous with the Master's preparation of the disciples for future dangers, as we learn about it in the other Gospels, though the phraseology is redolent of the Johannine idiom. But the last two verses of chap. xv. form the third[2] Paraclete logion, and have no clear connexion with what goes before or with what follows.

The five *logia* about the Paraclete, partly because of their completeness in themselves, partly because of their uncertain relation to the immediate context, have been called in question. But for two reasons we are disposed to think that the Evangelist is following an old tradition both in recording such teaching and in giving it in this context. First, the very great prominence given to the doctrine of the Spirit from the beginning of Christian history raises the question of Jesus' teaching on the subject. As Dr. H. A. A. Kennedy[3] reminds us, ' The data in the Synoptics are quite inadequate for the purpose. Those in the Fourth Gospel are an interpretation which presupposes Paulinism. And yet the place given by the writer to the conception of the Spirit is more intelligible if some traditions of Jesus' teaching on the subject were current in the Church. Cf. Luke xxiv. 48, 49; Acts i. 4 f.' In the second place, in that early

[1] *Introduction to the New Testament*, p. 259.
[2] Or, first, according to the rearrangement adopted. See Part II., chap. ii, p. 112.
[3] *Theology of the Epistles*, p. 114, *n*. 1.

collection of Sayings of Jesus used in common by Matthew and Luke we find the promise of guidance by the Spirit in the same context as that which surrounds this Paraclete logion in John xv. 26 f.; for it is in the hour when the disciples are brought before judicial tribunals by their persecutors that the Holy Spirit will teach them what they ought to say (Luke xii. 12). 'For it is not ye that speak, but the Spirit of your Father that speaketh in you' (Matt. x. 20). This is indeed the Advocate (Παράκλητος) of whom the Evangelist writes in John xv. 26, 27; 'But when the Advocate is come, whom I will send unto you from the Father, even the Spirit of truth, which proceedeth from the Father, he shall bear witness of Me: and ye also bear witness, because ye have been with Me from the beginning.'

That Jesus spoke in this strain of warning we know from the earliest tradition. That he should thus speak on the last night of His earthly life is surely not improbable. So we might take other thoughts and sayings in these chapters, and find that the Fourth Evangelist has given a Targum upon the text of some words of the Lord spoken on that memorable occasion. The Targum is sometimes an almost literal translation of the actual words that were spoken; sometimes a free paraphrase; sometimes an interpretative exposition.

Chapter IV

THE FOURTH EVANGELIST: HIS MESSAGE AND ITS ABIDING VALUE

SOME answer must now be attempted to the question which has haunted us all through this long investigation. However resolutely we may set ourselves to examine the structure of the Gospel, the manner of narration, the character of the sayings, without considering anything else than internal evidence and comparison with the Synoptic Gospels and the other so-called Johannine writings, we are driven back sooner or later to the question of authorship.

In the First Part the attempt was made to present in the form of a historical survey a fair and impartial statement of the very diverse opinions which have been held within the last generation upon the main questions that belong to the province of critical introduction. The more urgent questions have been followed up in the Second and Third Parts, and some indication of the present writer's personal conclusions has been offered. Before we pass on to the final summary of the Evangelist's message and its permanent value to the Christian Church we must try, in the light of all that has been said in these chapters, to give a brief answer to the question, Who, then, wrote the Fourth Gospel?

The Evangelist was almost certainly not the Apostle John. He was too dependent upon Synoptic records of incidents where personal memory would have made such reliance upon the words of others, not only unnecessary, but even unthinkable. He is silent regarding those very events where the Son of Zebedee was one of the three disciples chosen by the Master to share with Him some signal manifestation of His glory or His grief. It is most improbable that an intimate disciple, who had followed Jesus from the beginning of His ministry, should have found no place for a single parable or illustrative story, and should give no conception to his readers of the gradual disclosure in the self-revelation which occupied so large a place in the training of the Twelve. There is also the difficulty of accounting for the slow recognition of the Fourth Gospel, and for the absence of any reference to its apostolic authorship before the time of Irenaeus, if it were known to have come from the pen of the last survivor of the glorious company of the Apostles.

At the same time the Gospel claims to stand in some close relation to the Beloved Disciple, and the weight of internal evidence leans heavily towards identifying him with the Apostle John. If, as seems natural, we are to equate the titles ' the disciple whom Jesus loved ' and ' that other disciple,' the close association of this unnamed disciple with Simon Peter during the last days of the Gospel narrative corresponds remarkably with the relationship between Peter and John in the early chapters of Acts. Indeed, the identity of the Beloved Disciple was never called in question until the critical difficulties attending the Johannine authorship were felt acutely, and the denial of this identification seemed to offer a way of escape. The only strong reasons against the traditional view are that this disciple is said to have been ' known to the High Priest,' and that he is recorded to have taken the mother of our Lord after the Crucifixion ' to his own home from that hour.' But the vagueness of these two phrases, and our complete ignorance of the family relationships of the disciples, and of the homes that were open to them when visiting Jerusalem, leave ample room for suspending judgement on this issue. It is a pity that a statement which Eusebius quotes from a letter written by Polycrates, Bishop of Ephesus, late in the second century, is often used to help in the identification of the Beloved Disciple with an unknown ' John of Jerusalem.' The fact that, in this same letter, Polycrates confuses Philip the Evangelist with Philip the Apostle shakes one's confidence in his reliability as a historian of exact knowledge. Moreover, he writes that ' John who leaned on the Lord's breast was a priest wearing the mitre.' It is impossible to say what Polycrates meant by this cryptic phrase. The Greek word *petalon* is elsewhere used (in the LXX of Exodus) for the gold plate fastened in front of the High Priest's turban. The curious remark of Polycrates seems therefore to mean that this John was at some time High Priest. The absurdity of such an idea need hardly be pointed out. We may say with confidence that no ex-High Priest was present at the Last Supper. It is equally certain that no disciple of Jesus, who leaned on His breast at that Supper, ever afterwards became High Priest. If we may be allowed to extract any element of truth from this fantastic statement, it is just possible that one of the priests whose conversion to Christianity is recorded in Acts vi. 7 came profoundly under the influence of the Apostle John, and later in life settled in Ephesus and left a deep mark in the traditions of the local Church.

There is another theory to which frequent reference has been made in the historical survey. The Beloved Disciple, it is said, was not one of the Twelve, but a young Sadducee of good family, who as host entertained Jesus and the disciples at the Last Supper. Without actually being one of the Twelve, he was a supernumerary disciple, and was allowed special privileges, almost as though he were one of their number. There seem to be two fatal objections to this theory. It would have been the duty of the host, either to send his slave round with the basin of water and the towel, or else himself to have washed the feet of his guests. The mere fact that Jesus did this shows that He was host, and that none of His disciples had offered to take the place of His servant, and perform this menial office. Again, when it became necessary soon after to supply the vacancy left by the defection and death of Judas, would not the inevitable choice of the Eleven have fallen upon that intimate friend and disciple who had shared with them the sacred privilege of eating the Last Supper with the Lord on the night on which He was betrayed?

There is accordingly good reason to accept the obvious intention of the writer of the Gospel, and to regard the Beloved Disciple as John the Apostle. Nevertheless, if we separate the residuary element of possible truth in the legend reported by Polycrates from this idea of a young disciple who lived in Jerusalem and was present in the Upper Room at the farewell discourse, it is still possible for us to imagine a young man of priestly family, who did not become a disciple until after some years had passed. Such a witness of the debates in the Temple court, and of the councils held when plots were discussed for the arrest of Jesus, would have been a valuable source of information for any who were not satisfied with traditions of the Galilean ministry alone. There is nothing to prevent our thinking of such a convert from the Jerusalem priesthood as the actual writer of the Gospel. This might account for the legend which survived in Ephesus until the time of Polycrates.

But the tradition of Johannine authorship which Irenaeus held so strongly cannot be dismissed as valueless. A connexion between the Apostle John and the Gospel which so early became associated with his name is extremely probable. The silence of Ignatius about the venerable Apostle in the letter which he wrote to the Church at Ephesus about A.D. 115 is often felt to be a serious objection to the tradition that the aged John spent his last years in that city. Of recent years, moreover, an astonishing number of scholars have given their assent to a theory of the early martyrdom of John, so that his name is not deemed to have any but a fictitious connexion with the Gospel. It may seem presumptuous to speak lightly of arguments which are cogent to so many eminent writers. Here[1] it must suffice to quote, with entire agreement, some words written by Dr. A. S. Peake within a year or two of his death.[2] ' The alleged martyrdom of the Apostle John I still firmly disbelieve on grounds stated in my *Critical Introduction to the New Testament*. It has gained a credence which seems to me amazing in view of the slenderness of the evidence on which it is built, which would have provoked derision if it had been adduced in favour of a conservative conclusion. The difficulties about Papias' alleged statement mentioned in *Introduction*, pp. 144-6, still seem to possess their full weight. Yet it cannot be denied that this critical myth, as I consider it, is by dint of repetition hardening, temporarily I hope, into " an accepted critical result." '

We shall never know who wrote this Gospel. It can never be proved that the author was a personal disciple of the Apostle John. But the Evangelist obviously relies upon some sources of information which he deems sufficiently authoritative to justify him in departing in a number of important particulars from the earlier Gospels. The psychological factor counts for much when we find him confidently quoting sayings not elsewhere recorded as having been spoken by Jesus, and still more when he attributes to Jesus words which are clearly the result of reflection upon the teaching of Christ. It is much easier to understand such a procedure if behind this writer there stood the figure of one who had not only heard Jesus

[1] See further, Appendix A. [2] *Holborn Review*, xix (July 1928), p. 394.

speak in the intimate fellowship of the group of disciples and remembered actual utterances, but had also lived with Him and entered into His ways of thought. To this disciple 'the mind of Christ' would be a lifelong possession, both quickening memory and supplying guidance in the application of principles, learnt long before, to the new situations constantly arising in the Christian Church. When the Gospel was first published, those who guaranteed its truthfulness attested the witness of the Beloved Disciple. The Evangelist has given to the world the story of the ministry and message of Jesus as he knew it, based upon the Gospels current in the region where he lived and taught, but also based upon the meditations and instructions, the reminiscences and recollections, of one who had seen the glory of God in the face of Jesus Christ in the days of His flesh. Even though we stand at one remove from the eyewitness of the divine splendour, and hear his testimony from the lips of another, yet we know that the Evangelist was of the spiritual kindred of the Beloved Disciple. 'Everywhere in these writings we are impressed with the interior depth of the author. We feel sure that, either inwardly or outwardly, he has " lain on Christ's bosom," and that his personal testimony, " Of His fullness have we received," is profoundly true.'[1]

It is one of the misfortunes attending the necessity of the critical study of the Gospels that the singular beauty of the Johannine picture as a whole may be easily overlooked in the microscopic scrutiny of details. In the search for origins we may forget that our final task is to learn the meaning of the terms which he used and to grasp his message as a whole.[2]

---

[1] Rufus M. Jones, *E. R. E.*, ix, p. 90, art. 'Mysticism: Christian, N. T.'

[2] Cf. Inge, *Personal Idealism and Mysticism*, p. 38 : 'It is more important for us to know what St. John meant by calling Jesus Christ the Logos than what were the sources from which he drew the conception.'

The Gospel according to St. John was not a defence of Christianity to its cultured despisers. It was not a theological disquisition, although it is steeped in theology. It was a Gospel, a message of good news, born of an exultant experience of communion with the living God. Its doctrinal tone has led many to contrast it with the simple, humanitarian ethics of its predecessors. But this is to mistake the purpose of all the Gospels, for even Mark was written ' from faith unto faith.'[1] No Gospels would ever have been written but for the confident assurance of the Christian Church, from the very beginning, that in the life, the death, the resurrection of Jesus Christ, something of supreme importance had happened in the history of the world, something which had brought to them glad tidings of great joy. To some readers of the Fourth Gospel the narrative seems to be merely a diaphanous veil through which we are intended to see into the eternal world of truth. Goethe's dictum is often applied—' All that is transitory is merely a symbol.'[2] But one result of our studies throughout this book is the discovery how inadequate any interpretation of this Gospel is which ignores the Evangelist's interest in the actual events of the past. Hebrew history in the Old Testament has been described as ' prophecy teaching by example.'[3] There is a sense in which we might say that this Gospel offers us theology teaching by biography. But the vital factor is that the actual human life of Jesus gives substance to the theology. The essence of the Gospel is that the good news is true. In that age there was an abundant interest in speculations about God. In much of the popular

---

[1] J. Weiss, *Das älteste Evangelium*, p. 40 : ' Er schreibt aus seinem Glauben heraus für den Glauben, ihn zu erwecken, zu stärken oder zu klären.'

[2] Goethe, *Faust*, II. v. 1046 : ' Alles Vergängliche
 Ist nur ein Gleichnis.'

[3] G. F. Moore, *Encyc. Bib.*, ii. 2079. This is an adaptation of Bolingbroke's aphorism, taken from Dionysius of Halicarnassus, ' History is philosophy teaching by example.'

theosophy of the day, God was regarded as remote from this world, for matter itself was evil, and only a gradation of emanations linked the inaccessible God to this universe. On the other hand, the reflective minds which found a spiritual home in Stoicism inclined to pantheism. The Fourth Evangelist proclaimed to the Christian world of his time that the eternal Logos, the living and active Word of God, had become incarnate in Jesus. The Christian religion, the perfect revelation of God, was rooted in history. Paul, who also taught the Logos idea, without the term, had emphasized the providence of history. ' When the fullness of the time came, God sent forth His Son, born of a woman, born under the law, that He might redeem them which were under the law, that we might receive the adoption of sons' (Gal. iv. 4 f.). John also teaches that the line of providence runs through the historical revelation to Israel (iv. 22, i. 45, 49, v. 46 f., vi. 14, viii. 56, iii. 14, vi. 32). Yet there is a contrast between the old system and the new revelation. ' For the law was given by Moses; grace and truth came by Jesus Christ ' (i. 17). All this fresh knowledge came with Jesus, and a wide vocabulary of abstract terms is drawn upon to set forth the new conception of God. The supreme message of the Gospel, however, is that all these abstractions became concrete in the incarnate life of Jesus. ' The Word became flesh and dwelt among us (and we beheld His glory, glory as of the only begotten from the Father), full of grace and truth ' (i. 14). This revelation is unique, because it rests upon the filial consciousness of Jesus (i. 18). In the creative activity of the Logos there was evidence to inspire natural religion (i. 4 f.), but there is a divine exclusiveness in the Christian revelation. Not that the Evangelist denies the validity of the religious experience of the men of faith who have lived and died, or that he denies the reality of the prophetic message in the life of Israel (v. 39b, 46). ' I am the way, and the truth, and the life : no one cometh unto the Father, but by Me ' (xiv. 6). It is the Fatherhood of God which men learn from Him, and from Him alone.

There is a similarity between the teaching of the Fatherhood of God in the Synoptics and that given in the Fourth Gospel, and yet the difference also is marked. In the Sermon on the Mount we hear of the Heavenly Father whose undistinguishing regard is shown to all His children by the impartial distribution of sunlight and rain. In the latter Gospel those only are given the right to be called sons of God who have received Christ by faith, and have experienced the birth from above (i. 12, 13). The contrast between these two conceptions is self-evident. There is more, however, in common than appears at first sight to be there. The Synoptic Jesus is declaring man's ideal relationship to God. But the disciples know not how to pray, and prayer is surely the natural expression of the filial consciousness. Jesus shows that, where the sense of God's Fatherhood is present, prayer is the simple outpouring of the soul to God, springing from faith, and leading to that perfect trust which casts out care. In the Johannine teaching it is in the Upper Room that the disciples learn the meaning of prayer in Christ's name. Prayer that is in His spirit, according to His will, conceived after the pattern that He has taught them, is heard directly by the Father. This brings them into that freedom from the troubled heart which is attained by trust in God and trust in Christ. This stress upon Christ's name, and upon belief in Him, is part of the Johannine emphasis upon the historical revelation that has come through the Incarnation. The God to whom the Christian is taught to pray is the God and Father of our Lord Jesus Christ. Even in the Synoptics the simple sublimity of the Galilean teaching depends for its significance upon the Person of Him who taught. For this reason, faith has a prominent place in the Fourth Gospel. Not that the noun is used. By the time the Gospel was written, faith might easily have been understood as a body of doctrine. The verb is therefore always used, with a certain ethical force. It marks a moral attitude to Christ. It stands for an exercise of the higher judgement.

This important function given to moral discrimination illumined by the incarnate Word of God, accounts for the seeming contradiction between various statements about ' the world.' Since ' God is love ' (1 John iv. 8), it follows that ' God so loved the world that He gave His only begotten Son ' for it (John iii. 16). But it is also written : ' I pray not for the world, but for those whom Thou hast given Me ; for they are Thine ' (xvii. 9). The Spirit, ' when He is come, shall convict the world in respect of sin, because they believe not on Me ' (xvi. 8 f.). But ' God sent not the Son into the world to judge the world ; but that the world should be saved through Him ' (iii. 17). The love of God and the judgement of God are both affirmed, for the world is conceived sometimes as God's creation and the object of His beneficent care, and at other times as the baser nature of mankind organized in antagonism to the divine will. The struggle between darkness and light is the background of the drama of the life and death of Christ. Sin is the resolute refusal to walk in the light, now that the true light is already shining. ' And if any man hear My words and believe them not, I judge him not ; for I came not to judge the world, but to save the world. He that rejecteth Me, and receiveth not My words, hath one that judgeth him : the word that I have spoken, the same shall judge him in the last day ' (xii. 47 f.).

Judgement, however, is not the only result to follow from the wilful blindness of men in rejecting the Giver of life. The pain and humiliation inflicted on the Son of Man by an unbelieving world is accepted as an inescapable consequence of unfaltering obedience to the Father's will. 'The cup which the Father hath given Me, shall I not drink it?' (xviii. 11). The phrase 'lifting up' conceals a reference to His death. Exaltation is by way of the Cross (John iii. 14, viii. 28, xii. 32, 34). Even the 'glorifying' of the Son of Man is conditioned by the Cross (vii. 39, xii. 16, 23, xiii. 31). The paradox which runs through the Gospel is that life comes only through death (xii. 24 f.). But vindication will follow (xiii. 32), and the world will know that its dominion has been broken and its prince has been condemned by the very act that seemed at the time to be the crowning triumph of craft and force (xvi. 11).

The vindication of Jesus, the revelation to the world of His righteousness, can only follow His death, for until then His Spirit can not have free course (John vii. 39, xvi. 7, 10). So long as Jesus is present in the flesh with His disciples they are prevented from attaining to the higher experiences of spiritual communion. After the Death and Resurrection, comes the gift of the Spirit of Jesus (John xx. 22). The abiding presence of Christ in the hearts of His believers is represented as the sending of the Paraclete. This involves the Johannine doctrine of the Church. The word itself is not used, but the Evangelist represents Jesus as unfolding to His disciples a conception of a fellowship of believers united by the Holy Spirit who will dwell in their midst. The contrast between the Church and the world corresponds to that between the incarnate Logos and those who would not believe in Him (xvii. 14–16). The Church consists of those who recognize and welcome the Spirit of truth whom the world cannot receive (xiv. 17). Its members will be guided into the fuller truth for which the first disciples were not ready during the earthly life of Jesus. Yet there is a sacred continuity between the message of Jesus spoken on earth and the testimony of the Holy Spirit to the Church of believers. ' He shall bear witness of Me' (xv. 26); 'He shall glorify Me: for He shall take of Mine, and shall declare it unto you' (xvi. 14); 'The Holy Spirit, whom the Father will send in My name, shall teach you all things, and bring to your remembrance all that I said unto you' (xiv. 26). Through the Church, the Spirit will also bear witness to the world, and so the divine word of judgement and of love will go forth to those who are without. 'Ye also bear witness, because ye have been with Me from the beginning' (xv. 27). 'And He will convict the world in respect of sin, and of righteousness, and of judgement' (xvi. 8). 'Neither for these only do I pray, but for them also that believe on Me through their word; that they may all be one; even as Thou, Father, art in Me, and I in Thee, that they also may be in us: that the world may believe that Thou didst send Me' (xvii. 20-1). Through the Spirit, the Church will accomplish the work of Christ on a wider scale (xiv. 12). Through His influence, so close will be the moral union with Christ that the very prayers of Christians will be the prayers of Christ (xvi. 23).

It is sometimes objected to the Johannine message that all the stress is upon believing and knowing, and that the ethical note so characteristic of the teaching of Jesus in the Synoptics is strangely silent here. We have already seen that, in this Gospel, to believe is much more than to exercise the intellect in the acceptance of abstract truth. It connotes also moral choice and the obedience of faith. In the same way, knowledge is set forth as progress in learning the divine will, and it is conditioned by submission to that will. 'If any man willeth to do His will, he shall know of the teaching, whether it be of God' (vii. 17). But, even more directly, a moral value is given to that knowledge of God in which eternal life is said to consist by the addition of the significant words: 'and Him whom Thou didst send, even Jesus Christ.' All that was revealed in that fullness of grace and truth is the inheritance into which the believer is now to enter. 'God is love' (1 John iv. 8), and 'he that loveth not knoweth not God.' 'We know that we have passed out of death into life, because we love the brethren' (1 John iii. 13). These sayings from the First Epistle are entirely in the spirit of the Gospel. In the Synoptic records we learn that, when Jesus was asked to simplify the Commandments, He quoted two words from the Pentateuch: 'Thou shalt love the Lord thy God,' 'Thou shalt love thy neighbour as thyself.' So the Johannine ethic is summed up in these words attributed to Jesus on the night of the Last Supper: 'This is My commandment, that ye love one another' (John xv. 12). To those who persist in their objection by urging that this is a command restricted in its scope to the claims of fellow Christians, the answer is that the Christian Society was to be the school for the Christian character, not the exclusive field for its practice.

'These things are written that ye may believe that Jesus is the Christ, the Son of God; and that believing ye may have life in His name' (John xx. 31). This was the message of the Fourth Evangelist. Jesus the Son of God was the Life-giver, who came that we might have abundant life. And so the story of His life was told again that the true and living way might be found by those who thought of Jesus as a fading memory of the irrevocable past, and also by those whose religious speculations needed the control of the historic Christ.

'However the New Testament may have come into being,' wrote Dr. E. F. Scott not long ago, in an essay on 'Limitations of the Historical Method,' 'it has proved itself capable in a unique degree of meeting the religious needs of men. It has as much meaning for us now as it had in the first century. We have grown aware that it was written under given conditions, and that its teaching was affected at every point by existing modes of thought. But . . . behind all the contemporary factors there is an abiding message, and everything else is subsidiary to the discovery of its nature and meaning.'[1]

There is no book in the New Testament of which that may more truly be said than the Gospel according to St. John. On the one hand, it offers critical problems of unequalled complexity; on the other, it contains chapters which have endeared it, beyond other Gospels, alike to Indian mystic and to English peasant. With the possible exception of the Shepherd Psalm, the fourteenth of St. John is the best thumbed leaf in the cottar's Bible. Who can forget Lockhart's description of Sir Walter Scott, stricken unto death, when wheeled into his library, and placed before the window which commanded a view of the Tweed? 'Here he expressed a wish that I should read to him, and when I asked from what book, he said, "Need you ask? There is but one." I chose the 14th chapter of St. John's Gospel; he listened with mild devotion, and said when I had done—"Well, this is a great comfort."'[2] The same chapter was read night after night to James Adam, the famous Platonist, as he lay dying.[3] Sublime themes are handled with a simple dignity of language, and therein lies no small part of the universal appeal of the Gospel.

The abiding value of the Fourth Gospel consists chiefly in its mystical apprehension of the words and life of Jesus, for nothing can quench the eager interest of men, in every generation, in the teaching and character of our Lord. But there are several features in the method of presentation followed by this Evangelist which give it peculiar worth, even in an age like ours, when the vivid portrait in Mark is valued as never before.

---

[1] *Studies in Early Christianity* (ed. by S. J. Case), p. 17.
[2] *Life of Scott* (Standard Edition), p. 773.
[3] Memoir of James Adam, by his wife, in *Religious Teachers of Greece*, p. lv.: 'Every evening I read St. John xiv. before leaving him for the night, sometimes in English, sometimes in Greek.'

It was the Fourth Evangelist who set the teaching of Jesus free from the Jewish time-perspective in which the earliest Christians naturally preserved it. By transposing the thought of the return of Jesus from the dialect of Jewish apocalyptic into the universal language of mystical fellowship, he has given it a permanent place in Christian experience. By formulating the Logos doctrine, he taught the Church to stand firm on the historical revelation that came through Jesus, while relating the knowledge of Christ to the best available thought of the time. By his teaching of the Spirit as One who progressively guides the Church into new apprehension of the truth, he gave to Christianity the charter of freedom by which it has been saved from bondage to the past. His conception of inspiration is not static, but dynamic. Yet the continuity of Christian thought and experience has been secured by insisting that the Spirit of Truth is one with the Spirit of Jesus.

To the pilgrim seeking the way that leads to truth and peace the Evangelist brings his message that he who follows Jesus shall not walk in darkness, but shall have the light of life. To those who long for the assurance of eternal life there is given the open secret, ' Because I live, ye shall live also.' But the final word of the Gospel is ' that only those that love will ever understand.' To-day, as nineteen hundred years ago, it is still true that the disciple who loves his Lord and is loved by Him will discern His face through the morning mist. And now, as in the days of old beside the Galilean lake, the ardent defender of the cause of Christ is still met with the thrice-repeated challenge, ' Lovest thou Me ? '

CHAPTER V

INTERPRETATION OF THE FOURTH GOSPEL
1931–1953

THIS chapter will be confined to an outline of the views of three of the most notable expositors of the Gospel during the last twenty years. The limitation is regrettable, but necessary. If notice were to be taken of all discussions of John's meaning, and purpose in writing, the chapter would quickly grow to a book; and it has seemed better to give as full an account as possible of three outstanding expositions than a series of fragments dealing with a larger number.

Recent exposition as a whole has been marked by the recognition that John is a work of theology, and, further, of biblical theology. The commentator's work is seen to remain incomplete when he has laid bare the sources of the Gospel, rearranged it in its supposed original order, and on this basis estimated its historical value. Nor has he fulfilled a theological task when he has drawn out a series of parallels between John and other religious literature of the same period. John, no less than Mark or Romans, is a setting-forth of the Christian proclamation of the mighty acts of judgement and mercy wrought by God in Jesus Christ for the redemption of the world. The eternal counsels of God, his acts in history, and the consequences of these acts, are described, and described in relation to the biblical revelation as a whole—that is, in particular, to the Old Testament.

The three authors—E. C. Hoskyns, R. Bultmann, and C. H. Dodd—whose work is discussed in this chapter all recognize these points, but deal with them in different ways.[1] Hoskyns begins with the biblical world and Christian tradition and never moves outside that field. Professor Dodd—significantly—begins his book with an account of ' The Background ' and interprets the Gospel as an attempt to communicate the Christian message to the Hellenistic world. Dr. Bultmann goes farther still, and believes that material of non-Christian origin was incorporated into the Gospel, though he believes that it was ' Christianized ' in the process, and adapted to its new, biblical environment.

It ought to be said here that each of our three authors interprets the Gospel as a whole, and that each exposition is a whole, built up on the treatment of a vast number of details. To abstract and summarize a few sentences, therefore, or even a few themes, from such expositions means inevitably a measure of misrepresentation, if not of the general tenor of the author's thought, then at least of the way in which he arrives at and justifies his conclusions. Of all books, the commentary is the most difficult to summarize. In what follows, a short account is given of each author's general position, and then a summary of his exposition of a representative passage in the Gospel. For this purpose the discourse with Nicodemus (ch. iii.) has been chosen.

(1) E. C. Hoskyns. When Hoskyns died in 1937 he had completed the greater part of the Introduction of his Commentary, and had put into its final shape the commentary on the first six chapters. The commentary on chapters vii.–xxi. was drawn from earlier drafts which Hoskyns had intended to revise, and the whole was edited by Mr. F. N. Davey. The Introduction as we have it leaves out of account many of the routine matters which the reader looks for (such as external evidence regarding authorship and date, and the transmission of the text of

[1] For the works in question see the Bibliography.

the Gospel), but deals at length with the problem which emerges from the many attempts to locate and classify the Gospel in the world of ancient literature and religious thought. Of the last introductory chapter ('The Theological Tension of the Fourth Gospel') Mr. Davey writes in his preface (p. 8): 'As it now stands, this chapter is not as Hoskyns would have passed it for the press. . . . But in essence it undoubtedly presents the major conclusions about the exegesis of the Fourth Gospel to which his long study had led him.' Of this important chapter a brief account must now be given.

The Gospel is too complex to be patient of straightforward historical or psychological analysis. It does indeed purport to be history, yet itself declares that the flesh profiteth nothing and that the history of Jesus can be understood only by means of the Holy Spirit, who was not given till after the history had come to an end in the crucifixion and resurrection. Again, the Fourth Gospel is not to be regarded as a record of mystical experience, for it repeatedly emphasizes the central importance of the historicity, the ' flesh of Jesus the Son of man '. It is up to a point true that the Gospel contains both history and interpretation, but to separate the one from the other is an impossible task. ' In other words, the theme of the Fourth Gospel is the non-historical that makes sense of history, the infinite that makes sense of time, God who makes sense of men and is therefore their Saviour. The specific technique of the author has been wrought out in order to grapple with this theme. . . . The non-historical factor penetrates our supposed historical data and the historical factor is woven into what is manifestly non-historical ' (pp. 129 f).

The ' interpretation ' has no independent existence, and has not been superimposed upon the history. ' The meaning of the history of Jesus precedes and conditions its occurrence ' (p. 130). The Evangelist himself knew that in the life and death of Jesus he was confronted by what is infinite and eternal; and the truth of his perception is confirmed by the fact that it makes sense of the fragments recorded in the Synoptic Gospels. ' Though it is no doubt hard for us to understand, the themes of the Fourth Gospel in a real sense go before the contents of the synoptic sources in such a way as to rescue them from dissolving into mere fragments, or, better perhaps, in such a way as to show the wholeness which is lying hidden in the various Marcan episodes or in the separate, detached sayings that make up what is called the Q material; a wholeness not secured by the skilled literary arrangements of the same material which we possess in the Gospels of Matthew and Luke ' (pp. 130 f.).

The Gospel itself refuses any solution short of this, for the Evangelist is aware that the theological tension in which he stands can be resolved only in the resurrection, and in ' the advent of the Holy Spirit of God, who is the teacher of the final and ultimate Truth ' (p. 131). But it is because he has seen this tension in the flesh and blood of the Son of Man and believes in the resurrection and in the power of the Spirit, that he can bring out the meaning of whatever historical traditions were at his disposal. ' He saw the glory of God making sense of the history, for it is the Spirit who giveth life—by itself the flesh is meaningless and unprofitable. This is not metaphysics, though it is what the true metaphysician is in the end talking about. Rather, this is Apostolic Christianity, the rough material from which a philosophy may perhaps spring. This is the truth as it was seen by the Apostles of the Lord, by those who had been called into the theological tension of human life at its most acute point, at the place where the Christ was crucified. How many who were called by Jesus to be His apostles apprehended the meaning of His call and became Apostles, we do not know. Whether the man who wrote the Fourth Gospel was both an apostle and an Apostle we do not know. But it is almost impossible to escape from the conviction that the reader of the Gospel is at the very heart of that Apostolic Christianity which must be radically distinguished from mysticism on the one hand and from mere historical reminiscences on the other' (pp. 131 f.).

It follows that to interpret the Gospel is to 'hear and set forth the Meaning which the author of the Gospel has himself heard and seen in the concrete, historical life and death of Jesus of Nazareth, in His separate actions and in His audible words' (p. 132). To attempt to disentangle history and interpretation is to follow a false line, since without the interpretation the history is meaningless, and without the history the interpretation is a human notion or idea. Whether John truly perceived the truth in the history, or imported it into the history out of his own mind, may be tested by placing the Gospel in the context of the New Testament as a whole. 'The test that we must in the end apply to the Fourth Gospel, the test by which the Fourth Gospel stands or falls, is whether the Marcan narrative becomes more intelligible after reading the Fourth Gospel, whether the Pauline Epistles become more transparent, or whether the whole material presented to us in the New Testament is breaking up into unrelated fragments. If the latter be really and finally the case, we must then go back to speak of Johannine and Pauline theology. Once again we should be compelled to speak of the simplicity of the synoptic gospels, of the complexity of Pauline ideas, and of the unhistorical mysticism of the Fourth Gospel' (pp. 133 f.).

These problems, 'final problems' as he insisted that they were, are in mind throughout Hoskyns's exposition. In the light of them he perceived the theological unity of the New Testament with unusual clarity. We must turn now to his handling of John ii. 23–iii. 21, 'Jesus and Nicodemus the Rabbi'.

Hoskyns's discussion is in two parts, first an introductory exposition of the themes contained in the discourse, and next a 'Commentary', containing detailed notes, verse by verse. This latter may be neglected, for though it provides much useful information and many illuminating notes, it is the former that contains Hoskyns's original and distinctive contribution to the subject.

The themes of the discourse (says Hoskyns) are four.

(i) *Repentance*. The knowledge of God is not achieved by the acquisition of more and more information; of this, Nicodemus, the learned Jewish teacher, has already sufficient. It calls for a new, creative beginning; but this Nicodemus does not understand. In spite of his profession, in spite of his coming to talk with Jesus, he is a materialist, ' not because he takes visible human life seriously, but because he does not see what it means: he does not see that human birth is itself speaking of that which lies beyond it and above it; it is speaking of the creative act of God, of birth from above ' (p. 203). The discourse contains a second analogy, the baptism of John. ' The practice of religion, like the fact of birth, belongs to the structure of human life: both are necessary signs of the dominion of God ' (p. 204). But the signs are intelligible only to the man who is born of the Spirit. And ' there is no evolution from flesh to Spirit. What a man is in his own eyes or in the eyes of his religious companions is at best a parable of what he is as the creation of God: at worst it is a darkness from which he must escape at all costs ' (p. 204).

(ii) *Jesus Himself*, the visible, historical man Jesus. From signs, the discourse moves to the mission of Jesus Himself, the Son of Man. The theme of revelation is heaven; but the place of revelation, and of insight, is earth. No man has ascended into heaven; Nicodemus therefore can make no contribution to the conversation, but the situation is nevertheless not hopeless for it is precisely the situation Jesus has been sent to deal with. In Him and His descent to earth—a real descent in human flesh—the Danielic vision of the Son of Man found its fulfilment. 'A man among men, yet heaven is His home, and though deprived of glory, He is not deprived of ultimate and essential union with the Father' (p. 206).

(iii) *The Death of the Son of Man and the Love of God.* The Son of Man is to be lifted up. In the final perspective this means glory; but first it means death. 'For all those who have eyes to see, for those who believe, the place of death is the place of revelation. For this reason, the road to death, the death of the son of man, is the determined direction of the mission of the Son of God, determined, not by fate nor by mischance nor by the will of His enemies, but by the love of God for men' (p. 206). The place of revelation is also the place of faith. As men looked at the brazen serpent Moses made and were cured of their wounds, so must they look at the uplifted Son of Man—and live. Here however the discourse must end in tension. Jesus is the *only*-begotten Son of God, and what He does is (corresponding to His uniqueness) valid for *all*; yet it is effective for all—*who believe*; ' the thought of the love of God is still crossed by the thought of His judgement' (p. 207).

(iv) *Judgement and Salvation: Works and Faith.* The fact that the Son of God has come ' means that the opportunity of salvation has been provided, [but] it means also that to reject or to misunderstand the mission of the Son of God is to stand under the completed act of the judgement of God. And the generality of men do more easily reject than accept him: they prefer darkness to light; and this is to stand condemned in their whole behaviour, in all their works. But what are these dark, evil works? And what is the doing of the truth with which they are contrasted? And why should the line of demarcation between be so clear-cut and fraught with such terrible consequences? And, above all, why should Jesus be the place where both judgement and salvation occur?' (p. 208). 'To believe is to apprehend human action, all human action, in its relation to God: not to believe is not to recognize the only context in which human behaviour can be anything but trivial. The man who believes apprehends that every visible human act requires to be fulfilled by the invisible, corresponding and creative action of God. The man who believes recognizes that all human behaviour is by itself and in itself incomplete. The man who believes knows that God does fill up this incompleteness, and that, in filling it up, He makes of the human act a thing that has been wrought in God. . . . But the generality of men hate this exposure of their behaviour. They will not face the pain of it. They do not think that their actions require to be fulfilled, for their affections are set upon themselves. Or, if they do recognize their own inadequacy, they do not believe in the possibility of their behaviour being made good. These men are atheists: they remain in the darkness, and their whole behaviour is evil. They stand under the majestic judgement of God. This is the issue raised by the historical figure of Jesus, by His words and actions, and finally by His death. The death of Jesus is the supremely good action, since it is that work which above all others makes room for the creative action of the love of God' (pp. 208 f.). Out of this contrast arises the final metaphor of light and darkness.

(2) R. BULTMANN.[1] After examining John in relation to its environment, Dr. Bultmann draws the conclusion, which is fundamental to his exposition, that in this Gospel

---

[1] See not only the Commentary (mentioned in the Bibliography), but also *Theologie des Neuen Testaments* (Tübingen, 1948-53), II: '*Die Theologie des Johannes-Evangeliums und der Johannes-Briefe*' (pp. 349-439), from which, as the more convenient source for the purpose, the following account has in the main been taken. In the page references, *K.* stands for *Kommentar*, *T.* for *Theologie*.

Jesus is represented in terms of the gnostic Redeemer myth. This is not to say that the Gospel simply reproduces the myth in its non-Christian form—for John, redemption is not the liberation of pre-existent sparks of light, unfortunately imprisoned in the darkness by demonic powers—yet its framework in thought and language is essentially the gnostic framework. ' Jesus appears as in the gnostic myth as the pre-existent Son of God, whom the Father has endowed with authority and sent into the world. Here, appearing as a man, he speaks the words which the Father has given him, and accomplishes the works with which the Father has charged him. This does not mean that he is cut off from the Father; rather, as a faultless and truthful emissary, he stands in firm, lasting unity with him. He comes as the " Light ", as the " Truth ", as the " Life ", in that through his words and works he brings light, truth, and life, and calls his " own " to himself. In his discourses, with their " I am ", he reveals himself as the Emissary (*der Gesandte*); but only his " own " understand him. So his coming effects the division between those who hear his voice, and receive sight, and the others who do not understand his speech, who mistakenly suppose that they see and remain bound in their blindness. In the world, out of which he calls his own to himself, he is despised and hated. But he leaves the world; as he has " come ", so he " goes away " and takes leave of his own, whom he commits in prayer to the Father. But his departure also belongs to his redeeming work; for through his ascent he has opened for his own the way into the heavenly dwelling-places, into which he will bring them ' (*T.* 360). All this, and the very name Logos, comes out of the gnostic tradition; and the question which the interpreter of John must face is, what use the Evangelist has made of this originally non-Christian material.

In John, as in the gnostic writings, we meet the terms

Light and Darkness, Truth and Falsehood, Freedom and Slavery, Life and Death, but in John these dualistically conceived pairs are determined in their meaning by the biblical concept of creation. Thus Light, while signifying in general that which is good and healthful, means in particular the possibility which man possesses of exercising a true understanding of himself as God's creature. ' Darkness means that man does not grasp this possibility, that he shuts himself up (*verschliesst sich*) against the God who is manifest in creation, that he, instead of understanding himself as a creature, assumes a self-determination (*Selbstherrlichkeit*) such as is proper only to the Creator. To the question whence the darkness comes John does not answer with a myth. For the possibility of darkness—man's illusory understanding of himself—is implied by the possibility of light—man's true understanding of himself. Only because there is a revelation of God can there be enmity against God. Only because there is light is there darkness; it is nothing other than man's closing himself against the light, his turning away from the origin of existence, in which alone is found the possibility of the illumination of existence. In that the world closes itself against the light, it rebels against God, makes itself independent over against the Creator—that is, it attempts to be so, it imagines that it can be so ' (*T.* 364 f.). Similar remarks may be made about the other pairs. It follows that ' man stands—or stood—confronted by the decision for God or against God; and he is ever anew confronted with this decision through the revelation of God in Jesus. Out of the cosmological dualism of Gnosis there has emerged in John a dualism of decision ' (*T.* 367). This observation is fundamental to Dr. Bultmann's interpretation of Johannine theology.[1]

---

[1] That it is also closely related to Dr. Bultmann's views on ' Demythologizing ' is evident, but the matter cannot be pursued here.

So long as the world remains as it is the decision is scarcely an open one; the world abides in darkness and unreality, and man can be nothing other than he is. The significance however of Jesus' mission as the Revealer is precisely that He gives man the chance of becoming something other than he is. It is the coming of Jesus, the Light of the world, that realizes the possibility of decision; that is why His coming is the judgement ($\kappa\rho\iota\sigma\iota\varsigma$) of the world. His coming is described in both mythological and eschatological terms.[1] To the mythological language belong the ideas of pre-existence, of being 'sent', and of re-ascending to heaven (whence in the first instance the Revealer-Emissary had been sent). From the eschatological language of Judaism and early Christianity are borrowed such terms as Messiah, King of Israel, and Son of Man. But the eschatology is 'historicized' and thereby 'demythologized'. The day of the Messiah is the day of His incarnate ministry; judgement lies not in the future but in the present activity of Jesus—the shining of the light in the darkness.

This description of the work of Jesus does not mean that He appeared in a blaze of glory, universally acknowledged in the splendour of His proper relation with God. He came among men, not in the outward guise of a gnostic Redeemer, but in humanity, or rather as a particular man, Jesus of Nazareth. It is true that His career reveals (in the Johannine narrative) some of the characteristics of the Hellenistic $\theta\epsilon\hat{\iota}o\varsigma$ $\dot{\alpha}\nu\dot{\eta}\rho$ (divine man), such as supernatural knowledge and wonder-working; but, over against this, it is a well-known feature of the Gospel that both the words and works of Jesus are exposed to misunderstanding. So far from procuring honour for Him they lead to His rejection. In this, John marks a return to an aspect of the earlier Gospel tradition. 'It may be said that John, by his presentation of the activity of

[1] Eschatology is of course a kind of mythology.

Jesus as the Son of God who has become man, has in a unique way developed and deepened the Marcan theory of the "Messianic Secret". Over the figure of Jesus hangs a mystery, although he quite openly says who he is and what claim he makes. Although he says it? No! Because he says it. For, in full publicity, he is for the world a hidden Messiah, not because he conceals anything or orders the keeping of a secret, but because the world does not look with seeing eyes (xii. 40). His hiddenness is the consequence of his self-revelation; precisely this makes "those who see" "blind" (ix. 39) ' (*T*. 394).

To say this is not to deny that in Jesus God was veritably present. To express His presence John uses various figures of speech. For example, he borrows from the language of mysticism the notion of the mutual knowledge, and the reciprocal indwelling, of the Father and the Son, and he speaks mythologically of the love of the Father for the Son and of the Son's abiding in the Father's love. It is the language only that John borrows; he does not in fact teach either mysticism or mythology, any more than he offers a metaphysical doctrine of the 'two natures'.

The work Jesus carries out as God's envoy is His whole ministry, one salutary event; though this is summarized, as it were, in His death. This is complete in itself, and does not need the resurrection to complete it since it is already a manifestation of the glory of God. ' That the sacraments play no part in the Gospel[1] corresponds to the fact that the " saving events " in the traditional sense also play no part there and that the whole process of salvation—Incarnation, Death and Resurrection of Jesus, Pentecost and Parousia—is transposed into one event, the revelation of the ἀλήθεια of God in the earthly activity of the man Jesus, and the removal of the scandal [of such

---

[1] Dr. Bultmann believes all the Johannine allusions to the sacraments to be redactional glosses.

an act of revelation in unique circumstances of place and time] by faith " (*T*. 405).

In fact, the works of Jesus are His words. Revelation *is* the work of God; Jesus speaks what He has seen and heard in the presence of the Father, and this is His deed. This act of revelation however contains a surprise.

' What is surprising is that Jesus' words never communicate anything special or concrete which he has seen or heard with the Father. He never tells of things or events of which he was an eye- or ear-witness. The heavenly world is never the theme of his discourse; unlike the gnostic Redeemer, he communicates no cosmogonic or soteriological mysteries. The theme of his discourse is always the same, that the Father has sent him, that he has come as the Light, the Bread of Life, as witness for the truth, and so on, that he will go away, and that men must believe in him ' (*T*. 408 f.). Corresponding to this is the fact that the most characteristic sayings of Jesus are the ' I am ' sayings, and that He Himself is described as the Word. Moreover, although Jesus is the Revealer, He in fact reveals nothing more *than that He is the Revealer*, that He is Life and Light precisely in the moment of revelation that that is what He is. He offers no system of doctrine and no religious experience. He declares that He is the truth, and when men, hearing His word, turn from their own negative existence they discover that He is the reality which they most desire.

It is at this point that it becomes possible to understand the meaning of faith. To have faith is to hear and accept—to obey—the revelatory word of Jesus, to acknowledge that He is, as He claims to be, the Revealer, sent from God to whom He will return. Because the person and work of Jesus are identical with His word, it becomes possible to use not only the word ' hear,' but also the word ' see ', and out of this fact arises, as a concept parallel with faith, knowledge. '$\pi\iota\sigma\tau\epsilon\acute{u}\epsilon\iota\nu$ and $\gamma\iota\nu\acute{\omega}\sigma\kappa\epsilon\iota\nu$

cannot be distinguished as stages, as if there were in the Christian community, as in the gnostic, " pistics " and " gnostics ". Faith is not the acceptance of a dogma, upon which the opening out of esoteric knowledge or a mystic vision might follow; faith is everything. Knowledge cannot separate itself from faith and advance beyond it; yet faith is faith informed by knowledge (*ein erkennender*). As all knowledge must be a believing knowledge so in the same way faith realizes itself in knowledge. Knowledge is a structural element in faith ' (*T*. 420 f.).

Faith is the overcoming of the scandal inherent in the fact that the Word was made flesh; it means a decision against the world and for God. This further has as its result that the believer passes over into eschatological existence (*eschatologische Existenz*); he is still ἐν τῷ κόσμῳ, but he is no longer ἐκ τοῦ κόσμου (xvii. 11, 14, 16). From this condition flow the consequences which mark the Christian life—knowledge, freedom, peace and joy; and, at the same time, the obligation of love. These all are actuated within the Church by the Spirit, who is an eschatological gift.

This account of Dr. Bultmann's exposition of Johannine theology may be followed by a brief summary of his treatment of the conversation with Nicodemus. It should be noted that he regards iii. 31–6 as the immediate continuation of iii. 1–21.

The section as a whole (iii. 1–21, 31–6) is headed ' The Coming of the Revealer as the κρίσις of the World ' (*K*. 92). First is unfolded ' The Mystery of Rebirth ' (iii. 1–8). ' Man, as he is, is excluded from salvation, from the divine sphere of existence (*von der Sphäre Gottes*); for him, as he is, this is no possibility. But at the same time that is so said as to give rise to the suggestion that it may become a possibility for him, so far as there exists for him the possibility of becoming himself an other, a new man. And so the saying is also an admonition, not indeed a moralizing admonition, but the admonition that man should question his own being (*sich selbst in Frage zu stellen*).... For rebirth means (and Nicodemus's misunderstanding is intended to make this clear) not simply an improvement of man, but that he should receive a new origin (*Ursprung*); and this of course he cannot bestow upon himself.... His "whither" corresponds to his "whence"; and if his way is to lead to salvation then the "whence" of his way must become something other than it is; he must be able to make a break with his origin, to exchange his old origin for a new; he must be "born again"' (*K*. 95–8). The discourse moves forward to 'The Mystery of the Son of Man' (iii. 9–21). Here Dr. Bultmann believes the Evangelist to have taken over discourse material from the '*Offenbarungsreden*' source (see pp. 166, 171), and his comments on verses 12 and 13 make clear the way in which he believes the Evangelist to have handled this material, and what meaning he supposes the Evangelist to have attached to it. On verse 12 he says: 'In Gnosis, there corresponds to the soteriology a definite cosmology; he who does not accept the cosmology ... will also refuse to believe the doctrine of redemption. But in this field the doctrine of ἄνωθεν γεννηθῆναι, that is, of the pre-existence, the heavenly origin, of souls, belongs to the ἐπίγεια; for this doctrine is the essential point of the cosmology. And the chief point in the ἐπουράνια is the doctrine of the ascent of the soul.... The Evangelist also, who no longer understood ἄνωθεν γεννηθῆναι to refer to the heavenly origin of souls but applied it to rebirth, could make use of verse 12. The discourse on rebirth belongs to the ἐπίγεια in so far as it contains man's judgement upon his own situation in the world, the judgement, that is, that as one born of the flesh he is flesh, that he is lost.... So, as in the gnostic myth, τὰ ἐπίγεια means nothing other than the paradoxical situation in which man finds himself. . . . It would be possible to paraphrase: he who does not perceive the necessity of rebirth also fails to understand that in Jesus it has become possible' (K. 105 ff.). On verse 13 he says: 'What this clause meant in the source is plain: ascent into heaven is possible only for him who comes from heaven, for the ἄνωθεν γεννηθείς, that is, for pre-existent souls. . . . That for the Evangelist the meaning is different is clear. . . . The exaltation presupposes the incredible fact of the σὰρξ ἐγένετο, and faith in it requires that the man Jesus should be recognized as the 'Son of man' who comes down from heaven . . . this is the ἐπουράνια, in which the world refuses to believe' (K. 107–9). Verses 20 f., and indeed the whole paragraph up to this point, are summed up as follows: 'That a man, in meeting with the Revealer, decides for or against him on the ground of his own past, is only a bold, paradoxical way of saying that in his decision there comes to light what he really is. . . . For this reason the mission of Jesus is the eschatological Event, through which judgement is pronounced upon all the past. And this mission can be the eschatological event because in it God's love gives back to man his lost freedom to achieve his own proper self (*seine Eigentlichkeit zu ergreifen*)' (K. 115).

Verses 31–6 ('The Mystery of the Testimony') emphasize the point which has already been brought out (p. 255, *supra*) that Jesus reveals—that He is the Revealer! But for this very reason the mission of Jesus is the decisive eschatological event in which men are confronted by God and judged.

(3) C. H. DODD. Professor C. H. Dodd's book, *The Interpretation of the Fourth Gospel*, falls into three parts. The first deals with 'The Background' of the Gospel. In it the author discusses in turn 'The Higher Religion of Hellenism: the Hermetic Literature', 'Hellenistic Judaism: Philo of Alexandria', 'Rabbinic Judaism',

'Gnosticism', and 'Mandaism' as elements in the environment out of which the Fourth Gospel emerged. The second part of the book is headed 'Leading Ideas', and contains twelve chapters, on the following subjects: Symbolism; Eternal Life; Knowledge of God; Truth; Faith; Union with God; Light, Glory, Judgement; Spirit; Messiah; Son of Man; Son of God; and Logos. The third part of the book deals with the 'Argument and Structure' of the Gospel, and contains a complete and detailed analysis and exposition. For full measure, there are added in an appendix ' Some considerations upon the historical aspect of the Fourth Gospel '.

It will be impossible here to treat the first part of the book at all, except by quoting Professor Dodd's summary of his conclusions: ' While the Evangelist stands within the general environment of primitive Christianity . . . he also shows affinities with certain tendencies in non-Christian thought. He is well aware of the teaching of Rabbinic Judaism, but only partly sympathetic to it. He is more sympathetically in touch with Hellenistic Judaism as represented by Philo. Like Philo himself, he is in contact with the higher pagan thought of the time, as represented to us by the Hermetic literature. " Gnosticism " has in part the same roots as Johannine Christianity, and serves in some measure to illustrate Johannine conceptions, but more by contrast than affinity. Mandaism turns out to be too late in date to be of any direct importance for our investigation, though in so far as it retains elements of earlier Gnosticism it may afford some illustrative parallels. Rabbinic Judaism, Philo and the *Hermetica* remain our most direct sources for the background of thought, and in each case the distinctive character of Johannine Christianity is brought out by observing the transformation it wrought in ideas which it holds in common with other forms of religion ' (p. 133).

The second part of the book covers a very wide range.

It has been well described as a counterpart to the linguistic studies contained in Kittel's well-known *Theologisches Wörterbuch zum Neuen Testament*. Professor Dodd pursues not words in their various meanings, but concepts in the varying terminology in which they are expressed. Here the first chapter, on Symbolism, will be summarized; the scope, though unfortunately not the content, of the remainder of the part has already been indicated.

The Fourth is distinguished from the Synoptic Gospels in its use of symbolism. The synoptic parables are essentially stories from real life. They invite the hearer to make a judgement which, when made, can be applied to a fresh field of thought and experience. But the symbolic discourses of the Fourth Gospel are not drawn from real life, they are not stories, and they are essentially declaratory—that is, they make affirmations (notably about the person of Jesus) which the hearer is required to accept. Professor Dodd says of the 'allegory' of the Good Shepherd in ch. x.: 'Christ is the real subject of all the statements made, and shepherd and gate are cryptograms' (p. 135). There is here no story about a shepherd and his sheep (as there is in Matthew xviii. 12–14, Luke xv. 4–7), but a series of Christological pronouncements in symbolic form, the key to which is to be found in the Old Testament, the apocalyptic literature, the works of Philo, and the language of various cults in which deities are described as shepherds.

The allegory of the Vine in ch. xv. is similarly no story. 'The language indeed changes to and fro between the literal and the metaphorical in a way which would be bewildering, if the reader were not conscious all through that all the statements made really refer to Christ and His disciples, under the symbol of a vine and its branches, rather than to any earthly vine' (p. 136). Again, the explanation of the symbolism used is to be found in Old

Testament and Hellenistic religious language, and, still more significantly, in the primitive Christian use of vine-symbolism. 'The immediate point is that here, even more than in the shepherd "allegory", we are dealing with a kind of symbolism in which the images or figures employed, although they are taken from workaday experience, derive relatively little of their significance from the part they play in such experience. The symbol is almost absorbed into the thing signified. The meaning of the "allegory" is only to a slight extent to be understood from a knowledge of what vines are as they grow in any vineyard; it is chiefly to be understood out of a rich background of associations which the vine-symbol had already acquired' (p. 137).

'In like manner the images of bread and water retire behind the realities for which they stand, and derive their significance from a background of thought in which they had already served as symbols for religious conceptions' (p. 137). And, again, this background includes both Hellenistic and Jewish elements, together with a very important primitive Christian sacramental element. 'The Johannine statements, "I am the Vine", "I am the Bread", are intended to give expression to the mysterious truth uttered in the words of Institution, "*Hoc est corpus Meum; Hic est Sanguis Meus*"' (pp. 138 f.).

When John uses such terms as 'Bread' and 'Vine' in this significant way he often distinguishes them by the use of the adjective ἀληθινός. He uses this word in what may be called a Platonic sense (though his acquaintance with Plato was probably not at first hand). Thus by ἄρτος ἀληθινός 'he means that spiritual or eternal reality which is symbolized by bread' (p. 139).

Professor Dodd proceeds: 'From this we can understand his characteristic use of symbolism—I mean in particular the way in which the symbol is absorbed into the reality it signifies. Bread, vine, water, light, are not mere illustrations or analogies. A vine, in so far as it is a vine at all, bodies forth the eternal Idea of Vine; except in so far as it does so, it has no significance, indeed properly speaking no existence. Describe the eternal Vine, therefore, the ἄμπελος ἀληθινή, and you are describing every vine, in every respect which constitutes its vineness. What makes a shepherd a shepherd? The fact that he realizes in himself the eternal idea of shepherdhood, which is manifested in Christ. He enters by the door, knows his sheep, leads them to pasture, promotes their well-being, and risks his life to save them from danger' (p. 140).

Sometimes, as in the allegory of the Good Shepherd, the symbol is conveyed in a fictitious narrative or picture, sometimes however in a narrative ostensibly historical, such as the feeding of the multitude. Such incidents, though represented as historical, are none the less symbolic, and it is essential to John's thought that events in the life of Jesus both reveal and convey the eternal truths which lie behind them. At this point may be introduced another Johannine word—σημεῖον. This word calls to mind the symbolic actions of the Old Testament prophets; and in Philo it is actually used as a synonym of σύμβολον.

'In the prophets, the σημεῖον, or significant act, is usually a " sign " of something about to happen in the working-out of God's purpose in history. In Philo, the σημεῖον, or σύμβολον, points to a hidden meaning, on the abstract, intellectual level. The Johannine σημεῖον is nearer to the prophetic; only it refers, in the first instance, to timeless realities signified by the act in time. Yet not wholly so. As we shall see, while in the first intention the feeding of the multitude signifies the timeless truth that Christ, the eternal Logos, gives life to men, and the healing of the Blind that he is the Bearer of light, yet in the development of the argument we discover that

Christ's work of giving life and light is accomplished, in reality and in actuality, by the historical act of his death and resurrection. In that sense, every σημεῖον in the narrative points forward to the great climax. . . .

' I conclude that the events narrated in the Fourth Gospel are intended to be understood as significant events, σημεῖα. . . . To a writer with the philosophical presuppositions of the evangelist there is no reason why a narrative should not be at the same time factually true and symbolic of a deeper truth, since things and events in this world derive what reality they possess from the eternal Ideas they embody.

' Thus the very nature of the symbolism employed by the evangelist reflects his fundamental *Weltanschauung*. He writes in terms of a world in which phenomena—things and events—are a living and moving image of the eternal, and not a veil of illusion to hide it, a world in which the Word is made flesh. In the light of this, we proceed to the attempt to define as precisely as may be the leading ideas of the Gospel, having before us the book as a whole, narrative and discourse, bound together by an intricate network of symbolism ' (pp. 142 f.).

Such is the Evangelist's method, and such his *Weltanschauung*. It is in the light of both that the ' leading ideas ' of the Gospel are studied and its argument unfolded. ' The whole shape of the Gospel is determined by the idea expressed in the words, ὁ λόγος σὰρξ ἐγένετο, with the content of the term λόγος supplied by the Prologue as a whole ' (p. 285).

The Gospel itself reveals a sharp division at the end of ch. xii., and may accordingly be divided into three sections: The Proem (ch. i.), The Book of Signs (ii.–xii.), and The Book of the Passion (xiii.–xx., or xxi., if this ' appendix ' chapter be included).

The Proem corresponds to Mark i. 1–15. The Prologue is the counterpart of the opening Christological definition in Mark, and the remainder of the chapter is 'testimony', and recalls Mark i. 4–15: Jesus is set forth as the Lamb of God, the Messiah, the Son of God and the King of Israel. The relationship between John and Mark is not merely formal. 'The Prologue ... represents a thoroughgoing reinterpretation of the idea which in the later part of the chapter is expressed in terms of the "realized eschatology" of the primitive Church. The Logos-doctrine is placed first, because, addressing a public nurtured in the higher religion of Hellenism, the writer wishes to offer the Logos-idea as the appropriate approach, for them, to the central purport of the Gospel, through which he may lead them to the historical actuality of its story ...' (p. 296).

In the Book of Signs the first episode is ii. 1–iv. 42, The New Beginning. These chapters contain two σημεῖα, or significant actions, and two discourses developing their significance. Throughout, the dominant idea is that of 'the inauguration of a new order of life for mankind through the incarnation of the Logos' (p. 316). 'The two narratives are realistic and dramatic, ... this gives content to the term σάρξ in the fundamental proposition, ὁ λόγος σὰρξ ἐγένετο. At the same time the appended discourses point to the element of λόγος, the eternal reality embodied in the temporal events' (p. 317). Of these discourses we must glance at the former, that to Nicodemus.

'Jesus is confronted with a representative of the old order which is being superseded' (p. 303), and bluntly requires of him a new birth; no remote apocalyptic possibility, but a necessary condition of entering the kingdom of God, or eternal life, here and now. Nicodemus's bewilderment furnishes the occasion for a radical elucidation of rebirth in terms of the two levels of existence, σάρξ and πνεῦμα. 'On each level like produces like' (p. 304). 'The main theme of the discourse, then, is the passage of man out of the lower order of existence, the realm of σάρξ, into the higher order of existence, the realm of πνεῦμα in which alone ζωὴ αἰώνιος is his portion. It is this passage into the higher order of existence which has been symbolized by the changing of water into wine and by the cleansing (=transformation, or destruction and renewal) of the temple' (pp. 304 f.). This recalls one of the themes of the Prologue (cf. especially i. 13), and the monologue into which the conversation develops proceeds to speak of the Son of the Father, who is the bearer of life and light. 'The incarnation of the Logos is . . . the descent of the Son of Man, or heavenly Man, into the lower sphere, the realm of σάρξ. It is the heavenly Man alone (as a Hellenistic reader would at once concede) who, having descended, ascends to heaven again. His descent and ascent open to men the possibility of receiving eternal life, that is, of ascending to the sphere of πνεῦμα; in other words, the possibility of rebirth. The possibility becomes an actuality for those who have faith in the Son—which is tantamount (in terms of the Prologue) to "receiving the Logos", with the consequent ἐξουσία to be children of God' (p. 305).

Two further themes are introduced: first, the reference to the serpent in the wilderness and the 'lifting up' of the Son of Man. The explanation is not complete at this point, though the Hellenistic reader would at least understand that something more was being said about the ascent of the heavenly Man. Secondly, the theme of light is added to that of life. Since the incarnation can be compared to the shining of light it has the effect of judgement: 'It judges, in the sense that men pass judgement on themselves by their response to Christ' (p. 307).

Professor Dodd finds similar themes continued in iii. 22–36, and therefore sees no sufficient reason for separating this section, or part of it, from iii. 1–21.

The remainder of Professor Dodd's analysis of the

Fourth Gospel can only be hinted at. The remaining episodes in the Book of Signs are:

(2) The Life-giving Word (iv. 46–v. 47).

(3) Bread of Life (vi.).

(4) Light and Life: Manifestation and Rejection (vii.–viii.).

(5) Judgement by the Light (ix. 1–x. 21, with appendix, x. 22–39).

(6) The Victory of Life over Death (xi. 1–53).

(7) Life through Death. The Meaning of the Cross (xii. 1–36).

The Book of Signs is connected by a summary (xii. 37–50) with the Book of the Passion. Here there are two divisions: The Farewell Discourses, and the Passion-Narrative. The former is bound by many links with the Book of Signs, but offers a complete interpretation of the ascent and descent of the Son of God. It does so in terms that would be intelligible and acceptable to Hellenistic readers, yet in such a way as to bring out the distinctive features of the Johannine over against all Hellenistic teaching. '... In the Fourth Gospel the whole process of initiation takes place within a body of "friends" of Jesus. The corporate character of the transaction is essential.... That knowledge of God, or union with God, which is eternal life, is here interpreted in personal and ethical terms as ἀγάπη.... The knowledge of God which is life eternal is mediated by an historical transaction' (pp. 422 f.).

After this the Passion story itself, though showing traces of Johannine thought, is related in straightforward language. 'It is as though the Evangelist, having sufficiently set forth the meaning of the death and resurrection of Christ, turned to the reader and said, "And now I will tell you what actually happened, and you will see that the facts themselves bear out my interpretation"' (pp. 431 f.).

ADDITIONAL NOTES TO PART III

Page

192 Line 18. See the note on p. 100, line 5.

194 Line 15. For a detailed discussion of the problems raised by the narrative about Lazarus see Hoskyns, *op. cit.*, pp. 107–128.

204 Line 31. It is not quite clear whether Dr. Howard here quotes Lake's view of the text of Matt. xxviii. 19 with approval. It should be pointed out that many scholars disagree with it.

215 Line 16. See also M. Black, *op. cit.*

217 Line 21. It is doubtful whether the passage quoted on p. 204 is sufficient to establish this conclusion. ' In spite of the oft-quoted maxim, " The proselyte is like a new-born child ", and some similar *façons de parler*, the native Rabbinic Judaism seems to have had in this period no real doctrine of regeneration ' (C. H. Dodd, *The Interpretation of the Fourth Gospel* (Cambridge, 1953), pp. 303 f.).

# APPENDICES

Appendix A

THE AUTHORSHIP OF THE BOOK AND THE ALLEGED MARTYRDOM OF JOHN

THE external evidence has been discussed in recent years so fully, and the relevant passages have been quoted so often, that it will suffice to give the references to the original authorities, and to the best modern discussions, merely indicating the main points at issue.

PAPIAS (born *c*. 70, died *c*. 146). Eusebius preserved his testimony, *Hist. Eccles.* iii. 39:

> ' But if ever any one came who had followed the presbyters, I inquired into the words of the presbyters, what Andrew or Peter or Philip or Thomas or James or John or Matthew, or any other of the Lord's disciples, had said, and what Aristion and the presbyter John, the Lord's disciples, were saying. For I did not suppose that information from books would help me as much as the word of a living and abiding voice.'

The points under discussion are: 1. (*a*) Does Papias identify the presbyters with Andrew ... Matthew? Or (*b*) are the presbyters the link between the followers of the presbyters and the apostles? If (*a*) is his meaning, then ' what Andrew ... or any other of the Lord's disciples had said ' is simply in apposition with ' the words of the presbyters.' If (*b*) is the meaning, then ' what Andrew ... or any other of the Lord's disciples had said,' &c., is the content of the ' words of the presbyters.' Papias inquired from these followers what the presbyters had said to them about the teaching of their predecessors—the original disciples of Jesus.

2. (*a*) Are Aristion and the presbyter John distinct from the first group, so that Papias refers to two Johns? Or (*b*) is this clause resumptive? If 1 (*a*) is correct, then 2 (*b*) is admissible. But if 1 (*b*) is Papias's meaning, then the term ' the presbyter John ' is probably intended to distinguish him from one named in the apostolic group, even though the title ' the Lord's disciples '

covers not only Aristion and the presbyter John, but also the first group.

3. Is the change of tense from εἶπεν to λέγουσιν significant? In that case the apostolic group is thought of as in the past, whilst Aristion and John are thought of as still living when Papias made his inquiries.

Lightfoot (*Essays on Supernatural Religion*, p. 150) regards λέγουσιν as a historic present introduced for the sake of variety. Drummond (*Character and Authorship of the Fourth Gospel*, p. 199) thinks that it refers to the time of writing, not to the time of inquiry, and interprets it as a reference to books. They being dead yet speak.

IRENAEUS (*c*. 185). Three well-known statements have led to endless controversy.

1. *Contra Haereses*, III. 1: 'John the disciple of the Lord, who also reclined on his breast, he it is who gave out the Gospel, living on in Ephesus of Asia.'

2. *ibid.*, III. iii. 4 says that the Ephesian Church was founded by Paul, and that John lived on in Asia until the time of Trajan. (The second half of this statement is also given in II. xxii. 5.)

3. Eusebius preserves (*Hist. Eccles.*, v. 20) the famous letter to Florinus in which Irenaeus recalls his intercourse with Polycarp.

> 'For while I was still a boy I knew you in lower Asia in Polycarp's house, when you were a man of rank in the royal hall, and trying to stand well with him. I remember the events of these days more clearly than those which happened recently . . . so that I can speak even of the place where the blessed Polycarp sat and disputed . . . how he reported his intercourse with John and with the others who had seen the Lord, how he remembered their words. . . .'

It is urged that Irenaeus refers to John, but does not identify him with the Son of Zebedee. Nevertheless, he includes him among the apostles (*Contra Haereses*, I. ix. 2; II. xxii. 5).

For a careful examination of the testimony of Irenaeus, see H. A. A. Kennedy, *Expository Times*, xxix., pp. 103–7, 168–72, 235–8, 312–14.

The testimony of Irenaeus to the residence of John the Apostle in Asia Minor is strong. His evidence that John actually wrote the Gospel is weakened by the attribution of all five Johannine books to this John. The first writer to recognize the difficulty of ascribing Gospel and Apocalypse to the same hand was

DIONYSIUS of Alexandria (*c.* 250), who supported his critical theory of separate authorship by repeating the rumour which he had heard that there were two monuments at Ephesus bearing the name of John.

EUSEBIUS (260–340), who has preserved this fragment of Dionysius (*Hist. Eccles.*, vii. 24 f., *vide supra*, pp. 109 f.), combines this reference to the two tombs with an interpretation of the statement of Papias quoted above, which necessitates two Johns, in order to be able to affiliate the Apocalypse, with its millenarianism, to another than the Apostle.

The Ephesian residence of John the Apostle is denied, mainly on two grounds.

(1) *The Silence of Ignatius.*

The relevant passage is Ignatius, *Ad Eph.* xii. 2, in which Ignatius, on his way to martyrdom at Rome (*d.* 110–17), writes thus to the Church at Ephesus:

> 'You are the passage for those who are being slain for the sake of God, fellow initiates with Paul, who was sanctified, who gained a good report, who was right blessed, in whose footsteps may I be found when I shall attain to God, who in every Epistle makes mention of you in Christ Jesus.'

It is urged that Ignatius could not have been silent about John had that venerable Apostle passed his last years in Ephesus. But

(*a*) The preceding chapter ends: 'That I may be found in the lot of the Christians of Ephesus, who were ever of one mind with the Apostles in the power of Jesus Christ.'

(*b*) The point of the comparison is that Paul suffered great persecution at Ephesus, and finally died as a martyr at Rome. If John died in peaceful old age, we should not expect an allusion to him in this context.

(*c*) On the precariousness of this *argumentum e silentio* see the remarkable illustrations given by Drummond (*Character and Authorship*, pp. 157 f.) and Sanday (*Criticism of the Fourth Gospel*, p. 35 *n.*).

(2) *The Alleged Evidence that John the Apostle was Martyred.*

(*a*) Mark x. 35 ff. is a *vaticinium ex eventu*. But Mark ix. 1 is sufficient evidence that sayings of Jesus were preserved in the Gospel because they were remembered, not because they were framed afterwards to fit events in history.

(*b*) The alleged statement by Papias. This is found in two

late writers. In the De Boor fragment, a seventh or eighth century manuscript at Oxford giving an Epitome of the History of Philip of Side (c. 450), it is said :

> 'Papias in the second book says that John the theologian and James his brother were killed by Jews.'

George the Sinner (ninth century) states, on the authority of Papias, that John, the Son of Zebedee, ' has been deemed worthy of martyrdom, for Papias, in the second book of the Dominical Oracles affirms that he was slain by Jews.'

(c) An old Syriac calendar of martyrs, written in the year 411, gives for December 27, ' John and James the Apostles in Jerusalem.' This is supposed to record their death as martyrs.

A detailed examination would take too long. But four remarks may be offered.

(i.) The form of the statement in the Epitomist's alleged quotation from Papias is clearly an anachronism. John was not called ' the theologian ' so early as Papias—if so, it would imply his authorship of the Gospel.

(ii.) Eusebius was in full possession of all that was in Papias. Nowhere does he betray any knowledge of this statement. Neither does Irenaeus, who also knew the writings of Papias.

(iii.) James the Son of Zebedee was not slain by Jews, but by Herod Agrippa I. There has probably been confusion with James the Lord's brother, who was killed by Jews in Jerusalem in the year 62. There is no more reason to accept the other part of the statement than to accept this part, which is demonstrably unhistorical.

(iv.) It is more likely that Mark x. 35 gave rise to the idea that the two brothers must have suffered martyrdom than that not a trace of such an event should have survived in early Christian literature, if the story were based on fact.

Dr. B. W. Bacon writes (*Harvard Theological Review*, xxiii., p. 245), ' Why, then, not be satisfied with the conclusions of R. H. Charles, the unrivalled expert among English scholars in the history of apocalyptic literature, as patient and methodical in linguistic study as he is bold in critical discrimination ? A large and increasing proportion of the ablest scholars admit the claim of Charles to have placed the evidence of the martyr death of the Apostle John in Jerusalem between A.D. 62 and 66 on the level of demonstration.'

The reader is recommended, therefore, to study Dr. Charles's presentation of the case in *I. C. C.*, ' Revelation,' vol. i., pp. xlv.–l., and then to read the argument on the other side by Dr. Bernard, in *I. C. C.*, ' St. John,' vol. i., pp. xxxvii.–xlv. The literature in this debate is vast, but the main points on either side are put with clarity and fullness by these two writers. Dr. Bernard's earlier essay in *Studia Sacra*, p. 273, seemed to the present writer to have settled the case.

One further speculative assertion of a late scribe has aroused interest rather than discussion. Dr. A. Mingana (*Bulletin of the John Rylands Library*, xiv. 2, July 1930) reports the discovery of a Syriac manuscript of the Peshitta New Testament, written in the middle of the eighteenth century, but faithfully copying an original, a thousand years older. Before the Gospel of John there is a statement : ' The holy Gospel of our Lord Jesus Christ [according to] the preaching of John the younger.' At the close of the Gospel is the colophon, ' Here ends the writing of the holy Gospel [according to] the preaching of John, who spoke Greek in Bithynia.'

[An account of the evidence for the early use of the Fourth Gospel is given in J. N. Sanders, *The Fourth Gospel in the Early Church* (Cambridge, 1943); see pp. 165 f.

To the evidence for the existence of the Gospel early in the second century must now be added the two papyri, Rylands Papyrus 457 and Egerton Papyrus 2; see pp. 164 f. C. K. B.]

Appendix B

THE LINGUISTIC UNITY OF THE GOSPEL AND EPISTLES

I. CHARACTERISTICS OF JOHANNINE STYLE

(i.) *Transpositions into Johannine Style.*

JOHANNINE style may be illustrated by comparing a few passages where there is reason to suppose that the Evangelist has availed himself of earlier written sources.

(*a*) The Baptist's proclamation of the coming one.

Matt. iii. 11. Ἐγὼ μὲν ὑμᾶς βαπτίζω ἐν ὕδατι εἰς μετάνοιαν· ὁ δὲ ὀπίσω μου ἐρχόμενος ἰσχυρότερός μού ἐστιν, οὗ οὐκ εἰμὶ ἱκανὸς τὰ ὑποδήματα βαστάσαι· αὐτὸς ὑμᾶς βαπτίσει ἐν πνεύματι ἁγίῳ καὶ πυρί.

Mark i. 7-8. Ἔρχεται ὁ ἰσχυρότερός μου ὀπίσω μου, οὗ οὐκ εἰμὶ ἱκανὸς κύψας λῦσαι τὸν ἱμάντα τῶν ὑποδημάτων αὐτοῦ. ἐγὼ ἐβάπτισα ὑμᾶς ὕδατι, αὐτὸς δὲ βαπτίσει ὑμᾶς ἐν πνεύματι ἁγίῳ.

Luke iii. 16. Ἐγὼ μὲν ὕδατι βαπτίζω ὑμᾶς· ἔρχεται δὲ ὁ ἰσχυρότερός μου, οὗ οὐκ εἰμὶ ἱκανὸς λῦσαι τὸν ἱμάντα τῶν ὑποδημάτων αὐτοῦ. αὐτὸς ὑμᾶς βαπτίσει ἐν πνεύματι ἁγίῳ καὶ πυρί.

John i. 26-7. Ἐγὼ βαπτίζω ἐν ὕδατι· μέσος ὑμῶν στήκει, ὃν ὑμεῖς οὐκ οἴδατε, ὁ ὀπίσω μου ἐρχόμενος, οὗ οὐκ εἰμὶ ἐγὼ ἄξιος ἵνα λύσω αὐτοῦ τὸν ἱμάντα τοῦ ὑποδήματος.

(*b*) The Anointing at Bethany.

Mark xiv. 6-8. Ἄφετε αὐτήν· τί αὐτῇ κόπους παρέχετε; καλὸν ἔργον ἠργάσατο ἐν ἐμοί. πάντοτε γὰρ τοὺς πτωχοὺς ἔχετε μεθ᾽ ἑαυτῶν καὶ ὅταν θέλητε δύνασθε εὖ ποιῆσαι, ἐμὲ δὲ οὐ πάντοτε ἔχετε. ὃ ἔσχεν ἐποίησεν· προέλαβεν μυρίσαι μου τὸ σῶμα εἰς τὸν ἐνταφιασμόν.

LINGUISTIC UNITY OF THE GOSPEL

John xii. 7-8. Ἄφες αὐτήν, ἵνα εἰς τὴν ἡμέραν τοῦ ἐνταφιασμοῦ μου τηρήσῃ αὐτό· τοὺς πτωχοὺς γὰρ πάντοτε ἔχετε μεθ' ἑαυτῶν, ἐμὲ δὲ οὐ πάντοτε ἔχετε.

(c) Cure at Bethesda compared with healing of paralytic at Capernaum.

Mark ii. 11-12. Σοὶ λέγω, ἔγειρε ἆρον τὸν κράβαττόν σου καὶ ὕπαγε εἰς τὸν οἶκόν σου. καὶ ἠγέρθη, καὶ εὐθὺς ἄρας τὸν κράβαττον ἐξῆλθεν ἔμπροσθεν πάντων.

John v. 8-9. Λέγει αὐτῷ ὁ Ἰησοῦς· ἔγειρε ἆρον τὸν κράβαττόν σου καὶ περιπάτει. καὶ ἐγένετο ὑγιὴς ὁ ἄνθρωπος, καὶ ἦρεν τὸν κράβαττον αὐτοῦ καὶ περιεπάτει.

(ii.) *Idioms and Constructions.*

	Gospel	Epistles
Ἵνα.	Elliptical use of ἀλλ' ἵνα: John i. 8, ix. 3, xi. 52, xiii. 18, xiv. 31, xv. 25	1 John ii. 19
	Temporal use of ἵνα after a noun of time: John xii. 23, xiii. 1, xvi. 2, 32. N.B.—ὅτε is used iv. 21, 23, v. 25, xvi. 25. ἐν ᾗ is used v. 28	
	For explanatory infinitive after a demonstrative: John vi. 29, (?)50, 39, xv. 8, 13, xvii. 3, xv. 12	1 John iii. 1, 11, 23, iv. 17, 21, v. 3; 2 John 6a; 3 John 4
	For complementary infinitive after a verb: John iv. 47, viii. 56, ix. 22, xi. 53, xii. 10, xi. 37, xvii. 15, 21 *ter*, 24, xi. 50 (but note that acc. and inf. substituted when quoted in xviii. 14)	

For τό with inf. (or acc. and inf.) or inf. alone :
    John iv. 34, vi. 40, xi. 57, xiii. 34, xviii. 39

After χρείαν ἔχειν :
    John ii. 25, xvi. 30   1 John ii. 27

After adjective :
    John i. 27   1 John i. 9

<u>Πᾶς ὁ</u> c. *present participle :*
    John iii. 8, 15, 16, 20, iv. 13, vi. 40, 45, viii. 34, xi. 26, xii. 46, xvi. 2, xviii. 37, xix. 12   1 John ii. 23, 29, iii. 3, 4, 6 *bis*, 9, 10, 15, iv. 7, v. 1, 18; 2 John 9

<u>Πᾶν ὅ</u> or τό (collective masculine) :
    John vi. 37, 39, vii. 2 (cf. xvii. 24, ὅ without πᾶν)   1 John v. 4

<u>Ἄν</u> for ἐάν (*if*). Peculiar to John in New Testament—apart from reading of D at Matt. xxviii. 14 :
    John v. 19, xii. 32, xiii. 20, xvi. 23, xx. 23 *bis*

<u>Ὡς οὖν</u> (*now when*) also οὖν ὡς. Nowhere else in New Testament :
    John iv. 1, 40, xi. 6, 20, 32, 33, xviii. 6, xx. 11, xxi. 9

<u>Μέντοι.</u> Five times in John. Elsewhere in New Testament only thrice (2 Tim., James, Jude) :
    John iv. 27, vii. 13, xii. 42, xx. 5, xxi. 4

(iii.) *Synonyms interchanged in same sentence or context.*

Αἰτέω, ἐρωτάω
    John xvi. 23, 24 ; cf. 26   1 John v. 16

Λέγω, λαλέω
    John x. 6, xiv. 10, xvi. 18

LINGUISTIC UNITY OF THE GOSPEL

Ἀγαπάω, φιλέω
> John xi. 3 (cf. 5); iii. 35 (cf. v. 20); xxi. 15, 17

Ποιέω, πράσσω
> John iii. 20 (cf. 21); v. 29

Βόσκω, ποιμαίνω
> John xxi. 15, 16, 17
> N.B.—Interchange of nouns ἀρνία and προβάτια

Ἀποστέλλω, πέμπω
> John v. 36-7, vii. 28-9, xx. 21

Γινώσκω, οἶδα
> John xiv. 7; cf. viii. 19   (?) 1 John ii. 29

II. LINGUISTIC STUDY OF JOHN XXI.

(i.) *Vocabulary and Phraseology.*

John xxi.	John i.-xx.	Epistles of John
1, 14, φανερόω	i. 31, ii. 11, iii. 21, vii. 4, ix. 3, xvii. 6. Elsewhere only Mark iv. 22 (not of Jesus) and twice in Mark xvi. 12, 14	1 John i. 2, iii. 5
1, τῆς θαλάσσης τῆς Τιβεριάδος	vi. 1, τῆς θαλάσσης τῆς Γαλ. τ. Τιβεριάδος	Nowhere else in New Testament
5, παιδία (in address)	xiii. 33, τεκνία	παιδία, 1 John ii. 14, 18 τεκνία, 1 John seven times
9, 10, 13, ὀψάριον	vi. 9, 11. Nowhere else in New Testament	
14, ἐγερθεὶς ἐκ νεκρῶν	ii. 22 (*see note below*)	
18, ἀμήν, ἀμήν	In John i.-xx. twenty-four times. Nowhere else in New Testament	

19, τοῦτο δὲ εἶπεν   xii. 33, xviii. 32,
σημαίνων ποίῳ   τοῦτο δὲ ἔλεγεν σημαί-
θανάτῳ δοξάσει τὸν   νων, ποίῳ θανάτῳ
θεόν.   ἤμελλεν ἀποθνῄσκειν.

23, εἰς τοὺς ἀδελφούς   1 John iii. 14, 16
                                               3 John 3, 5, 10

(ii.) *Constructions in John xxi., with comparisons.*

John xxi.	John i.-xx.	Epistles of John
2, Ναθαναὴλ ὁ ἀπὸ Κανᾶ τῆς Γαλ.	i. 45, Ἰησ. υἱὸν τ. Ἰωσ. τὸν ἀπὸ Ναζ.	Elsewhere in New Testament : Matt. xxi. 11; Mark xv. 43 (and parls.); Acts x. 38
	xi. 1, Λάζαρος ἀπὸ Βηθανίας ἐκ τῆς κώμης Μαρίας	
	xii. 21, Φιλίππῳ τῷ ἀπὸ Βηθσ. τῆς Γαλ.	
	xix. 38, Ἰωσὴφ ὁ ἀπὸ Ἀριμαθείας	
2, καὶ ἄλλοι ἐκ τ. μαθητῶν δύο	i. 35, καὶ ἐκ τ. μαθητῶν δύο ix. 16, ἔλεγον .. ἐκ τῶν Φαρ. τινές xii. 42, καὶ ἐκ τ. ἀρχόντων πολλοί	
4, οὐ μέντοι ᾔδεισαν οἱ μαθηταὶ ὅτι Ἰησοῦς ἐστιν	xx. 14, καὶ οὐκ ᾔδει ὅτι Ἰησοῦς ἐστιν	
4, ἐξῆλθον καὶ ἐνέβησαν	Parataxis most noticeable in John. Subordination by use of aor. part. very common in Synoptics. Burney gives proportions per W-H page as Matt. 5; Mark 5.5; Luke 4.5; John 1	
8, ὡς ἀπὸ πηχῶν διακοσίων	xi. 18, ὡς ἀπὸ σταδίων δεκαπέντε	
14, τοῦτο ἤδη τρίτον ἐφανερώθη 16, λέγει αὐτῷ πάλιν δεύτερον	iv. 54, τοῦτο δὲ πάλιν δεύτερον σημεῖον ἐποίησεν	

Note on ἐγερθεὶς ἐκ νεκρῶν.
Scholten (cited by B. W. Bacon, *The Fourth Gospel*, p. 489), in calling the authenticity of John ii. 21 f. in question, says : ' The reanimation of Jesus is expressed passively as a *being raised* ; according to the Evangelist, on the contrary, Jesus *rises*, ἀνάστασις, ἀναστῆναι, xi. 25, xx. 9. Only in xxi. 14 do we have ἐγερθείς.'

The fact is that these two expressions are used in the New Testament as virtually interchangeable. Thus in Matt. xvii. 9, 23, xx. 19, and in Luke ix. 22, the MSS. vary between the two. In Matt. xiv. 2, xvi. 21, xxvii. 64, xxviii. 7 ἐγερθῆναι is used. Mark varies between ἀναστῆναι in ix. 9, xii. 25, and ἐγερθῆναι in vi. 14 ; Luke between ἀναστῆναι in xvi. 31, xxiv. 46, and ἐγερθῆναι in ix. 7 ; Paul between ἀναστῆναι in 1 Thess. iv. 14, 16, and ἐγερθῆναι in Rom. vi. 4, 9, viii. 34.

III. BIBLIOGRAPHICAL NOTE ON RELATION BETWEEN GOSPEL AND FIRST EPISTLE

The fullest examination of the relation in which the Gospel and First Epistle stand to one another was given by H. J. Holtzmann in a series of articles in *Jahrbuch für Protestantische Theologie* (1881, pp. 690 f., 1882, pp. 128 f., 136 f., 460 f.). This field has been harvested so well for English readers by R. Law, *The Tests of Life*, pp. 339–63, and by A. E. Brooke, *The Johannine Epistles* (I.C.C.), pp. i.–xxvii., that little is left for the gleaner. Law and Brooke both accept the common authorship, and date the Gospel before the Epistle. Holtzmann, who was against the identity of authorship, held that this common authorship would demand as its presupposition that the Epistle represents an earlier stage in the writer's theological position. A compact and useful summary of the points in common between the thought of the Gospel and that of the First Epistle is given by Windisch in his commentary on the Catholic Epistles in Lietzmann's *Handbuch zum N.T.*, ed. 2, vol. 15, pp. 109 ff. (1930 ; revised edition by H. Preisker, 1951).

[The question of the common authorship of the Gospel and Epistles (or rather, the first Epistle) of John was reopened by Professor C. H. Dodd in an article ' The First Epistle of John and the Fourth Gospel' (*Bulletin of the John Rylands Library*, xxi. (1937), pp. 129–56). Here, and in his *Moffatt Commentary* on the Epistles of John (London, 1946 ; pp. xlvii.–lvi.), he argued strongly on linguistic and theological grounds that 'the author of the Epistle was a disciple of the Evangelist'. Dr. Howard was not convinced by this view, and presented an opposite argument in an article 'The Common Authorship of the Johannine Gospel and Epistles' (*Journal of Theological Studies*, old series, xlviii. (1947), pp. 12–25). This article contains an impartial statement of Professor Dodd's opinions as well as Dr. Howard's own view, and by the courtesy of the Delegates of the Clarendon Press it is here reprinted. C. K. B.]

THE COMMON AUTHORSHIP OF THE JOHANNINE GOSPEL AND EPISTLES

The relation between the Gospel and Epistles of John is a question which has an important bearing upon our conception of the development of Christian thought and life towards the close of the first century. Whatever may have been the sources, oral or written, personal reminiscences and interpretative meditations, upon which the Evangelist drew, however gradually the material was put together, and through whatever phases it may have passed before it was published to the world, there can be little doubt that it went out into circulation (apart from the inevitable scribal modifications) as we have the text before us now. If the Evangelist was also the author of the Epistles, then we know something of the general situation. The Evangelist was a venerable man of considerable influence in the region to which these letters were addressed. There is a background of Church life with its Christian fellowship, but also its doctrinal dangers, the abuse of authority, yet the need of discipline. Passages in the Gospel take on a clearer meaning when read against this background of ecclesiastical life.

It is generally accepted that the Gospel and Epistles of John come from the same school of thought. In phraseology and general style, in the themes which are treated, and in the theological standpoint which distinguishes them from the other writings of the New Testament, they fall into a class of their own. Indeed, the similarities are so striking and so numerous that identity of authorship has generally been assumed. It is true that H. J. Holtzmann, after assembling a mass of data upon which the critic might form his own judgement on this question, gave his vote for a difference of authorship, and that such various writers as E. von Dobschütz, Hans Windisch, and A. H. McNeile have gone into the same lobby with him. But the grammatical instinct of J. H. Moulton and the minute investigations of R. H. Charles supported the weighty evidence which A. E. Brooke marshalled in favour of a common authorship.

Far away the ablest and most cogent presentation of the case against the unity of authorship has been made by Professor C. H. Dodd in the *Bulletin* of John Rylands Library for April 1937. As this examination of the evidence underlies his introduction to the Johannine Epistles in his recent brilliant exposition in the *Moffatt Commentary*, it seems a convenient opportunity to look more closely at this treatment of the problem. He recognizes the many points of resemblance, but after a close examination of literary style, vocabulary, and thought, he comes to the conclusion that the writer of the First Epistle cannot have written the Gospel, though he was quite possibly a disciple of the Evangelist and was certainly a diligent student of his work.

It would obviously be impossible to do justice without reproducing the essay in its entirety. All that can be attempted here is to indicate the main points in the argument, and to suggest that at certain points the linguistic evidence when examined in detail is less impressive than the statistical statement would lead one to suppose, whilst the argument from alleged divergences of theological outlook must be more carefully considered before they are finally accepted as conclusive.

The argument follows two lines of attack, the first by a linguistic analysis, the second by a comparison of thought.

I. The linguistic argument observes a number of stylistic contrasts. These consist of the richer resources of prepositions, of adverbial and conjunctive particles, and of compound verbs, shown by the writer of the Gospel over against the writer of the Epistle; of an excessive use in the First Epistle of idioms or rhetorical figures which occur rarely or not at all in the Gospel; and finally, of a list of six types of construction used in the Gospel which present at least a *prima facie* case for Aramaism, of which two are doubtfully represented in the Epistle.

Before giving this impressive list a closer scrutiny we ought to offer some general observations.

(a) The Gospel gives evidence of a long process of composition, whilst the Epistle seems to have been written to meet a special situation. The one is the result of a lifetime of thought and inquiry, of reflection and repetition, the other is a pastoral letter dealing with the practical needs of the hour.

(b) The subject-matter of a large part of the Gospel covers a far wider range than that of the Epistle. It contains narrative, dialogue, discourses, with particles appropriate to each. We must inquire whether many of these which come naturally in the course of the Gospel would have been appropriate in any part of the Epistle.

(c) It is generally recognized that the Evangelist drew largely on written and oral sources. Where this is apparently the case we always detect Johannine mannerisms or locutions, but we should expect a wider range of words than when the author was writing or dictating on the spur of the moment without the suggestion that comes from a previous statement of the same matter.

(d) The supposed Aramaisms in the Gospel may be due to the Jewish character of the tradition or of the written document followed by the Evangelist, whilst the letter is addressed in free Greek on a subject in which there is little or no quotation from any source, whether sayings of the Lord or testimonies from the Old Testament.

(e) There is one factor that has received far less consideration in all such discussions than it would seem to deserve. That is the less or greater degree of freedom allowed to the amanuensis in the composition of an apostolic letter. The apostolic authorship of 1 Peter becomes more likely if Silvanus be regarded as part author. Many of the difficulties that beset the acceptance of the Pauline authorship of Ephesians are removed if we allow to his companion Timothy a far freer hand in expanding the notes than, let us say, to Tychicus, to whom Paul may well have dictated the twin letter to the Colossians. Probably the limits which were allowed to another amanuensis, Tertius, were a single sentence in the list of cordial greetings to friends at Rome. Are we quite sure that this secretarial factor is one that can be ignored altogether?[1]

Under the heading *Style and Language* we must now examine the data assembled and classified by Dr. Dodd.

---

[1] Since the substance of this paper was read to the Society for Historical Theology at Oxford (November 1939), the subject of this paragraph has been more fully treated by J. A. Eschlinan in an essay 'La Rédaction des Épitres pauliniennes', in *Revue biblique*, Vol. LIII, pp. 185-96 (April 1946).

1. GRAMMATICAL WORDS AND PARTICLES

(a) Prepositions

1 Ep. uses 11 common prepositions, plus ἔμπροσθεν, ἐνώπιον, χάριν (14). The Gospel uses all these except χάριν, with 10 others. These are ἀνά (1, distrib.), ἀντί (1), ἐπάνω (2, in one verse), ὀπίσω (7), παρά (c. gen. 24, c. dat. 9), πέραν (8—all geographical phrases), πρό (9, including 3 c. artic. infin.), σύν (3—against μετά c. gen. 42, cf. 1 Ep. 7, 2 Ep. 2), ὑπό (c. gen. 1, c. acc. 1), ὑποκάτω (1).

E. A. Abbott points out that John's use of παρά c. gen. is almost always in the phrase 'from God (or the Father)', and that ὑπό (c. acc) occurs in the Gospel only at i. 48, ὑπὸ τὴν συκῆν, followed by i. 50, ὑποκάτω τῆς συκῆς. He also remarks that ὑπό c. gen. is avoided by John 'as he prefers to speak of an agent performing an action rather than of an act performed by (ὑπό) an agent. It occurs only in xiv. 21, ὁ ἔχων τὰς ἐντολάς μου κ. τηρῶν αὐτὰς ἐκεῖνός ἐστιν ὁ ἀγαπῶν με· ὁ δὲ ἀγαπῶν με ἀγαπηθήσεται ὑπό τ. πατρός μου, where perhaps the writer desires to repeat precisely the words ὁ ἀγαπῶν με so that they may constitute the two middle terms of the sentence. Perhaps the frequency of the nominatives ὁ ἀγαπῶν and ὁ μὴ ἀγαπῶν in the Epistle (1 John ii. 10; iii. 10, 14; iv. 7, etc.) may partly explain the shape of the sentence here. Had the verb been τιμάω we should have expected ἐάν τις ἐμὲ τιμᾷ τιμήσει αὐτὸν ὁ πατήρ similarly to xii. 26.' (J.G., pp. 278 ff.)

For a striking similarity we must notice the phrase εἶναι πρός c. acc.=*with*. Apart from Mark vi. 3, ix. 19, xiv. 49, and 3 Pauline passages (and 10 analogous ones), this use is peculiar to John i. 1 and 1 John i. 2. I have been able to find only one parallel in the inscrr. and no example in the papyri. (See Moulton, *Gram. of N.T. Greek*, vol. ii, p. 467. There are numerous papyrus parallels to Heb. iv. 13. See, e.g., Mayser, *Gram. d. gr. Pap.* II, ii, p. 505.)

(b) Adverbial Particles

In 1 Ep. there are 9, which occur also in the Gospel where there are also 27 others. Of these δεῦρο and δεῦτε are used imperatively, ἐκεῖ, ἐκεῖθεν, ἐνθάδε, ἐντεῦθεν, ἔπειτα, ἔσω, ἐχθές, πρωί, in their temporal and local sense would be more appropriate in narrative, and λάθρᾳ is hardly germane to the subject-matter of the Epistle. Ἄνω and ἄνωθεν belong to the dialogues with Nicodemus and Pilate.

(c) Conjunctive and Other Particles

All but one (ὅθεν) of the 18 are found in the Gospel with 19 others. The only remarks to be made here are (a) that against ἴδε and ἰδού we have ἴδετε in 1 John iii. 1; (b) Dr. Dodd observes that the Gospel prefers εἰ while 1 Ep. prefers ἐάν. The figures seem to be εἰ = *if*, Gospel 28, 1 Ep. 3; ἐάν = *if*, Gospel 39, 1 Ep. 18, 3 Ep. 1. Also ἐὰν μή, Gospel 18, 1 Ep. 1.

2. COMPOUND VERBS

1 Ep. has 11 verbs compounded with these prepositions: ἀνα-, ἀπο-, ἐπι-, ἐκ-, κατα-, μετα-, παρα-, περι-, ὑπο-. The Gospel has 9 of these verbs, also 87 other verbs of which the additional compounding prepositions are δια-, εἰσ-, ἐν-, προσ-, συν-. Here the vastly wider range of subject-matter in historical narrative gives the Gospel unquestionably a richer vocabulary.

3. IDIOMS AND RHETORICAL FIGURES

A. It is objected that of several characteristic idioms in the Gospel recurring in 1 Ep. 2 are used there to excess. (a) The articular participle used as a noun; (b) the articular participle strengthened by πᾶς. But this does not alter the fact that these locutions are specially frequent in the Johannine writings, and that (b) is almost a Johannine peculiarity in the N.T. (This is discussed later.)

B. Idioms preferred by the writer of 1 Ep., which are rare or non-existent in the Gospel. These are said to be: (a) The rhetorical question, e.g. 'Who is the liar?'; (b) the definition, introduced by 'This is . . .' or the like (G. 4, 1 Ep. 8); (c) a rhetorical use of the conditional sentence. Several examples of this figure are given, which have no parallel in the Gospel. But we should expect these rhetorical devices in an epistle which conforms to the style of the Diatribe rather than in the narrative or the polemical discourses of the Gospel.

C. Dr. Dodd gives 6 'conspicuous types of construction . . . which present at least a *prima facie* case for Aramaisms in the Gospel'. Of these only 2 are doubtfully represented in 1 Ep. The explanation may be that the sources and Palestinian traditions largely account for the greater prominence of these locutions in a Palestinian narrative.

Before passing from general considerations of idiom and style to lexical comparisons it seems reasonable to touch briefly upon the *similarities* in sentence construction which arrest the attention of every careful student of the Johannine writings.

Dr. Dodd refers to the list which A. E. Brooke supplies of phrases common to the Gospel and First Epistle. In its impressiveness it overwhelms the examples of contrast which have just been examined. To appreciate the degree of resemblance in phraseology the imposing list of over 50 phrases, set out in parallel columns for Gospel and First Epistle, should be studied in the *I.C.C., Johannine Epistles*, pp. ii.–iv. A few other idioms and constructions may be noted, all of which are given by Brooke in his compendious treatment, though as furnished here they were collected by the present writer in a detailed grammatical investigation made many years ago and published as an appendix to a critical introduction to the Fourth Gospel.[1]

1. *Characteristic uses of ἵνα.*
   (a) The elliptical use of ἵνα:
   Gospel, i. 8; ix. 3; xi. 52; xiii. 18; xiv. 31; xv. 25.
   1 Ep. ii. 19. (Elsewhere in N.T. only Mark xiv. 49.)
   (b) Used for the explanatory infinitive after a demonstrative:
   Gospel, vi. 29, 39, 50; xv. 8, 12, 13; xvii. 3.
   1 Ep., iii. 1, 11, 23; iv. 17, 21; v. 3; 2 Ep. 6a; 3 Ep. 4.
   (c) Used for the complementary infinitive after χρείαν ἔχειν:
   Gospel, ii. 25; xvi. 30; 1 Ep. ii. 27.
   After an adjective, Gospel, i. 27; 1 Ep. i. 9.

2. πᾶς ὁ c. present participle:
   Gospel, iii. 8, 15, 16, 20; iv. 13; vi. 40, 45; viii. 34; xi. 26; xii. 46; xvi. 2; xviii. 37; xix. 12; 1 Ep. v. 4.

3. πᾶν ὅ or τό (collective masculine):
   Gospel, vi. 37, 39; vii. 2 (cf. xvii. 24, ὅ without πᾶν); 1 Ep. v. 4.

4. The use of καθὼς ... καί:
   Gospel, xiii. 15; 1 Ep. ii. 18.

5. The elliptical use of οὐ καθώς:
   Gospel, vi. 58; 1 Ep. iii. 11–12.

6. The use of καὶ ... δέ:
   Gospel, vi. 51; viii. 16; xv. 27; 1 Ep. i. 3. (Elsewhere in the N.T. δέ comes as fourth word in a clause introduced by καί only in Matt. x. 18.)

We now come to the second part of Dr. Dodd's linguistic argument. This is something more than a matter of literary style. It is really a transitional link from the argument based upon

[1] *The Fourth Gospel in Recent Criticism and Interpretation* (ed.[1], 1931)

grammatical differences to that which rests upon important divergences in theological viewpoint.

There is no need to linger unduly over the statement that the First Epistle has 39 words which are absent from the Gospel, for Dr. Dodd admits that ' this is proportionately no greater than the number of words to be found in any given Pauline Epistle which do not occur in any other Pauline Epistle '. The strength of his contention lies in the surprising list of words ' which are either so frequent in the Gospel, or so intimately connected with leading Johannine ideas, that their absence from the Epistle is remarkable '.

The list is indeed impressive, but I have to acknowledge that after testing it with the concordance with some care I found that it assumed a less formidable appearance.

These words are grouped in 6 classes: (i.) general religious and theological terms; (ii.) references to the O.T. and Jewish background; (iii.) terms referring to the idea of Judgement; (iv.) Christological terms; (v.) terms special to the Johannine theology; (vi.) other terms characteristic of the Fourth Gospel.

In examining the number of occurrences of each word two considerations must be borne in mind: (a) the distribution throughout the Gospel, and (b) the relevance of such words to the subject-matter and purpose of the Epistle.

With regard to 4 of these classes, a sentence or two at this point must suffice. It is striking that (under ii.) 3 words relating to the O.T. and Jewish background should be entirely missing from the Epistle: the noun $\gamma\rho\alpha\phi\acute{\eta}$ (of the Scriptures) 12 times, the verb $\gamma\rho\acute{\alpha}\phi\epsilon\iota\nu$ (with the same reference) 10 times, and $\nu\acute{o}\mu os$ 14 times. This omission in the First Epistle seems to suggest a church, or group of churches, in which the Gentile element so predominated that for ethical exhortation the appeal to the O.T. was less effective than the enforcement of the ' new commandment '. More significant (iii.) is the entire absence in the Epistle of the verb $\kappa\rho\acute{\iota}\nu\epsilon\iota\nu$ (19 times) and the noun $\kappa\rho\acute{\iota}\sigma\iota s$ (11), apart from the occurrence in the Epistle once of the phrase $\dot{\eta}\mu\acute{\epsilon}\rho\alpha$ $\tau\hat{\eta}s$ $\kappa\rho\acute{\iota}\sigma\epsilon\omega s$, an exception which seems to prove the rule, since that term is foreign to the Gospel. This will come up later when we are considering the eschatology of John. In class (iv), Christological terms, we admit it is surprising that $\delta\acute{o}\xi\alpha$ (18 times) and the corresponding verb $\delta o\xi\acute{\alpha}\zeta\epsilon\iota\nu$ (21 times) should not be found in the Epistle. Perhaps we should notice that 19 times the verb is spoken by Jesus (or by the Father to the Son), twice it is used of the death of Jesus, and in xxi. 19 of the death of Peter. But when we are told that Κύριος is used of Christ 41 times in the Gospel, it ought to have been explained that in 31 instances the word is used in the vocative, which rules out three-fourths of the examples from any comparison with the Epistle. In class (v.), terms special to the Johannine theology, we have 4 spatial terms referring to the descent and ascent of Jesus, used in this special sense as follows: ἀναβαίνειν (5), καταβαίνειν (11), ἄνω and ἄνωθεν (4), and ὑψοῦν (5 times). It will be observed that nearly all these examples fall into one or other of 3 discourses, that at the close of ch. i., the conversation with Nicodemus in ch. iii., or the address at Capernaum in ch. vi. concerning the Bread of Life. The word ὑψοῦν is used in 3 separate passages about the lifting up of Jesus upon the cross, with a subtle suggestion of exaltation by way of crucifixion. It is always so used on the lips of Christ himself in a mysterious hint of the future.

There remain the first and last classes to be considered in rather fuller detail.

Class i., general religious and theological terms, has 10 words. Of these 3 rightly claim attention. Σώζειν (6 plus σωτηρία once), ἀπολλύναι (10 plus ἀπώλεια once), and the impersonal verb δεῖ (used of divine necessity, 8 times) are all well distributed. The only fact to put on the other side is that the idea of salvation is adequately expressed in one verse of the Epistle, ὁ πατὴρ ἀπέσταλκεν τὸν υἱὸν σωτῆρα τοῦ κόσμου, which is a good parallel to the words attributed in the Gospel to the men of Samaria, οὗτός ἐστιν ἀληθῶς ὁ σωτὴρ τοῦ κόσμου.[1]

When we turn to the remaining words in this class we discover how important it is to consider both distribution and relevance. Ἀνιστάναι is given as occurring 8 times. But 4 of these are its transitive use in the same refrain in ch. vi, 'I will raise him at the last day', and the three intransitive instances all come in the story of the raising of Lazarus. Similarly, the 4 occurrences of the corresponding noun ἀνάστασις are to be found in two successive verses in the same chapter, and twice in one verse

---

[1] Perhaps we shall be cautious in drawing inferences from the absence of these words in the First Epistle when we recall that σώζω, used in so many of the Pauline Epistles, is not found in Galatians, Philippians, or Colossians; that σωτηρία is not found in 1 Corinthians, Galatians, or Colossians; that σωτήρ occurs once each in Ephesians and Philippians, ten times in the Pastorals, and nowhere else in Paul. Again, δικαιόω, so characteristic of Romans, 1 Corinthians, and Galatians, does not occur in any other Pauline letters (save the Pastorals), and that δικαίωμα and δικαίωσις are found in Romans alone. Similarly, ἁγιάζω and ἁγιασμός are found each in but four of the genuine letters of St. Paul.

elsewhere. The verb ἁγιάζειν appears 4 times in the Gospel, always on the lips of the Lord, and 3 of these in the high-priestly prayer. Of the 11 occurrences of προσκυνεῖν all but 2 are in the dialogue with the Samaritan woman, whilst the remaining 2 are in narrative, recording the prostration of the man cured of his blindness and the visit of the Greeks to Jerusalem to worship. Ζωοποιεῖν is used only 3 times, twice in the same verse and once in the next chapter. The 2 other words in this class are εἰρήνη and χάρις. But of the 6 appearances of εἰρήνη 3 are in the farewell discourse, and the other 3 are the greeting of the risen Lord to his disciples in the closed room. This word is also used in the greeting in both the Second and Third Epistles. Again, the word χάρις is indeed found 4 times in the Gospel, but only in the closing verses of the Prologue, and never again. But it is found in the greeting in the Second Epistle.

There remains the last class of words (vi), terms characteristic of the Fourth Gospel. Most of these can hardly be called significant. Θέλημα heads the list, but by inadvertence, for it is also found twice in 1 Ep. The metaphorical use of καρπός is found 10 times. All but 2 of these, however, are in the allegory of the True Vine, whilst the other 2 come in the fourth and twelfth chapters, of the fields white for harvest and of the corn of wheat falling into the ground and dying. The fact that φιλεῖν (used in the Gospel 13 times) and πέμπειν (used 32 times) are absent from the Epistle requires an explanation. This calls attention to one or two interesting points in Johannine usage. Anyone who has studied closely the Greek of the Fourth Gospel must have been struck by one of the marked mannerisms of the Evangelist. This is his habit of ringing the changes on pairs of synonyms without any distinction of meaning.[1] When once this has been observed and allowed for, some of the subtleties of interpretation in Westcott's great commentary have to be dismissed as quite untenable. Good examples are the interchange of ἀγαπᾶν and φιλεῖν, and of ἀποστέλλειν and πέμπειν. Now φιλεῖν is used (perhaps to avoid monotony) in 13 places, but ἀγαπᾶν is used 35 times, i.e. nearly 3 times as often. It is the better Christian word, and is invariably used in the First Epistle. Here it comes 28 times, as well as twice in the Second and once in the Third Epistle. The cognate noun φίλος certainly comes 6 times in the

---

[1] See *The F.G. in Recent Criticism and Interpretation*, pp. 254 f. [in this new edition, pp. 278 f.]. To this list may be added θεραπεύειν and ἰᾶσθαι, John v. 10, 13, also (τὰς ἐντολὰς) ποιεῖν, τηρεῖν, 1 John v. 3. The following treatment of πέμπειν and ἀποστέλλειν anticipated the note by C. C. Tarelli in *J.T.S.*, xlvii., pp. 175 ff.

Gospel, but as it is used twice in the Third Epistle we need not regard its absence from the First Epistle as significant. The actual data for the use of πέμπειν and of ἀποστέλλειν deserve a rather more detailed statement. Of the 32 examples of πέμπειν, no less than 27 are accounted for by the articular aorist participle, and all but one of these are the all but technical term, ὁ πέμψας με, which, with one exception, is always spoken by Jesus of the Father. Otherwise it is found only in the present or future indicative active, with either Jesus or the Father as the subject. A good example of the juxtaposition of the synonyms is in John xx. 21: καθὼς ἀπέσταλκέν με ὁ πατὴρ κἀγὼ πέμπω ὑμᾶς. When we turn to the use of ἀποστέλλειν in the Gospel we find it 28 times, with this remarkable analysis: aorist indicative active 21 times, perfect indicative active 3 times, perfect participle passive 4 times. In none of these forms is πέμπειν ever found in the Gospel. Moreover, ἀποστέλλειν is used 3 times in the First Epistle, once in the aorist indicative active, twice in the perfect indicative active, just as the same verb is found in the Gospel, and as πέμπειν is never so found there. This may be a curious chain of coincidences, though it is more probably a linguistic usage which removes another word from Dr. Dodd's list.

It may seem like straining out a gnat and swallowing a camel to add that, from the standpoint of grammatical usage, the most startling fact is the very last word in this last list. Dr. Dodd points out that the Evangelist always uses the possessive adjective ἴδιος (15 times), whereas the First Epistle uses the genitive of the reflexive or of the personal pronoun (ἑαυτοῦ or αὐτοῦ). This raises a larger question, for two opposite tendencies were at work in the Κοινή with regard to possessive adjectives and pronouns. The possessive adjectives ἐμός and σός were on the wane, being largely superseded by ἐμαυτοῦ, σεαυτοῦ, and ἑαυτοῦ (which was widely used for the second person also). At the same time ἴδιος (in its 'exhausted' sense) was coming into use in the literary Hellenistic for ἑαυτοῦ, though the evidence of the papyri is not proportionately strong, in spite of Deissmann's claim. The following figures are illustrative:

Ἐμός. Gospel 41, 3 Ep. 1: (Rev. 1, Paul 23, Rest of N.T. 10).
Σός. Gospel 7, Epp. 0 (Paul 3, Rest of N.T. 17).
Ἡμέτερος. Gospel 0, 1 Ep. 2 (Luke–Acts 4, Paul 3).
Ὑμέτερος. Gospel 3, Epp. 0 (Luke–Acts 2, Paul 5).
Ἴδιος. Gospel 15, Epp. 0 (Gospels and Acts 24, Paul 42, Rest of N.T. 16).

By running the eye down the concordance one can see that almost every example given under this word shows that the Evangelist does not use ἴδιος in the exhausted sense, and it could be argued that as in every case emphasis was intended, we cannot institute a comparison here between Gospel and Epistle.

A still more remarkable grammatical peculiarity of the Gospel (not mentioned by Dr. Dodd) is the use of ἄν for ἐάν (*if*). This occurs 6 times and is found nowhere else in the N.T. except as a *v. l.* in two places, Matt. xxviii. 14 (D) and Acts ix. 2 (ℵE). It is found in the Ionicizing literary prose of the fifth century B.C. and in the Tragedians, but is very rare in the Attic inscriptions. In the papyri it is a symptom of illiteracy, yet it is common in Plutarch and Epictetus, and in modern Greek it has supplanted ἐάν. Moulton (*Gr.* vol. i, p. 43) says, ' Some peculiar local distribution is needed to explain why ἄν (*if*) is absent from the incorrectly written Rev., and reserved for the correct Jn.' May this peculiarity, which, though dialectic, looks more like an orthographic variant, be due to the habit of the amanuensis? The phraseology and the general structure of sentences is the mark of the author. Such minor variations between Gospel and Epistle might reasonably be attributed to the scribe who took down, or who later copied out, the Gospel.

Little has been said here about the Second and Third Epistles. The minute linguistic study furnished by R. H. Charles (*Revelation*, vol. i., pp. xxxiv. ff.) and A. E. Brooke (*Johannine Epistles*, pp. lxxiii. ff.) in the *I.C.C.* goes a long way to establish the case for unity of authorship of all four writings. The two short letters hardly provide enough material for a comparison on any considerations but those of phraseology and grammar. The suggestion of slavish imitation does not explain why the writer should attempt to disguise his identity from those who must have known him well.

II. The second part of the argument leaves the study of linguistic differences for a comparison of thought.

1. The Epistle is said to stand nearer than the Gospel to general or popular Christian beliefs, with respect to (*a*) eschatology, (*b*) the significance attached to the death of Christ, and (*c*) the doctrine of the Holy Spirit.

2. Passages are pointed out in the Epistle which are said to show that it stands closer than the Gospel to the Gnosticism against which both writings are directed. Such are ' God is light '; ' we know that, if he is manifested, we shall be like him; for we

shall see him even as he is '; ' Everyone who is born of God does not commit sin, because his seed abides in him; and he cannot sin, because he is born of God '; 'And *you* have an anointing from the Holy One, and all of you have knowledge.'

This statement fairly represents a difference of atmosphere and emphasis between the Gospel and the First Epistle. To not a few scholars this is decisive against the acceptance of a common authorship. Dr. Dodd in his essay has presented that side of the case with unsurpassed skill, and now in his latest commentary some of the most important passages have been more fully expounded in relation to their historical background. Gratitude is due for the clarity with which he has set out the respects in which the two writings are at variance. At the same time it is open to question whether this method does not suffer from two defects. It assumes too rigid a uniformity on the part of a religious teacher, and it overlooks the effect which a particular and critical historical situation may have upon the presentation of doctrine.

It is quite evident that the First Epistle was written at a time of crisis. According to Dr. Dodd's exposition some notable leaders had left the Church, and were attracting a large following. Half a century later Marcion's secession produced a rival Christian community which spread with unabated missionary fervour and for long years persisted side by side with the great Church. Gnostic teaching in the second century was to prove a more deadly peril than imperial persecution. Is it to be wondered at, that when meeting this danger on its first grave emergence the leader of the Church in Asia gave a special turn to some doctrines in his theological polemic?

This is peculiarly probable with regard to eschatology, and as a necessary result with reference also to the doctrine of the Spirit. It is natural to assume that the coming of the Spirit, foretold with such a wealth of instruction in chs. xiv.–xvi. in the Gospel, is the Johannine equivalent for the older apocalyptic conception of the coming of Christ represented by the discourse in Mark xiii. and the Synoptic parallels. The First Epistle then appears as a return to an earlier and more popular idea of an imminent return of Jesus, a return already heralded by the appearance of antichrists. In other words, in the Gospel the doctrine of the Spirit has sublimated the older apocalyptic conception into a mystical union with the glorified Christ and the Father. In the Epistle eschatology has returned, to the detriment of mysticism.

To discuss this properly it would be necessary to rehearse in full the eschatology of the Johannine writings, which is impossible here.[1] It must, however, be pointed out that there is a strongly eschatological element in the Fourth Gospel. Jesus as Son of Man is commissioned with the functions of Judge and Giver of Life. The old Jewish apocalyptic contrast between the world above and the world below, between the present age and the age to come, can still be found. Such sayings as 'I will raise him up at the last day', the thrice-repeated promise in ch. xiv. 'I come again', and 'If I will that he tarry till I come' must not be ignored. The term Son of Man occurs in eight different chapters, in some of which the title is associated with the idea of Judgement. This idea, even though in the Gospel it is often represented as a continual process in the present, is in two passages (v. 21 ff. and xii. 47 ff.) identified with a future domesday. The two conceptions of eschatology, partly as realized already, partly as still a future event, are both present in the mind of the Evangelist. It is the appalling spectacle of a successful apostasy that revives the memory of warnings of false prophets who would lead many astray. In earlier Christian teaching this was to be one of the tribulations that would herald the *parousia*, marking the darkest hour before the dawn. The word 'antichrists' calls to our minds some of the bizarre speculations connected with the antichrist legend. But A. E. Brooke's words should be remembered. 'The " spiritualization " of the idea of Antichrist in the Epistle is at least as complete as the spiritualization of popular eschatology in the Gospel. The *parousia* which the writer of the Epistle expected, perhaps more eagerly than when he wrote the Gospel, was nevertheless a spiritual fact rather than an apocalyptic display.'

The Paraclete in the Gospel is the Holy Spirit, in the Epistle he is the heavenly Christ. But in the Gospel the Spirit as 'another Paraclete' is to continue on the earthly plane what Christ had done for His disciples during the Incarnate life. In the Epistle that first Paraclete is continuing in heaven the ministry of intercession begun on earth (John xvii. 9, 15, 17, 19 f.). The special turn given to the work of the Spirit in the Epistle was occasioned by the deadly heresy which threatened the Church. The witness of the Spirit was needed to guarantee the reality of the fellowship with Christ in which the old yet new command of love was kept. Love of God depends upon love of the brethren, and it is the Spirit who gives inward assurance of this. The Spirit again is he who gives reality to the testimony of the Church

[1] I may be allowed to refer to the chapter on 'Eschatology and Mysticism' in *Christianity according to St. John*, pp. 106-28, and 201-4.

in its message and worship. Yet this very claim is made by the heresiarchs. They claim to be the true πνευματικοί as against the traditionalists. In reply the writer of the Epistle applies the Johannine teaching of the Paraclete. He bears witness to the revelation of the Incarnate life. He takes of the things of Jesus and recalls and interprets them. Jesus has come in the flesh. All that denies that is false, prompted by a 'spirit of error'. But the Paraclete is the Spirit of truth, guiding into all truth. Only those whose faith is rooted and grounded in the historical revelation of Jesus Christ can possess this Spirit. Well might E. F. Scott write about the teaching of the Spirit, ' so far from conflicting with that of the Gospel the doctrine of the Epistle is in full harmony with it and serves to elucidate and define it '.[1] Certainly it would be hard to find any words more truly in keeping with the teaching of the farewell discourse than the two verses, ' Hereby we know that he abideth in us, by the Spirit which he gave us ', ' Hereby we know that we abide in him and he in us, because he hath given us of his Spirit ' (1 John iii. 24; iv. 13).

As regards the death of Christ, there is no clear doctrine of the Atonement in any of the Johannine writings. The metaphors indeed are different, but is not the underlying conception the same? Dr. Dodd has himself done more than any other scholar to prove that ἱλασμός means not propitiation but expiation, the removal of the infection of sin that keeps man away from fellowship with God. Whatever original conception may lie behind the figure of the Lamb of God in John i. 29, He is there to ' take away the sin of the world '. So in 1 John iii. 5, ' Ye know that he was manifested to take away sins '. To clinch the matter we have but to set side by side John iii. 16, 1 John iv. 9 f., and ii. 2. ' God so loved the world that he gave his only begotten Son that whosoever believeth on him should not perish but have eternal life.' ' Herein was the love of God manifested in us, that God hath sent his only begotten Son into the world, that we might live through him. Herein is love, not that we loved God, but that he loved us, and sent his Son to be the means by which our sins might be removed.' 'And he is the means by which our sins are removed; and not ours only, but also those of the whole world.'

It is strange that the final argument should be that the Epistle stands nearer than the Gospel to the Gnosticism which is at the farthest remove from primitive Christianity, whilst it has just

[1] *The Spirit in the N.T.*, p. 211.

been described as nearer than the Gospel to the Judaic theology of earliest days. Yet the paradox is there. Here once more we can see the effect of Christian apologetic. Both Gospel and Epistle are strongly opposed to Gnosticism, whilst both use language intended to commend the Christian message to the contemporary world of Hellenism. In the Epistle the writer goes farther in the use of technical terms which the seceders may well have borrowed from the religious vocabulary of the Gnostics. But in the words of Dr. Dodd himself, he was 'using the weapons of the heretics against themselves'. No doubt the 'seed' and the 'chrism', possibly the very phrase 'God is light', were favourite terms on the lips of the heretics and had been used by them with a different reference. Dr. Dodd's excellent commentary shows with what a sound Christian content they are applied in this Epistle. And if assimilation to Christ by the vision of him (1 John iii. 2) might seem to owe something to the language of Hellenistic mysticism, at least the idea must have been familiar in Christian circles ever since St. Paul wrote 2 Cor. iii. 18 (cf. Rom. viii. 29–30). It is hard to think that the Fourth Evangelist was incapable of applying this great Christian conception as it appears in the Epistle.

To sum up: 1. There is so much that is common to Gospel and Epistle, both in language and in thought, that presumptive evidence favours the substantial unity of authorship.

2. Nevertheless, certain differences call for an explanation. This may be found partly in the difference of subject-matter, in the class of writing, in the manner of composition and of dictation, partly also in external events and their effect upon the mind of the Christian pastor or leader and upon the needs of the Church.

3. Possibly in our admiration of the superlative qualities that shine forth from the pages of the Fourth Gospel we are apt to overlook the extent to which it is a derivative. The creative mind of Him whose words are the nucleus of the discourses, and the Beloved Disciple who is the link between the Incarnate Word and the Evangelist, gave him his supreme opportunity. The pastoral disquisition has a beauty of its own, but it is not the splendour of the Incarnate Glory—the theme of the Gospel.

Appendix C

THEORIES OF PARTITION AND REDACTION

THE famous simile of the 'seamless robe' is to be found in D. F. Strauss, *Vorrede zu den Gesprächen von Ulrich v. Hutten*, vii., p. 556: 'Das alles, wie gesagt, wäre schon gut würde es nur offener ausgesprochen. Aber freilich, wie kann man deutlich heraussagen, dass man Erzählungen wie die von dem Wunder zu Kana, und vollends eine so bestimmte und umständliche wie die von der Auferweckung des Lazarus, nicht für historisch hält, wenn man dabei wie Ewald gegen die verhasste Tübinger Schule darauf beharren will, der Verfasser des Evangeliums in dem sie stehen, sei ein Augenzeuge, ja der vertrauteste Jünger des Herrn gewesen? Schon Weisse hat ihm vorgehalten, wie wenig das angeht, und sich daher, weil er doch die johanneischen Reden nicht ganz missen mag, seinerseits zur Teilung des vierten Evangeliums in einen apostolischen und einen nicht-apostolischen Bestandtheil entschlossen. Wäre nur nicht gerade dieses Evangelium selbst jener ungenähte Leibrock, von dem es uns erzählt, um den man wohl loosen, ihn aber nicht zertrennen kann. Davon sind nun leider alle die Ansichten und Darstellungen, die heutiges Tages zwischen dem streng kirchlichen und dem freiesten kritischen Standpunkte vermitteln möchten, das gerade Gegentheil: sie sind aus allerlei Fetzen der verschiedensten Stoffe zusammengeflickt, die unmöglich in die Länge zusammenhalten können.'

I owe this full reference to my friend the Rev. Dr. R. Newton Flew, of Wesley House, Cambridge.

A list is appended of some of the attempts that have been made either to separate an original *Grundschrift* from later additions quarried from a different tradition, or else to indicate redactional insertions into a document which has been extensively revised by a later hand.

Hugo DELFF [see *Th.R.*, ii. (1899), pp. 260 f. 'Die Behandlung der johanneischen Frage im letzen Jahrzehnt' (A. Meyer).] Delff distinguishes between (A) an original Gospel, containing the authentic narrative of an actual eye-witness, and (B) interpolations which aimed at bringing the Gospel nearer to the Galilean tradition, to the millenarian expectation of the age, and to the Alexandrian philosophy.

(A) i. 6–8, 19–51; ii. 12–16, 18–20, 23–5; iii. 1–iv. 43, 45; v. 1–16, 30–47; vi. 30–6, 41–3, 45–53, 55–8, 60–71; vii. 1–38, 45–52; viii. 12–xi. 57; xii. 1–15, 17–24, 31–2, 34–7, 42–50; xiii. 1–19, 21–38; xiv. 1–xviii. 40; xix. 1–19, 21–34, 38–42; xx. 1–8, 19–31.

(B) i. 1–5, 9–18; ii. 1–11, 17, 21–2; iv. 44, 46–54; v. 19–29; vi. 1–29, 37–40, 44, 54, 59; vii. 39; xii. 16, 25–30, 33, 38–41; xiii. 20; xviii. 19(?); xix. 20, 35–7; xx. 9–10, 11–18; xxi.

F. SPITTA (*vide supra*, pp. 62, 96) discriminates between (A) the *Grundschrift*, (B) the editor's additions from written sources, and (C) the editor's own reflections. Spitta's *Grundschrift* contains the following passages, which cannot always be indicated with perfect accuracy, as portions of verses are often attributed to (B) and still more often to (C).

i. 6–7, 9, 11–12, 14*bd*, 24, 26, 33–48, 50, 52; ii. 13, 15–20, 23–iii. 3, 9–11, 22–3, 25–7, 29–30; iv. 1, 3–7, 9–10, 19–25, 28–30, 40, 44–5; v. 1, 8–10, 13*b*–14, 18*a*, 19*a*; vii. 19–24; v. 30–40, 24, 41–7; viii. 39–43, 44*c*–45, 47–50, 56, 59; vi. 1*a*, 2–3, 26*a*, 27, 30*ab*, 31–2, 34, 35–7, 39, 41, 43, 45, 47*a*, 49, 51*b*; viii. 12*ac*, 13–14*a*, 16*b*–18, 21*a*, 25, 26, 28*b*–9, 31–6; vii. 1–4*a*, 6*a*, 9–17, 25–7, 31–3*a*, 34*a*, 35, 45–52; ix. 1–4, 6–13, 15*abde*, 24–8, 34*c*, 35*a*; x. 1–5, 11–14, 15*b*, 16*a*, 18*c*, 19–25, 29–42; xi. 1*a*, 3, 5–6*a*, 9*ab*, 16, 18, 20*a*, 21–2, 33*ac*, 34–7, 41*b*, 43–4, 45*ac*, 47–8*a*, 49*ac*, 50, 53–4*ab*, 55–7; xii. 1*a*, 2*a*, 3*ac*, 4*a*, 5, 7–8, 12–15, 19, 23*a*, 24–5, 27–9, 31–2, 35*b*, 36*b*, 37–8, 41–4, 46–7, 48*ab*, 49–50; xiii. 1–2*a*, 4–10, 21–3*a*, 24–30, 31*a*; xv. 2–3, 4*b*, 6*b*, 8–11, 16*ab*, 18–19, 21*ac*, 22, 25; xvi. 1, 2*a*, 3*b*, 4–8, 12, 13*ac*, 14, 16–17*a*, 18*bc*, 19–23*a*, 25*a*, 32–3; xvii. 1*a*, 4, 6*a*, 8*ac*, 9*a*, 11*b*, 12*ab*, 14–15, 17, 19, 23*ac*, 25, 26*ac*; xiii. 33*a*, 34–5; xiv. 1–3, 12–13*a*, 16*a*, 18, 27*ac*, 28*b*, 30–1; xviii. 1*a*, 2, 3*ac*, 4–6, 8, 12*bc*, 13*a*, 15, 16*a*, 19–23, 28–31, 35*bc*, 37*cd*, 38; xix. 9*bc*, 10–16*a*, 19, 21–3*a*, 26–7*a*, 28*c*, 29, 30, 31 (part), 32*a*, 33*a*, 34, 41*a*, 42*a*; xx. 1–11*a*, 14*b*–16, 17*ac*, 18*a*, 19 (part), 21*b*, 22–3.

Space forbids a list of the verses which Spitta attributes to (B) and to (C). But it is interesting to note that the narrative in John xxi. 1–12 is placed immediately after iv. 54. John xxi. 13 is assigned to (C), verse 14 to (B), with the words 'after that He had risen from the dead' regarded as the editor's own interpretation. Thus Spitta takes 14*a* as parallel to iv. 54. All references to 'the disciple whom Jesus loved' are ascribed to the reflections of the editor.

THEORIES OF PARTITION AND REDACTION

H. H. WENDT (*vide supra*, pp. 61, 96) prints in italics the following passages in the German translation of the Gospel given in *Die Schichten im vierten Evangelium*, pp. 112–58. They represent the secondary layer in the Fourth Gospel:

i. 6–8, 15, 19–52; ii. 1–13a, 17, 21–5; iii. 2c, 22–36; iv. 1–3, 10b, 11b, 15–18, 26, 27b–30, 39–54; v. 1, 8–15, 28–9, 33, 34b–36a; vi. 1–26, 39c, 40c, 44c, 54b, 59, 61b, 64, 70–71; vii. 8, 20–1a, 22b, 30–3a, 39, 44–52; viii. 20b, 27–8a, 30–1a; ix. 2–3, 6–38; x. 21b–2, 40–2; xi. 2, 4, 6b, 11–15, 19, 31, 33b, 36–7, 38b–57; xii. 1–19, 28b–30, 33, 36b–43, 47b, 48c; xiii. 11, 18–19, 21–31a; xvi. 13c; xviii. 1–32, 39–40; xix. 1–6, 11b, 13–42; xx., xxi.

B. W. BACON (*vide supra*, pp. 29 ff., 97 ff.) credits the Redactor with these passages:

i. 6–8, 15; ii. 1–12, 13–25; iii. 31–6; iv. 43–5, (46b), (54); v. 28–9; vi. 39b, 40b, 44b, (54b); vii. 1, 14, 37–9; x. 7, 8b, 9, 22, 23; xii. 29, 30, 33, 42, 43, 44–50; xiii. 16, 20, 36–8; xviii. 9, 14–18, 24–7; xix. 34, 35, 37; xx. 24–9; xxi.; (vii. 53–viii. 12); (xii. 8); (xxi. 25).

W. SOLTAU (*vide supra*, p. 65). Moffatt, *I. L. N. T.* (ed. 2, p. 560) gives from Soltau's earlier articles a twofold division. Under the original *Johannine Logia* were grouped:

i. 1, (35–42), 43–51; ii. 9–11; iii. 1–12, 22–31a; iv. 1–9, (16–19), 29–30, 39–42; v. 1–16, (18); vii. 1–viii. 1; viii. 2–11; ix. 23–41; xii. 20–33, (37–43); xiii. 2–15, (16–20), (31–6); xix. 25–37; xx. 14–18, 25–9. From the *Synoptic tradition* came i. 19–28, 31–4, (35–42); ii. 13–17, 19, 22; iv. 43–54; vi. 1–25, 66–71; ix. 1, 6–23; xi. 47–55, (57); xii. 3–8, 12–16; xiii. 26–7; xviii.; xix. 1–24, 38–42; xx. 1–2, 11–13, 19–23. In *Das vierte Evangelium in seiner Entstehungsgeschichte dargelegt* (1916), Soltau lays more stress on the various stages by which changes and alterations were introduced into the material from which the Gospel was formed. Without a table to show the final results the book is involved and confusing. But the following outline shows the main positions: L(egende), oral narratives of the Apostle John.

S(ynoptische Perikopen) added to L after A.D. 80. These were combined to form

G(rundschrift)=L+S. Out of this a new text was formed about A.D. 130 by

E(vangelist), who added some 'anti-Synoptic' apocryphal traditions, e.g. i. 35–51; iii. 22–30; ix. 1–3, 6–7; xx. 24–9; other narratives, e.g. ii. 1–11; v. 1–8; xviii. 25; xix. 25–33; xx. 11–18; many sayings from R (see below), e.g. vii. 6–7, 16–18, 28–9, 33–4; viii. 12, 19, 21, 31–2, 46–7, 50; ix. 4, 5, 39; xi.

25–6; xii. 23 f., 26, 28, 31–3, 35; xiii. 31–5; also many little explanatory insertions, e.g. ii. 16 f.; iii. 4–6; iv. 10–15, 30–9; v. 17–18; vi. 25–31; xii. 9–11 f.; xix. 42; xx. 22; and many additions in xviii.–xix. 1.

R(edestücke), or passages of Discourses, were inserted at length about A.D. 140, although many shorter sayings from it had been borrowed at an earlier stage. R is to be found almost exclusively in x. 1–18, 25–30; xiv.; xv.; xvi.; xvii.

C(ontinuator) after A.D. 150 added xxi. He is also credited in some parts of the book with xiii. 23–5; xix. 33–5; xx. 2–10.

I(nterpolationen) include xiii. 23, the story of Lazarus in xi., and possibly xx. 2 f.

A. E. GARVIE (*vide supra*, pp. 3, 40) divides the Gospel between:

The *Evangelist*.

i. 1–18, 48; ii. 17, 21–2, 24–5; iii. 31–6; iv. 18, 44; v. 18(?), 19–29; vii. 39; viii. 27; xi. 42, 51–2; xii. 33, 38–41; xiii. 1–3, 18–19; xiv. 29; xv. 25; xvii. 3, 12; xviii. 4, 9, 32; xix. 24, 28, 36, 37; xx. 30, 31. (Some of the comments of the Evangelist may come from the Witness.)

The *Redactor*.

iv. 43–54(?); vi.; xii. 20–36; xiii. 36–8; xviii. 17–18, 25–7; xix. 35; xxi. (Some of the matter in vi. and xii. 20–36 is probably reminiscence of the Witness.)

The *Witness*. For list of passages which Dr. Garvie traces to personal reminiscences of the Witness, see *The Beloved Disciple*, pp. xxvii. f.

R. H. STRACHAN (*vide supra*, pp. 37, 99, 173) attributes the following passages to the *Redactor*:

ii. 1, 12, 23–5; iii. 22–4; iv. 1–3, 43–6a, 54–v. 1; vi. 1, 2, 6, 15, 22–3; vii. 1, 10; x. 40–2; xi. 2, 15, 17, 19, 32 (part), 39 (part), 40, 42, 44 (part), 45–6, 54; xii. 1 (part), 9–11, 17, 18; xx. 2–10, 27; xxi. (left open).

Dr. Strachan offers important linguistic arguments on pp. 113 ff., 239 f. of *The Fourth Evangelist: Dramatist or Historian?*

Johannes WEISS (*R. G. G.*, ed. 1, iii. 2199) thought that the Gospel is an elaboration of the work of the Beloved Disciple, by the hand of the author of chap. xxi., to whom we owe both the designation of this disciple in xiii. 23, as well as the passages xix. 26 f., 35, xx. 2–10; further, i. 40 ff., xx. 24–9. This Redactor also enriched the text with additions, comments, expositions, and expansions of words of the Lord; e.g.

i. 24; iv. 2, 9b, 46, 54; i. 6–9, 14; i. 20, 21a, 25; iii. 28;

vii. 41a; viii. 24b; v. 34; iii. 5 f., 8c, 11c, 13c; vi. 36–40, 44–48; x. 6 f., 9 f., 16, 18, 26–9; xii. 39 f.; iv. 20–6, 37b; vi. 51b–58.

W. BOUSSET (*Th. R.*, xii., pp. 53–6) considered the author of the *Grundschrift* specially dependent on the Lucan writings, upon Acts as well as Luke (e.g. trial before High Priest, Acts xxiii. 2 ff., cohort and chiliarch, Acts xxi. 31 ff.). The self-indication of Jesus as ' Son,' ' Son of God,' is an excellent criterion for the determination of the redactional work. There are common phrases, references to the atoning work of Christ; the Son of Man has not come to judge the world, but to save it; judgement comes upon unbelievers already; there is a special emphasis on the heavenly origin and pre-existence of Jesus. The older stratum depends specially on the Lucan writings, then on Mark. A younger Interpolator works with Matthew.

Some scholars who do not favour the theory of composite authorship, or of redaction on any extensive scale, allow that a few verses are probably due to *editorial insertion*. Thus:

Martin DIBELIUS (*R. G. G.*, ed. 2, iii. 255 f.) who thinks that the author of chap. xxi. was probably not the author of the Gospel as a whole, mentions iv. 2 and vii. 39 as glosses, which may well be notes added by the author himself. He recognizes the difficulty of deciding in the following instances, but appears to favour the probability that they are all by the Evangelist.

i. 24 f., 28; vi. 46; x. 15a; xii. 33; xiii. 11; xv. 10b, 20a; xvi. 5b; xvii. 10a; xviii. 9, 32. (Whether i. 5–8, 15 should be included depends upon our judgement regarding the religious-historical origin of the Prologue.)

F. Warburton LEWIS (*Interpreter*, 1910, pp. 384 ff.) regards the following verses as short editorial insertions, interrupting the narrative. They show the same kind of misunderstanding of the Evangelist's point of view, and must be classed as misinterpretations by an editor.

ii. 21–2; v. 3 fin.–4; vi. 6, 64b; vii. 39; xi. 51–2; xii. 6, 16, 33; xviii. 9, 32; xx. 9; xxi. 19a, 24 (25 ?).

J. H. BERNARD (*I. C. C.*, ' St. John,' pp. xxxiii. f.) distinguishes between (*a*) *Non-Johannine Glosses*:

vii. 53–viii. 11; iv. 1–2; vi. 23; v. 4; xi. 2; xii. 16.

(*b*) *Evangelistic Comments*: appearing in the Prologue, i. 6 f. 12, 15; in the Appendix, xxi. 19; also in the body of the Gospel.

ii. 21; vii. 39; xii. 33; xvii. 3, explaining words of Jesus which may be misunderstood;

vi. 61, 64, calling attention to a point which may be missed;

vii. 22 ; viii. 27, pointing out misunderstanding on the part of Jews, and at xi. 13 of the disciples. See also xviii. 32 ; xii. 6, 43 ; iv. 9 ; vi. 71 (cf. ii. 24 ; vii. 5) ; xi. 51.

In xii. 36b–43, 'the Evangelist ends the narrative of the ministry of Jesus at Jerusalem and His rejection there by quoting, as part of his own comment, several verses from the Old Testament which show how Jewish unbelief had been foreordained in prophecy.'

Appendix D

THEORIES OF TEXTUAL DISPLACEMENT

F. Warburton Lewis. *Disarrangements in the Fourth Gospel* (1910), corrected from *The Interpreter* (1911, pp. 109 f., 331). The text of the Gospel is rearranged thus:

i.–ii. 12 ; iii. 22–30 ; ii. 13–iii. 21 ; iii. 31–6 ; iv. ; vi. ; v. ; vii. 15–24 ; viii. 12–20 ; vii. 1–14 ; vii. 25–52 ; viii. 21–59 ; ix. ; x. 19–29, 1–18, 30–9 ; xi. ; xii. ; xiii. 1–32 ; xv. ; xvi. ; xiii. 33–8 ; xiv. ; xvii. ; xviii. ; xix. ; xx. ; xxi.

A tentative suggestion which Mr. Warburton Lewis made in the Birmingham New Testament Seminar on May 17, 1929, is subjoined.

i.–ii. 12 ; iii. 22–30 ; ii. 13–25 ; iv. ; vi. ; v. ; vii. 15–24 ; viii. 12–20 ; iii. 1–21, 31–6.

James Moffatt. *New Translation of the New Testament.*

i.–ii. 12 ; iii. 22–30 ; ii. 13–iii. 21 ; iii. 31–6 ; iv. ; v. ; vii. 15–24 ; vi. ; vii. 1–14, 25–52 ; viii. 12–59 ; ix. ; x. 19–29 ; x. 1–18 ; x. 30–42 ; xi. 1, 2, 5, 3, 4, 6–17, 20–30, 18, 19, 31–57 ; xii. 1–36, 44–50, 36–43 ; xiii. 1–31a ; xv. ; xvi. ; xiii. 31b–38 ; xiv. ; xvii. ; xviii. 1–14, 19–24, 15–18, 25–40 ; xix. ; xx. ; xxi.

G. H. C. Macgregor. *Moffatt N.T. Commentary*, 'The Gospel of John.'

i.–ii. 12 ; ii. 13–iii. 13 ; iii. 31–6, 22–30 ; iv. ; vi. ; v. ; vii. 15–24 ; viii. 12–20 ; vii. 1–14, 25–36 ; viii. 21–59 ; vii. 45–52, 37–44 ; ix. ; x. 19–29, 1–18, 30–42 ; xi. 1–17, 20–30, 18–19, 31–57 ; xii. 1–32 ; iii. 14–15 ; xii. 34 ; iii. 16–21 ; xii. 35–6, 44–50, 36–43 ; xiii. 1–35 ; (xiii. 36–8) ; xv. ; xvi. ; xiv. ; xvii. ; xviii. 1–13, 24, 14–15, 19–23, 16–18, 25–40 ; xix. ; xx. ; xxi. (But Macgregor regards xviii. 13b–18, 24–7 as interpolations by R.)

J. H. Bernard. *International Critical Commentary*, 'St. John.'

i. ; ii. ; iii. 1–21, 31–6, 22–30 ; iv. ; vi. ; v. ; vii. 15–24, 1–14, 25–52 ; viii. 12–59 ; ix. ; x. 19–29, 1–18, 30–42 ; xi. ; xii. 1–36a, 44–50, 36b–43 ; xiii. 1–31a ; xv. ; xvi. ; xiii. 31b–8 ; xiv. ; xvii. ; xviii. ; xix. ; xx. ; xxi.

Greville P. Lewis (*vide supra*, pp. 126 f.) suggests the transposition of certain passages thus :

xii. 1–19 ; ii. 13–20 ; (ii. 21–22 by R) ; ii. 23–5 ; iii. 1–11 ; xii. 20–32 ; iii. 14–15 ; (omit xii. 33, R) ; xii. 34 ; iii. 12–13, 16–21 (continuing Judgement simile of xii. 31) ; xii. 35–6a (continuing Light simile of iii. 16–21) ; iii. 31–6 ; xii. 36b–41 ; xiii. 1–3 (cf. iii. 35 and xiii. 3).

Appendix E

EUCHARISTIC PARALLELS TO JOHN VI. IN IGNATIUS AND JUSTIN MARTYR

N.B.—The word ' flesh ' (σάρξ), not ' body ' (σῶμα), as in Mark xiv. 22, Matt. xxvi. 26, Luke xxii. 19, 1 Cor. xi. 23-5, Justin Martyr, *Apol.* I. lxvi. 3, is used in the following passages.

Ignatius:

Ad Rom. vii. 3 : ' I have no delight in the food of corruption or in the delights of this life. I desire the bread of God, which is the flesh of Christ, who was of the seed of David ; and for drink I desire His blood, which is love incorruptible.'

Lightfoot's note, *Apostolic Fathers*, II. ii. pp. 226 f. is : ' The reference here is not to the eucharist itself, but to the union with Christ which is symbolized and pledged in the eucharist. . . . " I desire," Ignatius appears to mean, " that heavenly sustenance which is derived from union with a truly incarnate Christ through faith and love." '

Ad Trall. viii. 1 : ' Do ye therefore arm yourselves with gentleness and be renewed in faith, which is the flesh of the Lord, and in love, which is the blood of Jesus Christ.'

Lightfoot's note, *ibid.*, p. 171 : ' The reference is only indirectly to the eucharist. The eucharistic bread and wine, while representing the flesh and blood of Christ, represents also faith and love. Faith is the flesh, the substance of the Christian life ; love is the blood coursing through its veins and arteries.'

Ad Phil. iv. 1 : ' Be ye careful therefore to observe one eucharist (for there is one flesh of our Lord Jesus Christ and one cup unto union in His blood ; there is one altar, as there is one bishop, together with the presbytery and the deacons my fellow servants), that whatsoever ye do, ye may do it according unto God.'

Lightfoot's note, *ibid.*, p. 258: ' The " one flesh " here is the one eucharistic loaf betokening the union in the one body of Christ.'

Ad Smyrn. vii. 1 (Lightfoot's text, vi.): ' They abstain from eucharist and prayer, because they do not acknowledge that the eucharist is the flesh of our Saviour Jesus Christ, which flesh suffered for our sins, and which the Father by His goodness raised up.'

Justin Martyr:
Apol. I. lxvi. 1–2: ' And this food is called by us "eucharist," and it is not lawful for any man to partake of it but he who believes our teaching to be true, and has been washed with the washing which is for the forgiveness of sins and unto a new birth, and is so living as Christ commanded. For not as common bread and common drink do we receive these; but like as Jesus Christ our Saviour being made flesh through the word of God had both flesh and blood for our salvation, so also were we taught that the food for which thanks are given by the prayer of His word, and from which our blood and flesh by conversion are nourished, is both flesh and blood of that Jesus who was made flesh.'

Appendix F

THE STYLE AND STRUCTURE OF THE TEACHING OF JESUS

(a) *Aphoristic Sayings in the Fourth Gospel.*

J. Drummond, *Character and Authorship of the Fourth Gospel*, pp. 17 ff., gives the following examples:

i. 51; ii. 16, 19; iii. 3, 6, 8; iv. 14, 21, 23, 31, 34, 44, 48; v. 14, 17, 19, 23, 30, 40, 44; vi. 27, 33, 35, 44, 63; vii. 7, 17, 24, 37; viii. 12, 26, 32, 34, 36, 51; ix. 4, 39, 41; xi. 25; xii. 24, 25, 26, 32, 36, 44, 47; xiii. 15, 20, 34, 35; xiv. 1, 2, 6, 9, 15, 21, 27; xvii. 1; xviii. 36, 37.

Many more can be found, particularly in chaps. xiii.–xvii. One of the most striking is xx. 29.

(b) *Johannine Parallels to Synoptic Sayings.*

In addition to those given above, Part III., chap. iii. (*vide supra*, pp. 216 ff.) note the following parallels.

John iii. 35	cf.	Matt. xi. 27 / Luke x. 22
iv. 35		Matt. ix. 37 / Luke x. 2
v. 23, xii. 48, xv. 23		Matt. x. 40 / Luke x. 16
v. 29		Matt. xxv. 46 / Luke xiv. 14
v. 47		Luke xvi. 31
xii. 27		Mark xiv. 34 / Matt. xxvi. 38 / Luke xii. 50
xii. 31		Luke x. 18
xiii. 13		Matt. xxiii. 8, 10
xiv. 13, 14, xvi. 23		Mark xi. 24 / Matt. vii. 7, xxi. 22 / Luke xi. 9

xiv. 26 }	{ Matt. x. 19, 20
xv. 7 }	{ Luke xii. 11, 12
xv. 14	{ Mark iii. 35 / Matt. xii. 50 / Luke viii. 21
xv. 21 } xvi. 2 }	{ Mark xiii. 12, 13 / Matt. xxiv. 9 / Luke vi. 22, xxi. 16, 17
xvi. 32	{ Mark xiv. 27 / Matt. xxvi. 31
xvii. 2	{ Matt. xi. 27 / Luke vi. 22
xviii. 11	{ Mark xiv. 36 / Matt. xxvi. 39 / Luke xxii. 42
xx. 23	Matt. xviii. 18

(c) *Poetic Structure in the Teaching of Jesus and in the Fourth Gospel.*

A good instance of the poetic structure of a saying of Jesus in this Gospel was brought out by Dr. Rendel Harris (*Expositor*, VIII., xx., p. 196), who restored the correct punctuation, and explained a *crux interpretum*, partly by showing how a confusion of words in Syriac accounts for the present meaningless form of the text, and partly by illustrating the ancient use of Testimonies.

John vii. 37–38:

> If any man thirst, let him come to Me:
> And let him drink, who believeth in Me:
> Even as saith the scripture, Rivers out of His throne shall flow of living water.

N.B.—The structure of the distich is a chiasmus. Cf. Matt. vii. 6:

> Give not that which is holy to the dogs:
> Neither cast your pearls before the swine:
> Lest haply they trample them with their feet:
> And turning rend you.

The Syriac word for 'belly' is *karsa*, and for 'throne' is *kurs^{e}ya*.

The scripture is a composite quotation from Zech. xiv. 8 'Living water shall go out of Jerusalem,' and Jer. iii. 17, 'They shall call Jerusalem the Lord's throne.'

C. F. Burney, in *The Poetry of our Lord*, has brought forward a mass of evidence to prove how much of the teaching of Jesus corresponds to the form and structure of Semitic poetry. By translating these passages from the Gospels back into the Aramaic of Palestine, and by transliterating the recovered original by means of English letters, Dr. Burney makes it perfectly clear that three notes of Semitic poetry are constantly found, viz. Parallelism, Rhythm, and Rhyme. For the last two the reader must be referred to chaps. iii. and iv. in the book named above. But a brief outline may here be given of Dr. Burney's illuminating treatment of Parallelism in the Gospels. The significant part of the argument is that exactly the same poetic forms clothe the teaching of Jesus in John as in the Synoptics.

Synonymous Parallelism. Cf. Mark x. 38 ff.; Matt. xx. 22 ff. John iii. 11:

> That which we know we speak,
> And that which we have seen we testify.

Cf. John iv. 36; vi. 35, 55; vii. 34, 37; xii. 26, 31; xiii. 16; xiv. 27; xv. 26; xx. 17, 27.

Antithetic Parallelism. Cf. Matt. vii. 17; vi. 14, 15. John iii. 6:

> That which is born of the flesh is flesh,
> And that which is born of the spirit is spirit.

Cf. John iii. 18, 20–21, 31, 36; iv. 13–14, 22; v. 29, 43; vi. 27, 32; vii. 6; viii. 23, 35; ix. 39, 41; x. 10; xi. 9, 10; xii. 8, 24, 25; xiv. 19; xv. 2, 15; xvi. 33.

Special form *a minori ad maius.* Cf. Matt. vii. 3–5; Luke vi. 41–2. John iii. 12:

> If I told you earthly things, and ye believed not,
> How shall ye believe if I tell you of heavenly things?

Cf. John v. 47.

Synthetic (or constructive) *Parallelism.* Cf. Matt. xxiii. 5–10; Luke xii. 49–51.

John viii. 44.

Step-Parallelism. Cf. Mark ix. 37; Matt. xviii. 5; Luke ix. 48. John xiii. 20:

> He that receiveth whomsoever I shall send, receiveth Me;
> And he that receiveth Me, receiveth Him that sent Me.

Cf. John vi. 37; viii. 32; x. 11; xi. 25; xiv. 2–3, 21; xv. 13–14; xvi. 7, 20, 22. So in prose, John x. 26–7; xviii. 36.

Another feature common to the Synoptics and John is the

explanatory line turning a parallel distich into a tristich. Sometimes the line is poetic, sometimes it is a prose comment upon the distich. Cf. Mark ii. 27.

John iii. 11 :

> That which we know we speak,
> And that which we have seen we testify,
> Yet ye receive not our testimony.

Cf. John iii. 14, 18, 19, 34 ; iv. 22, 36 ; vi. 32.

Structure of the Prologue.

It is generally recognized that the Prologue has many of the characteristics of a Hebrew poem. This is brought out well by a German rhythmical rendering, which is given in Johannes Weiss's *Das Urchristentum*, p. 614 (E.T., p. 790).

Two elaborate attempts to set forth the system of its composition deserve mention here.

(*a*) Mr. Cecil Cryer (*Expository Times*, xxxii., pp. 440 ff.) claims that the Prologue embodies a poem or hymn of a Hebraic type on the Logos, written by the author of the Gospel and prefixed by him as an introduction to the narrative proper. Verses 1–5, 9–14, 16–18 fall into a series of tristiches (α), and distiches (β), while verses 6–8 and verse 15 are in prose narrative. He argues also that verses 6–8 and verse 12*d* were added by the author when incorporating the poem into the Gospel, while verses 13*c* and 15 are marginal glosses which have been absorbed into the text.

$$\alpha\alpha\beta\beta : \alpha\alpha\beta : \alpha\alpha\beta : \alpha\alpha\beta : \alpha$$

(*b*) Dr. C. F. Burney (*Aramaic Origin of the Fourth Gospel*, p. 40) accepts the Prologue as taking the form of a hymn, written in eleven parallel couplets, with comments introduced here and there by the writer. Thus :

1*a b* : 1*c* 2*a* : 3*a b* : 4*a b* : 5*a b* : 10*b c* : 11*a b* : 14*a b* : 14*c d* : 14*e* 16*a* : 17*a b*. :

The comments are verses 6–10*a*, 12–13, 16*b*, and 18.

Appendix G

THE ALLEGED SYMBOLISM OF NUMBERS IN THE FOURTH GOSPEL

NUMBERS, WORDS, AND SYMBOLS IN GREEK

Numbers were expressed in Greek by letters of the alphabet, with the help of three additional signs. Generally a horizontal straight stroke distinguished the cipher from the letter. ' The dropping of the horizontal line, which in ordinary arithmetic was not needed, made these series of ciphers exactly like words, the more so as their order did not matter, and they could be arranged very often so as to be pronounceable. Hence arose, no doubt, the link between numbers and names, which on the one side produced mystic words like $αβρασαξ$, the number of the year (since $1 + 2 + 100 + 1 + 200 + 1 + 60 = 365$), and on the other made a name numerically significant, as 'Ἰησοῦς=888 ' (see Moulton, *Grammar of New Testament Greek*, ii., p. 169). This number 888 is not symbolical to begin with, it is the sum total of the numerical values of the letters which form the name Jesus in Greek. But, as soon as this numerical value of the name was discovered, its symbolical meaning would be recognized at once. The sacred number seven is surpassed in each of the three digits. ' The number of the Beast,' 666, may well have been influenced by this consideration. The Antichrist is a parody, which just fails to reach perfection all along the line. Deissmann (*Light from the Ancient East*, ed. 2, p. 278) thinks that the form of the number given in Irenaeus is original, viz. 616. He writes : ' If I may here venture to propose a solution, 616 (=Καῖσαρ θεός, " Caesar god ") is the older secret number with which the Jews branded the worship of the emperor. 666 is perhaps a Christian adaptation of the Jewish number to bring it into (subordinate) harmony with 888 (='Ἰησοῦς, " Jesus ").'

The point to observe is that the symbol is found in something *given*.

The Rev. Dr. W. F. Lofthouse has kindly furnished the following notes.

THE ALLEGED SYMBOLISM OF NUMBERS

NOTES ON NUMBERS IN FOURTH GOSPEL

(a) It is difficult for us to appreciate the significance and fascination of numbers in the ancient world, where, for long, mathematics was the only pursuit worthy of the name of science. Pythagoras held that all things are numbers; and Anaximander, earlier, had noticed the numerical values that emerge in the study of the stars and the musical intervals (Burnet, *Greek Philosophy*, Pt. I., 1914, pp. 52 ff.). Plato carries this further in his myth of Er and his half-serious, half-playful, and wholly baffling exposition of the proper number of citizen births in his perfect State (*Plato's Republic*, viii. 546. Cf. Jowett, *Plato's Republic*, pp. cxxxi. ff.; also Nettleship, *Lectures on Plato's Republic*, pp. 302 ff., and A. E. Taylor, *Plato*, pp. 289 ff.). It is noticeable that some of our most recent thinkers are hinting at a not wholly un-Platonic emphasis on number and pattern as the ground of reality. Babylonian speculation had not advanced nearly as far; but the Babylonian savants knew enough of astronomy and mensuration to attribute an importance to numbers and their curious and fascinating relations to one another which was not wholly fanciful. On the other hand, to the rabbinic Old Testament scholars, observation of numbers in the sacred text became a kind of intellectual diversion (e.g. the question, Why are certain words, like 'Comfort ye, comfort ye,' Isa. xl. 1, repeated? Might not the same question be asked as wisely of ' Jerusalem, Jerusalem,' Luke xiii. 34 ?). But the author of the Fourth Gospel never answers such questions, nor, to the plain reader, suggests them. If arithmetical correspondences are found in some sections of his book, they are conspicuously absent in others. He would appear to have been as little of a Rabbi as of a Neo-Platonist, but to have been rather attracted by the idea of a certain symmetry and orderly construction which is noticeable in more ways than one in Ezekiel (if the latest exponents of that prophet will allow us to say so) and which so deeply influenced (in directions in which our author was not at all interested) the writer of the Apocalypse.

(b) If our allegorists had been aware of the life of the members of the Jewish colony at Elephantine in the fifth century, they might have found a further suggestion in the five deities worshipped in the temple there, Jau (Jehovah), Anath-Bethel, Anath-Jau, Asham-Bethel, Herem-Bethel. It is generally held that there was some connexion between the worship at that outlying post and the earlier Samaritan cults (see Cowley, *Aramaic Pap. of Fifth Cent.*, 1923).

BIBLIOGRAPHY

Note. To Dr. Howard's Bibliography a number of recent books have been added, but the list as a whole has been shortened, in the hope that a selective account of the literature might be of greater use to younger students. Only books which bear directly upon the Fourth Gospel have been included.

ABBOTT, E. A.: *Johannine Vocabulary* (London, 1905)
    Johannine Grammar (London, 1906)
BACON, B. W.: *The Fourth Gospel in Research and Debate* (New Haven, 1910; ed. 2, 1918)
    The Gospel of the Hellenists (edited by C. H. Kraeling; New York, 1933)
BAUER, W.: *Das Johannesevangelium* (Handbuch zum Neuen Testament; ed. 1, 1912; ed. 2, 1925; ed. 3, 1933)
BEHM, J.: Der gegenwärtige Stand der Erforschung des Johannesevangeliums. *Theologische Literaturzeitung*, lxxiii. (1948), 21–30
BERNARD, J. H.: *The Gospel according to St. John* (International Critical Commentary; Edinburgh, 1928)
BORNHÄUSER, K.: *Das Johannesevangelium eine Missionsschrift für Israel* (Gütersloh, 1928)
BÜCHSEL, F.: *Johannes und der hellenistische Synkretismus* (Gütersloh, 1928)
    Das Evangelium nach Johannes (*Das Neue Testament Deutsch*, Göttingen, 1934)
BULTMANN, R.: *Das Evangelium des Johannes* (Kritisch-exegetischer Kommentar über das Neue Testament; ed. 11, 1950)
BURNEY, C. F.: *The Aramaic Origin of the Fourth Gospel* (Oxford, 1922)
CARPENTER, J. E.: *The Johannine Writings* (London, 1927)
CASSIEN, B.: *La Pentecôte johannique* (Valence-sur-Rhône, 1939)
CHARNWOOD, LORD: *According to St. John* (London, 1925)
COLWELL, E. C.: *The Greek of the Fourth Gospel* (Chicago, 1931)
CULLMANN, O.: *Les Sacrements dans l'Évangile johannique* (Paris, 1951)

DODD, C. H.: *The Interpretation of the Fourth Gospel* (Cambridge, 1953)
DRUMMOND, J.: *An Inquiry into the Character and Authorship of the Fourth Gospel* (London, 1903)
DUBOSE, W. P.: *The Gospel in the Gospels* (New York, 1907)
DUPONT, J.: *La Christologie de Saint Jean* (Bruges, 1951)
EISLER, R.: *The Enigma of the Fourth Gospel* (London, 1937)
GARDNER-SMITH, P.: *St. John and the Synoptic Gospels* (Cambridge, 1938)
GARVIE, A. E.: *The Beloved Disciple* (London, 1922)
GOGUEL, M.: *Introduction au Nouveau Testament*, II: Le Quatrième Évangile (Paris, 1923)
GREEN-ARMYTAGE, A. H. N.: *John who Saw* (London, 1952)
HARRIS, J. R.: *The Origin of the Prologue to St. John's Gospel* (Cambridge, 1917)
HEITMÜLLER, W.: *Das Johannes-Evangelium* (Die Schriften des Neuen Testaments; Göttingen, ed. 1, 1906; ed. 3, 1918)
HIRSCH, E.: *Studien zum vierten Evangelium* (Tübingen, 1936)
HOARE, F. R.: *The Original Order and Chapters of St. John's Gospel* (London, 1944)
HOLLAND, H. S.: *The Fourth Gospel* (London, 1923)
HOLTZMANN, H. J.: *Das Evangelium des Johannes* (Hand-Commentar zum Neuen Testament; Tübingen, ed. 3 by W. Bauer, 1908)
HOSKYNS, E. C.: *The Fourth Gospel* (London, ed. 1, 1940; ed. 2, 1947; reprinted, 1954)
HOWARD, W. F.: *Christianity according to St. John* (London, 1943)
JACKSON, H. L.: *The Problem of the Fourth Gospel* (Cambridge, 1918)
JEREMIAS, J.: *Die Wiederentdeckung von Bethesda* (Göttingen, 1949)
KNOX, W. L.: *Some Hellenistic Elements in Primitive Christianity* (Schweich Lectures, 1942; London, 1944)
LAGRANGE, M.-J.: *L'Évangile selon Saint Jean* (Paris, ed. 1, 1925; ed. 8, 1947)
LEE, E. K.: *The Religious Thought of St. John* (London, 1950)
LEIPOLDT, J.: Johannesevangelium und Gnosis, in *Neutestamentliche Studien: Festgabe für G. Heinrici* (Leipzig, 1914)
LIETZMANN, H.: *Ein Beitrag zur Mandäerfrage* (Berlin, 1930)

LIGHTFOOT, J. B.: *Biblical Essays* (London, 1889)

LOEWENICH, W. VON: *Das Johannes-Verständnis im zweiten Jahrhundert.* Beiheft zur Zeitschrift für die neutestamentliche Wissenschaft, 13 (Giessen, 1932)

LOFTHOUSE, W. F.: *The Disciple whom Jesus loved* (London, 1934)

LOISY, A.: *Le Quatrième Évangile* (Paris, 1903)
Le Quatrième Évangile, deuxième édition refondue: Les Épitres dites de Jean (Paris, 1921)

MACGREGOR, G. H. C.: *The Gospel of John* (Moffatt New Testament Commentary; London, 1928)

MANSON, T. W.: The Life of Jesus, V. *Bulletin of the John Rylands Library*, xxx (1947), 312–29

MANSON, W.: *The Incarnate Glory* (London, 1923)

MAURER, C.: *Ignatius von Antiochien und das Johannesevangelium* (Zürich, 1949)

MENOUD, P. H.: *L'Évangile de Jean d'après les Recherches récentes* (Neuchâtel and Paris; ed. 1, 1943; ed. 2, 1947)

MERX, A.: *Die vier kanonischen Evangelien nach ihrem ältesten bekannten Texte:* II. ii. b, *Das Evangelium des Johannes* (Berlin, 1911)

MICHAELIS, W.: *Die Sakramente im Johannesevangelium* (Bern, 1946)

MURRAY, J. O. F.: *Jesus according to St. John* (London, 1936)

ODEBERG, H.: *The Fourth Gospel interpreted in its Relation to Contemporaneous Religious Currents* (Uppsala and Stockholm, 1929)

OEHLER, W.: *Das Johannesevangelium, eine Missionsschrift für die Welt* (Gütersloh, 1936)
Zum Missionscharakter des Johannesevangeliums, Beiträge zur Förderung christlicher Theologie, xlii. 4 (Gütersloh, 1941)

OMODEO, A.: *La Mistica Giovannea* (Bari, 1930)

PALLIS, A.: *Notes on St. John and the Apocalypse* (Oxford, n.d.)

PERCY, E.: *Untersuchungen über den Ursprung der johanneischen Theologie* (Lund, 1939)

PRIBNOW, H.: *Die johanneische Anschauung vom 'Leben'*, Greifswalder Theologische Forschungen, 4 (Griefswald, 1934)

REDLICH, E. B.: *An Introduction to the Fourth Gospel* (London, 1940)

ROBERTS, C. H.: *An unpublished Fragment of the Fourth Gospel in the John Rylands Library* (Manchester, 1935)

RUCKSTUHL, E.: *Die literarische Einheit des Johannesevangeliums.* Studia Friburgensia, Neue Folge, Heft 3. Freiburg in der Schweiz, 1951.

SANDAY, W.: *The Criticism of the Fourth Gospel* (Oxford, 1905)

SANDERS, J. N.: *The Fourth Gospel in the Early Church* (Cambridge, 1943)

SCHLATTER, A.: *Der Evangelist Johannes* (Stuttgart; ed. 1, 1930; ed. 2, 1948)

SCHWEIZER, E.: *EGO EIMI . . . Die religionsgeschichtliche Herkunft und theologische Bedeutung der johanneischen Bildreden, zugleich ein Beitrag zur Quellenfrage des vierten Evangeliums*, Forschungen zur Religion und Literatur des Alten und Neuen Testaments, Neue Folge, 38 (Göttingen, 1939)

SCOTT, E. F.: *The Fourth Gospel: Its Purpose and Theology* (Edinburgh, 1906)

SPITTA, F.: *Das Johannesevangelium als Quelle der Geschichte Jesu* (Göttingen, 1910)

STANTON, V. H.: *The Gospels as Historical Documents: I, The Early Use of the Gospels; III, The Fourth Gospel* (Cambridge, 1903, 1920)

STRACHAN, R. H.: *The Fourth Gospel, its Significance and Environment* (London; ed. 3, revised and rewritten, 1941)

STRACK, H. L., and BILLERBECK, P.: *Kommentar zum Neuen Testament aus Talmud und Midrasch: II* (Munich, 1924)

STRATHMANN, H.: *Das Evangelium nach Johannes* (Das Neue Testament Deutsch, Göttingen, 1951)

STREETER, B. H.: *The Four Gospels* (London, 1924)

TEMPLE, W.: *Readings in St. John's Gospel* (London, 1945)

TORREY, C. C.: The Aramaic Origin of the Gospel of St. John. *Harvard Theological Review*, xvi (1923), 305–44

WELLHAUSEN, J.: *Erweiterungen und Aenderungen im vierten Evangelium* (Berlin, 1907)

Das Evangelium Johannis (Berlin, 1908)

WESTCOTT, B. F.: *The Gospel according to St. John* (Speaker's Commentary: London, 1880)

The Gospel according to St. John: The Greek text, with introduction and notes, 2 vols. (London, 1908)

WETTER, G. P.: *Der Sohn Gottes: Eine Untersuchung über den Charakter und die Tendenz des Johannes-Evangeliums*, Forschungen zur Religion und Literatur des Alten und Neuen Testaments, Neue Folge, 9 (Göttingen, 1916)

WINDISCH, H.: Die Johanneische Erzählungsstil, in *Eucharisterion: Studien zur Religion und Literatur des Alten und Neuen Testaments Hermann Gunkel dargebracht* (Göttingen, 1923)

Johannes und die Synoptiker (Leipzig, 1926)

Die fünf johanneische Parakletsprüche, in *Festgabe für Adolf Jülicher* (Tübingen, 1927)

Jesus und der Geist im Johannesevangelium, in *Amicitiae Corolla* (London, 1933)

WREDE, W.: *Charakter und Tendenz des Johannesevangeliums* (Tübingen, 1903); reprinted in *Vorträge und Studien*, pp. 178–231 (Tübingen, 1907)

WRIGHT, C. J.: *Jesus, the Revelation of God* (London, 1950)

ZAHN, T.: *Das Evangelium des Johannes* (Kommentar zum Neuen Testament, IV; Leipzig, 1908)

INDEX OF SCRIPTURE REFERENCES

(This does not include passages referred to in the Appendices)

THE OLD TESTAMENT

DEUTERONOMY.
ii. 14 182

2 KINGS.
xvii. 24–34 . . . 183

NEHEMIAH.
viii. 7 . . 224n

PSALMS.
xcv. 10 . . . 182

PROVERBS.
viii. 22–36 . . . 223

ISAIAH.
i. 16–20 . . . 205

THE APOCRYPHA

ECCLESIASTICUS.
xxiv. 21 . . . 210

2 BARUCH.
xxix. 8 . . . 210

THE NEW TESTAMENT

MATTHEW.
v. 11–12 . . . 150
x. 17–22 . . . 226
x. 20 . . . 227
x. 24 . . . 216
x. 39 . . . 216
x. 40 . . . 151, 216
xi. 25–7 . . 78, 219
xiv. 19 . . . 209
xvi. 25 . . . 216
xvii. 3, 4 . . . 217
xviii. 3 . . . 206
xviii. 5 . . . 216
xviii. 12–14 . . 260
xxv. 31–46 . . . 151
xxvi. 1 . . . 137
xxvi. 19 . . . 137
xxvi. 21 . . . 209
xxviii. 14 . . . 106
xxviii. 18 f. . 78, 204

MARK.
i. 1–15 . . . 263
i. 4–15 . . . 264
i. 14 . . . 135
i. 35–ii. 17 . . . 123
ii. 11 . . . 216
ii. 12 . . . 103
ii. 18–iii. 6 . . 123
iii. 7–8 . . . 123
iii. 7–vi. . . . 123
vi. 32–44 . . 130, 150
vi. 41 . . . 209
vi. 48, 49 . . . 189n
vii. . . . 124
vii. 24 . . . 124

viii. 1–10 . . . 130
viii. 6 . . . 209
viii. 10 . . . 124
viii. 27 . . . 124
viii. 35 . . 150, 216
viii. 38 . . . 150
ix. 37 . . 216, 218
x. 5, 6 . . . 223
x. 15 . . . 217
xi. 30 . . . 222
xiv. 1 . . . 137
xiv. 2 . . . 137
xiv. 6, 8 . . . 102
xiv. 16 . . . 137
xiv. 18 ff. . . 209
xiv. 29 . . . 143
xiv. 42 . . 64, 216
xiv. 43 . . . 137
xiv. 53 . . . 137
xiv. 58 . 132, 142, 216
xiv. 61–4 . . . 136
xv. 9–10 . . . 136
xv. 29 . . . 142
xv. 46 . . . 137
xvi. 16 . . . 204

LUKE.
ii. 25 . . . 217
ii. 38 . . . 217
iii. 2 . . . 130
iii. 15 . . . 131
iv. 24 . . . 216
iv. 29 . . . 131
iv. 44 . . . 125
v. 1–11 . . 129, 143
vi. 40 . . . 216

vii. 38 . . . 131
ix. 16 . . . 209
ix. 18 f. . . . 124
ix. 24 . . . 216
ix. 48 . . . 216
ix. 51 . . 124, 131
x. 16 . . . 216
x. 21–2 . . . 219
x. 38 . . . 131
xii. 12 . . . 227
xv. 4–7 . . . 260
xvii. 33 . . . 216
xviii. 17 . . . 217
xxii. 13 . . . 137
xxii. 15, 16 . . . 137
xxii. 21 ff. . . 209
xxii. 27 . . . 134
xxii. 32 ff. . 131, 143
xxii. 38 . . . 137
xxii. 39 . . . 131
xxii. 50 . . . 131
xxiii. 3 . . . 131
xxiii. 4 . . . 131
xxiii. 14 . . . 131
xxiii. 22 . . . 131
xxiii. 52 . . . 131
xxiii. 56 . . . 137
xxiv. 48, 49 . 131, 226

JOHN.
i. . . . 72, 263
i. 3 . . . 198
i. 4 . . 82, 235
i. 6–8 . . 79, 118
i. 9 . . . 198
i. 12 . . 199, 202, 236

317

Reference	Pages
i. 13	236, 265
i. 14	132, 195, 201, 235
i. 15	73n, 79, 118
i. 17	79, 235
i. 18	235
i. 19, 20	131
i. 28	133
i. 30	185
i. 35	123
i. 44	133
i. 45	235
i. 49	235
ii.	126
ii. 11	73n, 132
ii. 12	123
ii. 17	73n
ii. 18–20	133
ii. 19	141, 216
ii. 19–21	185
ii. 20	143n
iii.	126, 203, 244
iii. 2	126
iii. 3	185, 205
iii. 5	204, 205
iii. 8	185, 202, 205
iii. 11	202
iii. 12, 13	257
iii. 13	174, 258
iii. 14, 15	185, 235, 238
iii. 16 ff.	202, 237
iii. 17	219, 237
iii. 20 f.	258
iii. 21	200
iii. 24	130, 135
iii. 29	185
iii. 34	219
iii. 36	152
iv.	71, 120, 123, 126, 182
iv. 1–3	205
iv. 1, 2	100, 117
iv. 2	204
iv. 10	185
iv. 14	153, 201, 202
iv. 18	185
iv. 22	235
iv. 31	219
iv. 35	185
iv. 38	215
iv. 42	159
iv. 46	191
iv. 54	73n
v.	25, 71, 113, 115, 117, 120, 124, 125, 222
v. 1	125
v. 2 ff.	153
v. 4	100
v. 8	216
v. 9	103
v. 16	112, 120
v. 18	112
v. 19 f.	136
v. 20 f.	153
v. 22	220
v. 24	174, 219
v. 25	185
v. 27 f.	148, 220
v. 28 f.	73n
v. 30	219
v. 36	219
v. 37	219
v. 38	219
v. 39	164, 235
v. 43	20, 71
v. 45	164
v. 46 ff.	235
vi.	10, 25, 39, 40, 72, 113, 120, 123–5, 202, 203, 205, 266
vi. 4	125
vi. 11	209
vi. 14	235
vi. 15	125
vi. 19	189n
vi. 23	100, 209
vi. 29	219
vi. 32	235
vi. 35	201
vi. 38 f.	219
vi. 39	73n
vi. 40	73n, 220
vi. 44	73n, 201, 219
vi. 45 f.	220
vi. 53, 54	130, 185
vi. 56	152
vi. 57	219
vi. 58	201
vi. 60–3	139, 211
vi. 62	174
vi. 66	125
vi. 70	130
vi. 70, 71	209
vii.	114, 124
vii. 3	63, 64, 174
vii. 16	219
vii. 17	239
vii. 18	219
vii. 19	112, 113
vii. 28 f.	219
vii. 30	164
vii. 31	73n
vii. 32	164
vii. 33	219
vii. 37–9	153, 202
vii. 38	185, 202
vii. 39	73n, 132, 152, 238
vii. 44	164
viii.	25
viii. 16	219
viii. 18	219, 222
viii. 19	220
viii. 26	219
viii. 28	238
viii. 29	219
viii. 35	215, 220
viii. 38	220
viii. 42	219
viii. 51	152
viii. 56	235
viii. 58	223
viii. 59	131, 164
ix.	71, 112, 121
ix. 4	215, 219
ix. 7	185, 218
ix. 29	164
ix. 31 f.	73n
ix. 39	254
x.	260
x. 6	225
x. 7	158
x. 11	158, 215
x. 15	220
x. 21	112
x. 25	164
x. 27 f.	199
x. 29 ff.	136
x. 30	220
x. 31	164
x. 36	219
x. 38	220
x. 39	131, 164
xi.	71, 122, 192–4
xi. 1 f.	131
xi. 2	100
xi. 4	132
xi. 5	112
xi. 6	192
xi. 11	185
xi. 15	189
xi. 18	112
xi. 19	112
xi. 25, 26	152, 202
xi. 40	132
xi. 42	189, 219
xi. 49	187
xi. 51	187
xii.	112, 119, 122, 126, 127
xii. 1	137
xii. 2 f.	131
xii. 3	131
xii. 6	100
xii. 7	102
xii. 16	238
xii. 23, 24	153, 238
xii. 24	185, 238
xii. 25	216
xii. 27	130
xii. 32	185, 238
xii. 34	126, 238
xii. 36	112, 131

INDEX OF SCRIPTURE REFERENCES 319

xii. 37	. .	. 73n
xii. 40	. .	. 254
xii. 42	. .	. 106
xii. 44 ff.	202, 216, 219	
xii. 47	. .	. 237
xii. 49	. .	. 219
xiii. 1	. 131, 134, 137, 174	
xiii. 2	. .	. 63
xiii. 7–8	. .	. 153
xiii. 8	. .	. 203
xiii. 8–10	.	158, 185
xiii. 10	. .	. 204
xiii. 16	. .	. 216
xiii. 18–20	. .	. 134
xiii. 20	.	216, 219
xiii. 21 ff.	62, 63, 209	
xiii. 23	. .	. 65
xiii. 27	.	63, 131
xiii. 28 f.	. .	. 63
xiii. 29	. .	. 137
xiii. 31	.	113, 238
xiii. 32	.	132, 238
xiii. 36	. .	. 112
xiii. 36–8	. .	. 131
xiv.	65, 112, 241	
xiv. 2	. .	. 215
xiv. 5	. .	. 112
xiv. 6	. .	. 235
xiv. 12	.	153, 239
xiv. 13	. .	. 220
xiv. 15–17	. .	. 72n
xiv. 16	. .	. 147
xiv. 17	. .	. 238
xiv. 19	. .	. 203
xiv. 20	. .	. 203
xiv. 21 ff.	. .	. 203
xiv. 24	. .	. 219
xiv. 25 f., 26	.	. 72n
xiv. 26	. .	. 239
xiv. 30, 31	. .	. 64
xiv. 31	.	174, 216
xv.	65, 112, 115, 199, 226, 260	
xv. 3	. .	. 203
xv. 7	. .	. 203
xv. 10	. .	. 203
xv. 12	. .	. 240
xv. 13	. .	. 75
xv. 15	. .	. 220
xv. 20	. .	. 216
xv. 21	. .	. 219
xv. 26, 27	72n, 227, 239	
xvi.	65, 112, 115	
xvi. 5	.	112, 219
xvi. 7	.	152, 238
xvi. 8	.	237, 239
xvi. 10	. .	. 238
xvi. 11	. .	. 238
xvi. 12	. .	. 64
xvi. 12, 13	. .	. 152
xvi. 14	. .	. 239
xvi. 15	. .	. 220
xvi. 21	. .	. 215
xvi. 23	. .	. 239
xvi. 25	. .	. 225
xvi. 29	. .	. 225
xvi. 33	. .	. 78
xvii.	.	48, 198
xvii. 1	.	132, 220
xvii. 2	. .	. 220
xvii. 3	. .	. 219
xvii. 4	. .	. 132
xvii. 5	. .	. 132
xvii. 8	. .	. 219
xvii. 9	. .	. 237
xvii. 11, 14	. .	. 256
xvii. 14–16	. .	. 238
xvii. 15	. .	. 78
xvii. 16	. .	. 256
xvii. 17	. .	. 203
xvii. 18	. .	. 219
xvii. 20, 21	. .	. 239
xvii. 21	152, 203, 219, 220	
xvii. 21 f.	. .	. 155
xvii. 22 f.	. .	. 198
xvii. 23	. .	. 219
xvii. 25	.	219, 220
xviii.	63, 64, 71, 111, 113, 119	
xviii. 1	. .	. 134
xviii. 2	. .	. 131
xviii. 6	.	128, 135
xviii. 8	. .	. 63
xviii. 10	. .	. 131
xviii. 11	.	130, 238
xviii. 12	.	130, 134
xviii. 13	. .	. 187
xviii. 15	. .	. 51
xviii. 24	113, 117, 130, 136	
xviii. 28	134, 136, 137	
xviii. 30	. .	. 136
xviii. 31–3	. .	. 164
xviii. 33	. .	. 136
xviii. 36	. .	. 215
xviii. 37, 38	. .	. 164
xviii. 38	. .	. 131
xviii. 40	. .	. 137
xix.	. .	. 63
xix. 4	. .	. 131
xix. 6	. .	. 131
xix. 7	. .	. 136
xix. 12	. .	. 136
xix. 14	.	134, 137
xix. 30	. .	. 180
xix. 34, 35	. .	. 153
xix. 35	31, 55, 73n, 89	
xix. 36	. .	. 137
xix. 39	.	128, 134
xix. 41	. .	. 131
xx.	.	48, 63
xx. 2	. .	. 65
xx. 17	. .	. 174
xx. 21	. .	. 219
xx. 21–3	. .	. 153
xx. 22	. .	. 238
xx. 30	.	55, 73n
xx. 31	.	9, 55, 240
xxi.	30, 32, 37, 39, 40, 48, 51, 55, 62, 63, 65, 67, 68, 71, 85, 89, 96, 98, 100, 104, 263	
xxi. 1 ff.	. .	. 189n
xxi. 14	. .	. 99
xxi. 19	. .	. 55
xxi. 20 ff.	. .	. 31
xxi. 24	8, 56, 73n, 107	
xxi. 25	. .	. 107

Also the following passages:

i.–ii. 12	. .	. 120
i. 46–51	. .	. 185
ii.–iv. 42	. .	. 264
ii.–vi.	. .	. 64
ii.–xii.	. .	. 263
ii. 1–11	74, 123, 153, 189	
ii. 13–iii. 21	. .	. 120
ii. 23–iii. 21	. .	. 247
iii. 1–8	. .	. 256
iii. 1–21	.	256, 265
iii. 3–8	. .	. 218
iii. 9–21	. .	. 257
iii. 14–21	. .	. 126
iii. 22–30	112, 120, 123, 126	
iii. 22–36	. .	. 265
iii. 31–6	116, 120, 126, 214, 256, 258	
iv. 1–3	.	126, 127
iv. 15–26	. .	. 185
iv. 34–8	. .	. 153
iv. 46–v. 47	. .	. 266
v. 19–26	. .	. 220
vi. 1–15	.	130, 153
vi. 16–21	. .	. 153
vi. 31–5	. .	. 147
vii., viii.	. .	. 266
vii. 1–14	113–15, 121, 125, 133	
vii. 15–24	112, 113, 115, 121, 222	
vii. 25–36	. .	. 115
vii. 25–52	. .	. 121
vii. 37–44	. .	. 115
vii. 45–52	. .	. 115
vii. 53–viii. 11	34, 114, 115	
viii. 12–20	114, 115, 121, 125, 222	

INDEX OF SCRIPTURE REFERENCES

viii. 21–59	115, 121, 222, 223
ix. 1–11	153
ix. 1–x. 21	266
x. 1–18	121
x. 19–29	112, 121
x. 22–39	266
x. 24–38	222
x. 30–42	121
x. 40–2	133
xi. 1–53	266
xii.–xiv.	63
xii. 1–32	126
xii. 1–36	266
xii. 35–36a	126
xii. 36b–43	126
xii. 37–50	266
xii. 44–50	112, 126
xiii.–xx.	263
xiii. 5–10	200
xiv. 6–11	220
xv.–xvii.	63, 64
xv. 18–xvi. 2	226
xvi. 5–11	72n
xvi. 12–15	72n
xviii. 12–28	136
xviii. 14–18	117
xviii. 19–23	113
xviii. 24–7	117
xix. 34–7	179
xx. 3–5	200
xxi. 1–13	129
xxi. 7–19	200

ACTS.

i. 4 f.	226
vi. 7	230
x. 37	123, 125
xii. 2	70
xviii. 24	146

ROMANS.

vi. 4	218
viii. 3	218

1 CORINTHIANS.

v. 7 f.	140
x. 16 f.	208
xi. 23	136
xi. 24	210
xi. 26	208
xi. 29	208

2 CORINTHIANS.

v. 1–4	207

GALATIANS.

ii. 20	31, 199
iv. 4	218, 235

EPHESIANS.

v. 22 ff.	207
v. 26	156n, 206

COLOSSIANS.

ii. 6	106
iii. 3	203

1 THESSALONIANS.

i. 1	203

2 THESSALONIANS.

i. 1	203

TITUS.

iii. 5	156n, 206, 218

1 PETER.

v. 5	134

2 PETER.

iii. 13	220n

1 JOHN.

i. 1–3	195, 201
ii. 1	147
ii. 5	203
iii. 2	149
iii. 6	203
iii. 9	201, 206
iii. 13	240
iii. 14	174, 207
iii. 23	202
iv. 1–6	195
iv. 8	237, 240
iv. 10	201
iv. 13	152
iv. 19	201
v. 1	202
v. 5	202
v. 6–8	153
v. 8	204

REVELATION.

i. 4	184
iii. 1	184

INDEX OF NAMES AND SUBJECTS

(References to the Bibliography are not included)

A

Abbott, E. A., 20, 35, 38, 105, 187, 191, 223, 225, 285
Abingdon Commentary, 3
Abraham, 121, 223
Abrahams, I., 221 f.
Adam, James, 241
Aenon, 120
Agony, 8
Agrippa I, 70, 274
Alexandria, 165
Alexandrian mysticism, 195; philosophy (*see also* PHILO), 33, 61, 86, 145 f.
Allegory, 13, 27, 35, 68, 74, 86, 163, 186, 188, 190, 192
Alogi, 21
Ambiguities in F. G., 185, 207
American work on F. G., 29, 90
Andrew, 133, 271
Androcles and the Lion, 4
Angela of Foligno, 197
Annas, Trial before, 113, 130
Anointing at Bethany, 102, 129, 131, 137, 276 f.
Antichrist, 310
Antioch, 89
Aphoristic sayings in F. G., 306
Apocalypse of John, 31, 33 f., 42, 66, 70, 104, 109, 160, 182, 272 f., 311
Apocalyptic. *See* ESCHATOLOGY
Apologetic aim of F. G., 55, 58, 59, 132
Apostolic Constitutions, 205
Appel, H., 66
Appendix (chap. xxi.), 30, 31, 32, 34, 55, 62 f., 67 f., 76, 85, 89, 96 f., 98, 100, 104, 107, 116
Aramaic colour of F. G., 12, 41, 80, 107, 215, 308
Aristion, 271 f.
Arnold, Matthew, 45, 213 f.
Asclepius, 83
Askwith, E. H., 29
Augustine of Hippo, 184
Authorship of F. G., 39, 73, 228, 271ff.

B

Bach, J. S., 154
Background of thought, 59, 144–59, 244, 250 f., 258 f.
Bacon, B. W., 2, 4 f., 29–32, 33, 97–9, 106, 116 f., 140, 181, 226, 274, 281, 299

Baldensperger, W., 24, 57
Baptism, 145, 151 f., 158, 203 f.
Baptism of Jesus, 123, 130
Baptist, John the, 8–10, 24, 57 ff., 87, 118, 120, 129 f., 135, 162, 190, 213 f.
Barabbas, 129, 137
Bar-Cochba, 20, 71
Bardaisan, 158
Barnabas, Ep. of, 218
Baruch, Apoc. of, 150, 210
Basilides, 86
Bauer, W., 54, 78, 80, 109, 158, 171 f., 191
Beethoven, L. von, 154
Belief, 108, 237, 239
Bell, H. I., 164
Beloved Disciple, 4, 8, 30 ff., 37 f., 40, 54, 56, 70, 85, 98 f., 108, 119, 185, 229 f., 233, 300
Bernard of Clairvaux, 197
Bernard, J. H., 51 f., 100, 117, 125 f., 143, 193, 206, 222, 275, 301, 303
Bert, G., 81, 83
Bethany. *See* ANOINTING AT
Bethany beyond Jordan, 133
Bethesda, Cure at, 67, 71, 103, 120, 129, 132, 182, 277
Bethsaida, 133
Betrayal. *See* JUDAS ISCARIOT
Bett, Henry, xi., 188
Bezae, Codex, 34
Biblical Commission, 88, 90
Billerbeck, P., 217
Birmingham N. T. Seminar, v., x., 126, 303
Black, M., 173, 267
Blind, Man born, 67, 121, 129, 132
Body of Christ (mystical), 207
Bornhäuser, K., 81
Boswell, James, x.
Bousset, W., 66 f., 76, 95, 109, 148 f., 203, 301
Box, G. H., 140
Bread of Life, 2, 59, 120, 139, 202, 209 ff., 261
Bretschneider, C. T., 53
Brooke, A. E., 3, 28, 104, 137, 180, 281, 283, 287, 292, 294
Büchsel, F., 81, 172
Bultmann, R., 10, 78–80, 166 f., 171 ff., 250–8
Burch, V., 48, 141 f.
Burkitt, F. C., 11, 24, 29, 137, 157, 180, 220, 222 f.

321

INDEX OF NAMES AND SUBJECTS

Burnet, J., 311
Burney, C. F., 41, 80, 81, 215, 307, 309
Burton, E. D., 114

C

Cadoux, C. J., 143
Caiaphas, 187
Caiaphas, Trial before, 113, 129, 136
Calmes, Th., 87
Cambridge Biblical Essays, 28, 198, 221
Cana, Miracle at, 67, 74, 82, 120, 123, 129, 132, 184, 189, 191
Cana, Officer's son, 120, 129, 133
Capernaum, 103, 120, 129
Capernaum, Discourse at, 139, 200, 202, 205, 210 f. See also BREAD OF LIFE
Case, S. J., 241
Characteristics of Johannine style, 104 ff., 276 ff.
Charles, R. H., 38, 104, 210, 274, 283, 292
Charnwood, Lord, 45
Chiliarch, 134 f.
Christ-Mysticism, 149 ff., 203
Chronological order, 111–43
Chronology of F. G., 34, 37, 44, 63, 87, 97, 99, 119 f.
Church in F. G., 24, 238 f.
Clark, A. C., 115 f.
Cleansing of Temple, 57, 120, 126, 129, 133, 138, 141–3, 161
Clement of Alexandria, 13, 195
Clementine Homilies, 205
Codex-form of F. G., 116
Comments, Explanatory, 58, 301
Continuator, 65, 300
Cowley, A. E., 311
Cryer, C., 309
Cullmann, O., 175

D

Dalman, G., 138 f.
Daniel, Eschatology of, 150
Date of Crucifixion, 138, 161
Date of F. G., 20, 71, 85, 86, 89, 165
Date of Last Supper, 55, 137 ff., 161, 174 f.
Davey, F. N., 244
Death of Christ, 249, 266
Dedication, Feast of, 112, 121 f.
Deification, 156
Deissmann, G. A., 41, 154, 199, 310
Deissmanns Festgabe, 75
Delafosse, H., 89
Delff, H., 22, 60, 98, 297
Demoniacs, Cure of, 130, 132
Denney, James, 2, 147
Dialogues with Jews, 25, 27, 220 ff.

Diaspora, 12, 146
Diatessaron of Tatian, 30. See also TATIAN
Dibelius, M., 39, 75 ff., 301
Didache, 210
Dionysiac mysteries, 74, 83, 191
Dionysius of Alexandria, 109, 273
Disarrangements in F. G., 30, 32 f., 39, 46 f., 67, 91, 100, 160, 166–8, 303
Discourses in F. G., 25, 27, 30, 65, 82, 87, 96, 214, 220
Dislocations, 111–27. See also DISARRANGEMENTS
Displacements in Text. See DISARRANGEMENTS and DISLOCATIONS
Dobschütz, E. von, 282
Docetism, 172
Dodd, C. H., 128, 157, 159, 168 f., 171, 173 f., 219, 258–66, 267, 281, 283
Dods, Marcus, 2
Door, The, 158
Dramatic Element in F. G., 6, 33, 44, 63, 71, 85, 187, 192
Drummond, James, 22, 147, 214 f., 272, 306
Dualism, 147, 198, 252

E

Easton, B. S., 29
Ecclesiasticus, 210
Ecstasy, 196
Eisler, R., 220
Elder of Ephesus, 30. See JOHN THE PRESBYTER
Elephantine, 311
Emmerich, Anne Catherine, 197
Enoch, Eschatology of, 150
Ephesus, 8 ff., 23, 31, 34, 38, 42, 54, 82, 89, 146, 165, 230 ff., 273
Ephraim, 122
Epiphany, Feast of, 191
Epistle, First, 57 ff., 61, 69, 82, 107 ff., 132, 155, 195, 204, 213, 240, 281–96
Epistles. See JOHANNINE EPP.
Eschatology, 62, 80, 107, 149 f., 207, 242, 253, 256
Eschlinan, J. A., 284
Eternal Life, 155, 206
Ethical Teaching, 203, 240
Eucharist, 10, 25, 39, 83, 130, 132, 136, 145, 152
Eucharistic discourse. See CAPERNAUM, DISCOURSE AT
Eucharistic parallels, 304
Eucharisterion, 79
Eusebius, 26, 110, 204, 230, 271 ff.
Eyewitness, 134
Ezekiel, 311
Ezra, Fourth Bk. of, 150

INDEX OF NAMES AND SUBJECTS

F

Faith in F. G., 9, 108, 155, 236 f., 239, 256
Faith and Miracles, 58, 189
Farewell Discourse, 112, 118, 154
Fatherhood of God, 236
Feeding of Multitude, 25, 71, 120, 122, 129 f., 136, 150, 209
Feet-washing, 130, 134, 153, 158
Feine, P., 146
Fernley Lecture, 1
Festivals in F. G., 30, 62, 64
Fiebig, P., 158 f.
Flesh (Eucharistic term), 210 f., 304
Flew, R. N., 297
Florinus, 272
Forbes, H. P., 29
Form-criticism, 39, 69, 71, 74, 141
Formgeschichte. See FORM-CRITICISM
Fourth Evangelist, 228 ff. *et passim*
French books on F. G., 84, 90

G

Galilean Ministry, 122 ff., 143, 161 f.
Galilee, 31, 120, 122
Galilee, Sea of, 71
Gardner, P., ix., 36, 194, 209
Gardner-Smith, P., 169, 173 f.
Garvie, A. E., 3, 40, 99, 193, 300
Gennesaret. *See* GALILEE, SEA OF
George the Sinner, 274
German books on F. G., 53–84
Gethsemane, 130, 132, 134
Glory of Jesus, 132, 190
Glosses in text of F. G., 67 f., 76, 89, 118, 301
Gnosis, 9, 145, 158
Gnosticism, 9, 11, 21, 24, 59, 76 f., 85, 87, 132, 145, 156 ff., 162, 170 ff., 198, 200, 206, 235, 251 f., 257 f.
Gnostics, 165
God-mysticism, 149 ff., 203
Goethe, J. W., 68, 234
Goguel, M., 81, 88, 131, 133 f., 157
Gore, C., 3
Gospel and First Ep., 107 f., 276–96
Grammatical characteristics of F. G., 105 ff., 276 ff.
Grandmaison, L. de, 88
Gregory, C. R., 66
Grill, J., 82, 146
Grubb, E., 193
Gunkels Festschrift. See *Eucharisterion*

H

Harnack, A. von, 55 ff., 157, 199
Harris, Charles, 3
Harris, J. Rendel, 41, 223, 307
Hebrews, Ep. to, 83, 101
Heitmüller, W., 13, 44, 66, 68, 190 f.
Hellenistic mysticism, 11, 145, 151, 156, 162
Hellenistic syncretism, 76, 148
Hellenizing influence in F. G., 145, 149, 155
Heraclitus, 146
Hermes (Thoth-Hermes), 157
Hermetic writings, 77 f., 157, 165, 259
Historical element in F. G., 25, 27 f., 33, 35 f., 40, 46 f., 54, 56, 58, 62, 71, 84 f., 86 f., 96, 128, 144, 179, 195, 234
History and Interpretation in F. G., 245 ff.
Hoare, F. R., 166 f.
Hoernle, E. S., 49
Holland, H. Scott, 42
Holtzmann, H. J., 44, 54, 57, 81, 196, 281, 282
Homiletic amplification, 67
Hoskyns, E. C., 168, 170, 172 ff., 244–50, 267
Hügel, F. von, 7, 34, 200

I

'I am' sayings, 77 f.
Ignatius, 77, 80, 86, 151, 156, 165 f., 211, 304
Ignatius, Silence of, 231, 273
Inge, W. R., 13, 27, 146, 156, 195, 198
Interpolations in F. G., 29, 39, 63
Interpolator, 65, 300 f.
Interpretation of Jesus in F. G., 5, 11, 43, 144
Iranian redemption-mystery, 10, 77
Irenaeus, 7, 54, 229, 231, 272

J

Jackson, H. Latimer, 37, 45
James, Son of Zebedee, 70, 274
Jeremias, J., 174 f.
Jerome, 184
Jerusalem, John of, 22, 40, 230
Jerusalem, Visits to, 161
Jewish standpoint of F. G., 38, 84, 101, 155
Jews in F. G., 25, 124, 133, 220
Johannine Epistles, 14, 20, 30 ff., 37, 42, 45, 61, 63, 67, 82, 85, 96, 103 ff., 148, 160
Johannine grammar, 38, 105 ff., 277 ff.
Johannine parallels to Synoptic sayings, 216 ff., 306 f.
John the Apostle, 85 f., 89, 96, 99, 228 ff.
John the Baptist. *See* BAPTIST, JOHN THE
John Mark, 67

John the Presbyter, 31, 33 f., 38, 40, 43–5, 55 f., 65 f., 70, 76, 81, 85 f., 89, 271
John, Son of Zebedee. *See* JOHN THE APOSTLE
Johnson, Samuel, x.
Jones, Rufus M., 200 f.
Jowett, Benjamin, 311
Judaean ministry, 122 f., 126, 162
Judas Iscariot, 131, 134, 187, 209, 212
Judgement, 249
Julian of Norwich, 197
Jülicher, A., 54, 57, 196
Jülicher-Festgabe, 72
Justin Martyr, 7, 98, 151, 205, 211, 214, 304 f.

K

Kennedy, H. A. A., 146, 185, 188, 224, 226, 272
Kenyon, F. G., 174
Kiddush, 140
Kingdom of God, 155
Kittel, G., 84
Knopf, R., 66
Knowledge, 256
Koine, Greek, 12, 105

L

Lagrange, M.-J., 88, 117, 184
Lake, Kirsopp, 144, 204 f., 267
Last Supper, 25, 40, 129, 134 f., 208 f., 212, 230. *See also* DATE OF L. S.
Law, Robert, 281
Law, The, 153
Lazarus, Raising of, 25, 27, 44, 56, 67, 71, 122, 129, 141, 189, 192
Lepin, M., 87
Lewis, F. Warburton, xi., 33, 114 f., 119 f., 125 f., 143, 301, 303
Lewis, Greville P., xi., 126 f., 303
Lidzbarski, M., 79
Lietzmann, H., 157
Life, 82, 157, 201 f., 213
Light, 82, 157, 202, 213
Lightfoot, J. B., 6, 19, 272, 304 f.
Lightfoot, R. H., 175
Linguistic usage in Johannine writings, 38, 41, 46, 97, 99, 110
Lock, W., 3, 194
Lockhart, J., 241
Lofthouse, W. F., xi., 310 f.
Logos, 5, 11, 28, 33, 39, 41, 49, 54, 57, 59, 71, 76, 82 f., 86, 144, 146, 152, 157, 191, 198, 235, 242
Lohmeyer, E., 81, 109
Loisy, A., 84, 86, 156, 196
Lord's Supper. *See* EUCHARIST
Luke Gospel of, 35, 100, 102, 130 ff., 143, 187, 192, 217, 301

M

McClymont, J., 50 f.
Macgregor, G. H. C., 51, 115 f., 126 303
Mackintosh, H. R., 188
McNeile, A. H., 47, 282
Mandaism, 10 f., 77 ff., 81, 157, 159
Manicheeism, 10, 77, 198
Manna, 147, 212
Manson, W., 44
Marana tha, 148
Marcion, 87, 89, 158, 199
Mark, Gospel of, 32, 35, 98, 100, 102 f., 129 f., 142, 161 f.
Martha and Mary, 131, 189, 193
Martineau, J., 22
Martyrdom of John, 23, 26, 32, 38, 42, 45 f., 55, 66, 70, 232, 273 f.
Matthew, Gospel of, 138, 182
Maurer, C., 166
Mayeda, G., 165
Mayser, E., 285
Melchizedek, 83, 191
Menoud, P. H., 173
Messiah, 8
Messianic Secret, 254
Meyer, A., 297
Meyer, Eduard, 68
Michaelis, W., 155
Millenarianism, 85, 273, 298
Milligan, G., 110
Mingana, A., 275
Ministerial gradations, 200 f.
Miracles, 58, 62, 188, 193
Miraculous draught, 129, 143, 201
Misunderstanding of Jesus, 58
Moffatt, James, 32, 36, 111–13, 125 f., 146, 206, 208, 299, 303
Moore, G. F., 204, 234
Moses, 121, 224
Moulton, J. H., 41, 105, 116, 283, 285, 292, 310
Mozley, J. B., 190
Muirhead, L. A., 2, 13, 44
Murry, J. Middleton, 4
Mysteries, 83, 148, 156
Mysticism, Acting and reacting, 199
Mysticism of F. G., 34, 44, 70, 86, 151, 195–203, 220
Mysticism, Jewish, 158 f., 206
Mysticism of Paul, 30, 151, 154, 162, 199, 201, 203
Mythology, 253

N

Nestle, E., 183
Nettleship, R. L., 311
Nicodemus, 112, 117, 120 f., 126, 130, 132, 134, 142, 161, 200, 204, 214

INDEX OF NAMES AND SUBJECTS

Nolloth, C. F., 45
Novellen, 75
Numbers in F. G., 182, 310 f.

O

Odeberg, H., 49, 84, 158, 183, 206
Odes of Solomon, 74, 77 ff., 80, 83, 157
Oehler, W., 170 f.
Oesterley, W. O. E., 140
Oppian, 184
Origen, 13

P

Palestinian outlook of F. G., 12, 19, 27, 31, 41, 84
Papias, 23, 55, 85, 98, 232, 271, 273 f.
Papyrus roll, 116
Papyrus, Egerton, 164, 275
Papyrus, Rylands, 164, 275
Parabolic teaching, 8, 229
Parallelism in Gospels, 308 f.
Paraclete, 28, 59, 65, 72, 131, 147, 226 f., 238
Parousia, 65, 72, 101, 208
Parseeism, 83
Partition, Theories of, 60, 98, 297 ff.
Passover, Feast of, 120, 122 ff., 137, 162
Pausanias, 191
Paul the Apostle, 42, 46, 86, 140, 145, 150, 273
Pauline doctrine, 5, 33, 37, 54, 206, 226
Pauline mysticism. *See* MYSTICISM
Pauline sacramentalism, 151, 204, 218
Peake, A. S., 3, 29, 183, 232
Pentecost, Feast of, 123 ff.
Peraea, 31, 122
Percy, E., 172
Pericope Adulterae, 34, 114, 116
Pericope structure, 72
Peter, Simon, 32, 98, 118, 120, 130, 135, 143, 183, 201, 229, 271
Peter's confession of faith, 129
Peter's denial, 32, 63, 113, 131
Philip, 133, 271
Philip of Side, 274
Philo, 20, 35, 54, 74, 76 ff., 82, 85, 156, 165, 182 ff., 191, 259
Philo and F. G. compared, 146 f., 185 f., 195
Phlegon, 68 f.
Pilate, Trial before, 71, 129, 136
Pistis Sophia, 11
Place of writing of F. G., 165
Plato, 311
Platonic ideas, 101
Pliny, 191
Poetical form of sayings, 215, 307
Polemical aims of F. G., 24, 132
Pollitt, T. H., 190

Polycarp, 7, 98, 272
Polycrates, 26, 230
Potentiality of numbers, 184
Prayer, 236
Presbyter. *See* JOHN THE
Prologue of F. G., 11, 39 f., 57, 61, 79, 82, 85, 96 f., 118, 146, 156, 213, 215
Prologue, Structure of, 309
Proselyte's initiation, 204
Proto-Luke theory, 43, 138, 141
Psychological attitude of Evangelist, 27, 232
Psychology of Mysticism, 34, 197
Purpose of F. G., 9, 33, 59, 170, 240 ff.
Pythagoras, 311

Q

Q (Non-Marcan Source of Matt. and Luke), 73
Quartodeciman controversy, 21

R

Rabbi Jose ben Halafta, 204
Rabbinic ideas, 42, 49, 158 f., 217, 259
Rabbis, Debates with, 221 ff.
Rawlinson, A. E. J., 219
Re-arrangements of text, xi. *See* DISARRANGEMENTS
Redactor, 3, 31 f., 38, 40, 63, 65, 67, 69, 75, 86, 98 f., 116 ff., 127, 299 f.
Regeneration, 145, 152, 156 f., 206, 218, 236, 248, 256 ff., 264 f.
Reitzenstein, R., 78, 148
Religious-historical treatment, 76
Renan, E., 186
Repentance, 248
Resurrection, 203
Revealer, The, 255, 258
Réville, J., xii., 84-6, 128, 196
Revision, Theories of, 34, 37, 97
Reynolds, H. R., 19 f.
Richmond, W. J., 42
Riggs, J. S., 27
Roberts, C. H., 164, 174
Robinson, B. W., 29
Robinson, J. Armitage, 42 f.
Rohde, E., 156
Rome, 31 f., 98

S

Sabbath, Discussions about, 120 f., 222 f.
Sacramentalism, 9 f., 14, 25, 152 f., 200 ff., 204, 254
Sadducee, 26, 230
Sadhu Sundar Singh, 197
Salmon, G., 26

Samaria, 64, 120, 123, 130
Samaritan woman, 71, 182
Sanday, W., 7, 19, 22
Sanders, J. N., 165 f., 275
Sanhedrin, 121 f., 134
Sayings of Jesus, 32, 96, 306 ff.
Schlatter, A., 84, 145, 158 f.
Schmiedel, P. W., 20 f., 29, 54, 57, 99, 128
Schmidt, K. L., 39, 74 f., 220
Scholten, J. H., 99, 281
Schwartz, E., 62, 64, 68 f., 70, 95
Schweitzer, Albert, 11, 149–56, 162, 175, 199, 203
Schweizer, Alexander, 95
Schweizer, E., 167, 172 f.
Scott, C. Anderson, 5, 208, 212
Scott, E. F., 23, 28, 36, 108, 146, 240, 295
Scott, Sir Walter, 241
Seamless robe, 95, 201, 297
Seed, 201, 206
'Sent,' The, 77, 210, 218, 251
Septuagint, 42
Shaw, G. B., 4
Shepherd, Allegory of Good, 59, 112, 121, 158, 225, 260–3
Siddons, V. D., xi.
Signs, 12, 30, 63, 75, 132, 185, 262 f.
Siloam, 218
Sin in F. G., 237
Sinaitic Syriac, 111, 113
Skeat, T. C., 164
Solomon. *See* ODES OF
Soltau, W., 65, 299
Son, The, 220
Son of Man, 148, 248 f., 265
Song of Songs, 186
Sources of F. G., 166, 171
Spirit, Doctrine of, 107, 226, 238 f. *See also* PARACLETE
Spitta, F., 33, 62, 95 ff., 111, 115, 298
Stanton, V. H., 21 f., 39, 211, 220
Stoicism, 5, 11, 33, 146, 235
Strachan, R. H., 27, 37, 46, 99, 168, 173, 192, 300
Strack, H. L., 217
Strauss, D. F., 183, 297
Streeter, B. H., 43, 138, 197
Style and Structure of teaching, 214, 306 ff.
Stylistic tests for F. G., 80, 213, 277 ff.
Supplement to Synoptics, 59
Symbol, symbolism in F. G., 12, 14, 27, 35, 44, 54, 56, 81, 85, 87, 163, 179–94, 260
Synagogue, Worship of, 224
Syncretism, 46, 78, 81
Synonyms, Interchange of, 106, 278 f.
Synoptic parallels to Johannine logia, 216, 306 f.
Synoptics, Relation to, 14, 37, 40, 43, 47, 55, 63, 65, 67, 72, 123, 128–43, 161, 169, 197, 214, 219
Syntax of Johannine writings, 105 ff., 276 ff.
Syriac martyrology, 26, 274
Syrian Church, 158

T

Tabernacles, Feast of, 121 ff., 127
Tarelli, C. C., 290
Targum, 225, 227
Tatian, 7, 30, 32, 111, 126 f.
Tayler, J. J., 22
Taylor, A. E., 188, 311
Taylor, V., 138, 174
Telford, J., 181
Temple. *See* CLEANSING OF
Temple, W., 170
Temptation of Jesus, 123, 130, 132, 189
Tennant, F. R., 188
Teresa, Santa, 197
Testimonia, 180
Theology of F. G., 28, 235 ff., 243–66
Theologische Rundschau, 60, 67, 81, 297, 301
Thomas, Acts of, 78
Thomas, Appearance to, 130
Thompson, J. M., 71, 114 f., 125
Thucydides, 69
Toplady, A., 181
Topographical details in F. G., 31
Transfiguration, 8, 130, 132
Triumphal Entry, 129, 137
Truth in F. G., 157

U

Underhill, Evelyn, 44, 196–8
Unity of authorship, 73, 76, 86, 109
Unity of Gospel, 95–110
Unity of ideas, 67
Unity of style, 97, 160, 213, 276–81
Universalism, 249
Upper Room, 112, 208, 211 f., 225 f., 236

V

Valentinus, 86 f.
Vine, Allegory of, 199, 202, 208, 260 f.

W

Walking on sea, 72, 129, 188
Water and blood, 179 ff., 200
Watts, G. F., 5
Weinel, H., 202 ff.,
Weiss, B., 54, 57, 66
Weiss, J., 66, 109, 213, 234, 300, 309
Weisse, C. H., 95
Wellhausen, J., 62, 66, 68 f., 70, 95–7, 106

Wendland, J., 188
Wendland, P., 68
Wendt, H. H., 20, 61, 82, 95-7, 98, 299
Westcott, B. F., 19
Windisch, H., 71 ff., 81, 132, 135 f., 146, 281
Wisdom of Ben Sira. See ECCLESIASTICUS

Wisdom of God, 9, 80, 146, 223
Wood, H. G., xi.
Works and faith, 249 f.
Wrede, W., 58
Wright, C. J., 188

Z

Zahn, Th., 6, 53, 57, 66

www.ingramcontent.com/pod-product-compliance
Lightning Source LLC
Chambersburg PA
CBHW061426300426
44114CB00014B/1554